MW00777801

Alpha Male Bible

Charisma. Attract Women with Psycology of Attraction. Art of Confidence, Self Hypnosis, Art of Body Language. Small Talk, Eye Contact. Habits & Self-Discipline of a Real Alpha Man

---

Dale Wayne

© Copyright 2021 - All rights reserved.

The content contained within this book may not be reproduced, duplicated or transmitted without direct written permission from the author or the publisher.

Under no circumstances will any blame or legal responsibility be held against the publisher, or author, for any damages, reparation, or monetary loss due to the information contained within this book, either directly or indirectly.

Legal Notice:

This book is copyright protected. It is only for personal use. You cannot amend, distribute, sell, use, quote or paraphrase any part, or the content within this book, without the consent of the author or publisher.

Disclaimer Notice:

Please note the information contained within this document is for educational and entertainment purposes only. All effort has been executed to present accurate, up to date, reliable, complete information. No warranties of any kind are declared or implied. Readers acknowledge that the author is not engaged in the rendering of legal, financial, medical or professional advice. The content within this book has been derived from various sources. Please consult a licensed professional before attempting any techniques outlined in this book.

By reading this document, the reader agrees that under no circumstances is the author responsible for any losses, direct or indirect, that are incurred as a result of the use of the information contained within this document, including, but not limited to, errors, omissions, or inaccuracies.

1

TABLE OF CONTENTS

INTRODUCTION: --- 9
TYPES OF MAN AND HOW TO AVOID NOT BEING AN ALPHA ------------ 9
Good Guys --- 10
Problem With Being His "Friend" -- 13
Avoid the Beta Male Posture --- 14
Talk To Other Girls. -- 16
Alpha Male -- 18

CHAPTER ONE: CHARISMA --- 20
Charisma? What's That? --- 20
The Charisma Is It Learned Or Born With It? ---------------------------- 21
Here Are The Techniques That Will Grow Your Charm. --------------- 22
The Scientific Basis For Charisma -- 25
A Charismatic Person -- 29
Seduce with Charisma --- 36
Charisma for introverts and shy people --------------------------------- 39

CHAPTER TWO: ATTRACT WOMEN WITH THE PSYCHOLOGY OF
ATTRACTION. --- 47
The First Impression Is Decisive. --- 47
Hair And Smell, Key Elements --- 48
Beauty Is Not Everything. --- 49
Other Physical Factors That Arouse Sexual Attraction ---------------- 49
We Are Not So Different From Animals ----------------------------------- 50
The Wrinkle Is Also Beautiful --- 50
Love And Attraction Are Not The Same. --------------------------------- 51
The Five Definitive Laws Of Attraction: ---------------------------------- 51
How We Choose Our Partner --- 51
Attraction --- 54
The Consequences Of Association And Reinforcement. --------------- 54
Proximity -- 55
Negative And Positive Affect -- 56
Personality Traits -- 57
Similarity -- 58
Reciprocity -- 60
Physical Attractiveness --- 61

Attractiveness, Perception And Social Behavior ------------------------- 63
Attractiveness Factors --- 64
Attractiveness And Evolutionary Explanations ------------------------- 65
Love --- 66
Types of Love -- 67
Functions Of Love And Evolution --------------------------------------- 69
Universal Character Of Love And Cultural Influence ------------------- 72
Socio-Structural Factors And Intimate Relationships ------------------- 74
Cultural Factors And Intimate Relationships ---------------------------- 75
Types of Love And Social-Cultural Factors ----------------------------- 77
Types of Love And Gender Differences ---------------------------------- 79
Marriage And Social-Cultural Factors ----------------------------------- 80
Great Behaviors That Instantly Lead To Low Status -------------------- 82
The Most Important Attitude Of Power You Can Have ----------------- 84
Creating Your Own Reality --- 86

CHAPTER THREE: THE ART OF CONFIDENCE AND TRUST ----------- 89
How To Appear Confident To Women ----------------------------------- 89
Ten Keys To Project Safety --- 91
How To Be A Confident Person? --- 92
Acting And How To Show Confidence Or Security ----------------------- 93
Signs That Show Confidence And Others That Denote Insecurity ----- 94
Tips To Promote Trust In Your Partner --------------------------------- 100
How To Project More Confidence -- 104
Are You Insecure? How To Gain Self-confidence ---------------------- 105
Self-Confidence -- 106
False Ideas About Self-confidence -------------------------------------- 106
Doubts Away -- 107
The Fear Of The Future -- 108
The Pillars Of Self-safety -- 109
The Art Of Flirting Based On Confidence And Good Self-esteem ---- 112
Boost Your Self-confidence From Improvisation ----------------------- 114
The Fear Of Rejection Is Based On An Illusion ------------------------- 115
Without Practice, There Is No Progress --------------------------------- 116
Trust Is The Key To Attracting Women --------------------------------- 116
Confidence Attracts Women, Discover How To Show Confidence -- 118

CHAPTER FOUR: HYPNOSIS AND SELF HYPNOSIS ------------------- 120
Terminology -- 120
The Self-concept --- 122

There Are Three General Rules For Taking On A Role: ---------------- 223

"Getting The Game" --- 227

Playing Roles --- 231

Start Now! --- 232

How To Flatter A Woman Effectively-------------------------------------- 232

CHAPTER SEVEN: THE POWER OF EYE CONTACT -------------------- 235

What Is Eye Contact?--- 235

The Importance Of Eye Contact-- 236

Types Of Looks In Psychology-- 236

The Types Of Gazes In Psychology And Their Meaning --------------- 237

What We Say Through The Gaze, By Science. -------------------------- 238

Contact Excites --- 238

Eyes Reveal The Honesty Of A Smile --------------------------------------- 239

Pupil Dilation Is A Sign Of Interest -- 239

The Reciprocal Gaze Is A Sign Of Love ------------------------------------- 239

Eye Contact Gives Rise To Deception--------------------------------------- 239

Keys To Non-verbal Language: The Four Views That Work --------- 240

What Your Looks Say --- 240

The Four Looks Of Power --- 242

Make A Good Impression--- 245

Establish Trust --- 246

Present --- 246

Show Interest--- 247

Reduce Anxiety--- 247

The Best Ways To Conquer Her With Just One Look------------------- 249

Maintain Eye Contact For 4.5 Seconds ------------------------------------ 249

Look At It, Look Away, And Look At It Again! --------------------------- 250

The Triangle -- 250

Blink -- 251

Sting Her Eye--- 252

The Secrets Of Eye Contact-- 252

The Duration Of Eye Contact, A Fundamental Factor------------------- 253

Eye Reading -- 253

Seduction And Instinct--- 254

According To Body Language Experts, Interest In Another Person Is

Measured In Eye Contact.-- 254

The Power Of The Gaze -- 255

How To Seduce Someone With Your Eyes --------------------------------- 259

Characteristics Of The Self-concept------------------------------------125
Frequently Asked Questions About Hypnosis --------------------------127
Hypnosis, Will, And Conscience--129
Hypnosis And Self-hypnosis ---130
Varieties Of Auto Hypnotic Techniques: -------------------------------131
Engraved Rite ---135
Things --138
Erotic Hypnosis And Seduction ---------------------------------------138

CHAPTER FIVE: THE ART OF BODY LANGUAGE ---------------------- 149

What Is Communication? --149
Non-verbal Communication ---150
Seduction--153
The language of seduction --155
What Is Body Language? --161
Body Language Clues To Watch Out For--------------------------------162
How To Improve Your Body Language----------------------------------164
Body Language Changes Us.---165
What Should You Look For In Your Partner's Body Language? ------168
Body Language As A Weapon Of Seduction ----------------------------176
A Goddess Of Eroticism --178
The Unconscious Signals That Show That You Attract Her-----------179
Non-verbal Signs That Scream "I'm Not Dominant. "And How To Avoid
It! --182
Practicing the Body Language of an Alpha Male ---------------------188

CHAPTER SIX: SEDUCTION --- 192

Serious Mistakes You Probably Make That Keep Her From Your
bedroom. ---193
The Main Reason Why Men End Up In The Friendzone --------------194
Creating a Sex Character--197
Getting To Sex In 3 Steps: The System -------------------------------199
Step 1: The C Rating Button --200
The Classification of C Button ---------------------------------------200
Step 2: Express Your Sexual Interest --------------------------------204
"The Playful Look"--207
Step 3: Intensify the Flirting --208
Going forward --215
The Ultimate advice--217
Fear Of Breaking Comfort ---218

CHAPTER EIGHT: INTIMATE RELATIONSHIPS: ATTRACTION, LOVE, AND CULTURE --- **261**

Attraction --261
Proximity --263
Negative And Positive Affect--264
Personality Characteristics --265
Likeness ---265
Reciprocity --268
Physical Attractiveness --268
Attraction And Culture ---271
Socio-cultural And Attractive Factors---------------------------------272
Appeal and Evolutionary Explanations ---------------------------------273
Love--274
Types Of Love --274
Functions Of Love And Evolution --------------------------------------277
Socio-Structural Factors And Intimate Relationships ------------------281
Cultural Factors And Intimate Relationships --------------------------283
Types Of Love And Socio-cultural Factors -----------------------------285
Types Of Love And Gender Differences ---------------------------------286
The Truth About Women's Love and Sex ... It May Surprise You-----288
What All Women Fear To Live---288
What Women Like --290
Do Not Talk Explicitly About What You Are Going To Do --------------292
The Number One Mistake Men Make In Dating, And How To Avoid It
--293
The Secret Of Knowing How To Listen ---------------------------------296
The Magic Word That Reinforces A Woman's Good Behavior--------298
Non-Verbal Signs That Say, "I'm Adorable"----------------------------299
Evoke Mercy--300

CHAPTER NINE: HABITS & SELF-DISCIPLINE OF A REAL ALPHA MAN --- **302**

Why Should You Become A Better Male?---------------------------------302
Look Better Than You Ever ---302
Shoes --303
Hair ---304
The Skin ---305
The Shave --305
Stretch --306
Combining --308

Accessories --- 309

Your Style -- 310

Your Body -- 311

A Basic Guide To Work The Body ------------------------------------ 312

What It Means To Look Good -- 315

Important Techniques To Control Your Mindset And Build Your Ideal

Personality -- 315

Your Powers Affect Your Conduct. --------------------------------- 316

Simple Alpha Male Exercise- -------------------------------------- 318

Your Thoughts --- 319

Develop Positive Thinking -- 320

Overcoming Your Insecurities ------------------------------------ 322

Easy Alpha Male Exercises --------------------------------------- 323

Drowning Your Fears About Rejection --------------------------- 323

How to Eliminate Your Fears ------------------------------------ 325

Making A New Way You Talk To Yourself Through Statements ----- 329

An Easy Alpha Male Exercise ----------------------------------- 333

Simple Secret To Being Dominant ----------------------------- 336

Seven-Step System -- 340

Being Persistent -- 341

The Boarding --- 342

CHAPTER TEN: HOW TO SUCCESSFULLY SEDUCE A WOMAN FROM

ZERO --- 343

The Approach And How To Do It --------------------------------- 343

Making The Appointment -------------------------------------- 349

Telephone Success --- 350

The Only Place You Should Take a Woman on a First Date ---------- 353

How to Convert an Easy Conversation Successful on a Date --------- 355

Differences between men and women. ------------------------------ 356

Shoes. --- 356

The Importance of Laughter ------------------------------------- 362

Signs Of Attraction --- 363

Why You Must Assume the Attraction --------------------------- 367

Your Behavior -- 368

How To Make A Woman Feel Happy And Very Hot For Sex ---------- 373

Easy Alpha Male Exercise: ------------------------------------ 374

The Non-verbal Signal That Yells Kiss Me! -------------------- 378

Tomorrow After -- 381

7

CLOSING WORDS--- **383**

BECOMING AN ALPHA MALE --383
   Be the Boss! --383
   Project Your Ideal Ego By Controlling The Way You Are Seen -------384
   Beta Male Behaviors to Avoid ---384
   Simple Alpha Male Practice - Fixing the Mindset About You. ---------388

INTRODUCTION:

TYPES OF MAN AND HOW TO AVOID NOT BEING AN ALPHA

The Three Kinds of Men — Alpha Male, Beta Male "Good Guy," and Idiots

Beta Male "Good Type"

When growing up, moms, aunts, and other older ladies always told me that you had to be a nice guy to get a girlfriend. A man had to constantly buy her flowers, gifts and take her out to eat.

And unfortunately, if you used their advice. Trying to be the good guy through high school and college, the one that women supposedly wanted. Girls would always say how much they appreciated what I did, but the biggest reward I got was a kiss on the cheek.

Then in college and later, the council changed. It was suddenly common knowledge that to be successful with women, and one had to act like an asshole rather than a good boy.

I tried to follow that advice and found that some women responded more to me when acting like an idiot. However, I still wasn't getting the wanted success. Although I did get to have my first sexual relationship, I had a case of low self-esteem in my head. And I still had issues with a lot of women who preferred other guys over me.

So I took a good look at the guys who were successful with women, those who were unsuccessful, and others who were in between, and I deduced that there are three kinds of men. And there is an order as far as women are interested.

Good Guys

At the bottom of the list are the good guys who make up most of the male population. A good guy is a man who begs for sex. He appears at the door of a woman with flowers, leads her to an elegant restaurant, and buys her filet mignon and a glass of good wine.

After taking her home, he gets the blue balls because she doesn't even invite him inside. And the downside is that he doesn't learn from this — he uses the same tactics again on the next woman.

And you want to know what is ironic here? Believe it or not, women consider nice guys to be manipulative.

It's pretty obvious to the woman why the nice guy buys her so many things. "They are only after one thing!" It is a common phrase that women repeat about good guys. However, she thinks that he could have the potential for a good relationship, so she can secretly have him as a backup, and in the future, she can have sex with him.

And boy, does she make him wait a long time! Some women set at least three dates: winning the lottery for the guy, while many other women make them wait months until "the day" comes.

And when sex comes, it's a big event, and the woman makes a fuss about it. There's just one problem, he won't be able to get sex as long as he wants. He will have to accept her terms and when she is in the mood to do so.

Why are good guys not successful? The nice guy's problem is that not only do women see him as manipulative, they also see him as boring. The nice guy talks about logical things like politics or how his car engine works. Sometimes he brags about himself and how much money he makes, making it clear that he can buy things for the woman. How pathetic, she thinks.

Going into a rational conversation and trying to impress a woman with your intelligence and financial potential is a mistake 99% of guys make. This kills a woman's attraction to you because it communicates destitution and lower value.

If you weren't seeking her approval, you wouldn't be trying to impress her. If you were instead a man of high value (an Alpha Male), then she would be the one who would seek your approval.

The other problem is that a woman in the middle of a ritual with a guy in a rational conversation brings her awake from the trance. So refrain from talking about the Chinese trade policies that you read about in The Economist.

Don't get me wrong, though. It would be best if you didn't pretend to be some fool around women. Women find it attractive when a guy is an expert at something. It would be best to talk about interesting things within your area of expertise, not things that clutter the mind.

You should start immediately, if you haven't already, become an expert at something. No matter what, real estate, rock music, South Park trivia, religion, history, etc.

A man who is an expert is automatically an alpha male in that area. Just be sure to captivate her with the knowledge you share. Don't bore her. (When sharing facts, ask yourself, "Would this information be in 'Ripley's Believe It or Not' or would it be something a boring college professor would say?)

As the song says, women want to have fun, and nice, boring guys aren't fun. Go to the places where singles congregate, and you can do an interesting exercise by observing and analyzing them.

If the girl looks bored or is constantly talking on her cell phone, she is with her boyfriend. That's because her boyfriend is a nice guy who isn't playing with her and doesn't turn her on.

If, on the other hand, she is laughing and seems to be having a good time, then what you are seeing is most likely an attempted seduction by an Alpha male.

Note, too, that the Alpha male who seduces a woman has an easy relationship with her. The two speak as if they have known each other for a long time.

The problem with being the nice guy is the startling posture. A man who pleads with a woman does so out of insecurity and desperation for sexual approval and attention.

Do you want to sleep with hot girls? So keep this in mind above all else: The quickest and easiest way to kill any attraction a woman may be starting to feel is feeling insecure, demonstrating need (being needy), or seeking approval. When you take the pose of being desperate to please. It's like you're begging.

There is an old saying about banks: They only want to lend you money when you don't need it. If you need money, forget about the bank.

Problem With Being His "Friend"

A man has settled by being friends with a girl, orbiting her as the months go by, hoping that she will tell him something one day. Many guys do this, particularly the shy ones.

These guys end up acting as emotional buffers for women. They listen carefully as her friends tell him about how idiotic the men in her life are. We sat in her living room, and like a nice guy, I was listening for 2 hours to everything she was meticulously telling me about what her next-door neighbor had told her at lunch days ago. He laughed and called me a fool. Do you think he likes me? "

I did my best — I told her that I thought he was an idiot and that she deserved better. I gave her all the legitimate and logical reasons why that was true. She told me that she agreed with me. (Women with the "bad guy" always agree that he is bad. So, of course, they ignore this and have sex with those "bad guys." As she did.)

If there is any justice in the world, women will end up with good guys one day. Tell the truth, sometimes they do, usually when they are older. By that time, they have usually already had children of some Idiot who abandoned them, and the thought of setting up with a man to pay the bills begins to be attractive.

Women don't like men with no guts for more than just friends. And when you act like a nice guy and follow the woman's plan, accepting that she makes the decisions, she doesn't respect you.

Good guys want the woman to decide where they will eat and when they will have sex. They have no idea that this difference automatically drops them into the permanent category of "just friends."

And that's why the nice guy doesn't have sex. As I said, women don't like to take responsibility for sex. You, like a man, need to take that responsibility and lead the way. That's what women want you to do, believe me, they love when you do this!

Avoid the Beta Male Posture

Besides being too indecisive, nice guys tend to be passive-aggressive. Women are often passive-aggressive too, which turns off when that particular trait shows up in a man.

What is passive-aggressive? You are passive until you have been pushed too far, then suddenly becoming aggressive. Have you ever had a woman who expected you to read her mind and then got upset when you read it wrong? That's passive-aggressive.

Instead of being grounded in between the passive and aggressive, which is assertive, the nice guy will constantly give in and do whatever the woman wants.

When the woman finds this unattractive and in the future leaves him for a more exciting guy, the good guy will complain about how he "did everything for her." Good guys also have a problem with jealousy, born out of their insecurity.

They are too dependent on the outside; all his happiness is in that woman. They don't want her to talk to other guys because he is afraid that she will leave and lose his source of happiness.

Now you see, the problem with the feelings of jealousy that so many betas have towards their women is that it comes from a position of deprivation or need. So whenever you feel like this with a girl, soak it up and let those feelings go.

When a girl detects a jealous guy, it's like he's saying, "Hey, I feel inferior to those other guys you're talking to.

And having that lack of confidence in you makes the girl trust you either. She begins to wonder if the grass is greener on other grasses.

I know it's hard not to feel jealous, but look at it this way: If you knew that you were the ultimate and that you could attract hot babes and could easily sleep with them, would you take care that your girl was leaving or talking to some other guys? Of course not, because the loss would be hers (and you could get another girl)

Okay, here's a new attitude I want you to adopt: "I'm becoming a High-Value Alpha Male." Keep repeating that to yourself throughout the day as an affirmation.

By the way, you're probably still wondering what you should do if your girl is talking to other guys. Well, the worst thing you can do (ironically) is trying to intervene to stop her from doing it. That makes her the highest value, not you.

Instead, the best way to counter such behavior is to say, "Have a good time!" With a tone of complete nonchalance when she says that she is going out with some other guy. Let her see that it doesn't affect you in the least.

Talk To Other Girls.

That changes the situation so that now she is the one who worries about whether you will leave her for the competition. That makes her understand that you have a higher value.

Another way to avoid getting upset about a woman's behavior is not to take individual women seriously or pay close attention to their thinking. Worrying too much about a woman's thoughts and feelings is a waste of time because the bottom line is that you cannot control what a woman thinks or feels. You can only control yourself.

Rather than taking women too seriously (giving them power over you, making you needy and unattractive), view them as collective sources of fun and pleasure in your life. That's it. Try something:

The next time you are with a woman, try saying "NO" to her at some point.

Saying "NO" can be powerful with women, but do it gently, like this:

She: *Let's rent a movie. "*

You: *"No, not yet. Let's go in an hour."*

By saying no, you establish authority and establish it as a challenge to the woman. If she sees it as a challenge, she will be turned on by you instead of boring.

If you say YES to everything she says, then she will soon say NO to you, and in the worst place of all, the bed.

What you need to know, more than anything, is that women notice any need. The Alpha male is exciting to women because their happiness comes from within, so he does not burden her with any responsibility for her emotional state.

Let me emphasize one thing here: your internal state is the key with women. For them to love you, you have to love yourself first. It would be best if you had a passion for your life, and you have to go for what you want. There are too many nice guys out there who are insecure. So when it comes to loving, the good guys finish last.

At a medium level, above the good guy is the asshole or idiot. For the most part, assholes attract women more than good guys because assholes aren't boring.

Although the asshole creates an emotional roller coaster of drama with his girlfriend, the girl is going through the ride's emotional high points along with the low points. In other words, he can make her cry, but he also makes her laugh. And the uncertainty of what will create excitement in your life.

Here's what you need to know about women: To be sexually aroused, women need to tune in to their emotions rather than logic. The good guy makes the fatal mistake of eliminating his logic, considering that one good thing the idiot does is eliminate a woman's emotions.

Idiots get sex because they manage to turn women on by being so persistent and driving them to the act. They are sexually aggressive, unlike the good guys who are sexually passive. As long as the idiot creates negative emotions within women, they are still creating emotions instead of the good guy who bores women.

However, it is not all good for idiots. The types of women who seek out idiots are low self-esteem, depression, and other emotional problems. Such women often act weird and insecure when it comes to relationships, so they aren't the kind of women a well-adjusted man would want to get.

Although idiots get laid, I'm not suggesting that you are one of them. The good news is that there is a higher level of men I call the Alpha Males who induce positive emotions within women without a negative side.

Alpha Male

In society, Alpha males are the leaders; people admire them. The alpha male is confident, socially powerful, outstanding, funny, a leader, self-confident, has high self-esteem and integrity. He is capable of joking around with women and being playful.

When a woman says something sarcastic, the Beta takes offense, while the Alpha laughs because he knows that girls are like his silly little sister. And when a woman later feels his sarcasm and learns that it wasn't a big deal to the Alpha, she gives him good marks for it.

Many social interactions in which we engage have the undercurrents of domination and submission. Studies of social situations have shown that dominant people will mark their territory in various non-verbal ways, such as gaining space with their bodies, using a louder voice, controlling conversations, and using strong eye contact.

The Alpha people are absorbed in their reality because he is interesting and makes them feel comfortable.

The Alpha does not feel possessive or jealous of the woman because he is not needy. He also does not suffocate women by putting them on a pedestal. Because of this, he knows that any woman would be lucky to have him, so if any particular woman is not looking for him, then she is the loser, not him.

In contrast, the Beta is nervous, has low social status, is typically a follower rather than a leader, normally feels clandestinely resentful of successful guys, has low self-esteem, and is annoying and desperate with women.

The real confession: I was Beta. I was depressed and resentful. I wanted a girlfriend because I thought having one would add value to my life. I once got a girl and could have as much sex as I wanted, and I thought my life would be wonderful. It wasn't until later that I learned that it was exactly the other way around.

It wasn't until I developed from within and had a life worth living that I began attracting amazing girlfriends that I have had through the years and the wonderful woman I am currently in a relationship with.

Please join me in figuring out the different aspects that make an alpha male a worthy companion for a woman and how to get the woman you want at your feet.

CHAPTER ONE

CHARISMA

If I ask you what charisma is, you may not be able to instantly give me a definition, but if I ask you to think of some charismatic person, surely one of them comes to mind.

And it is that charisma is like creativity; difficult to measure but impossible to deny.

Charisma? What's That?

What is the meaning of charisma? Good question. If we go to the strictly grammatical point, you can find various definitions. An official one, and with whom I disagree, is the following:

"Gift that God gives to some people for the benefit of the community."

I don't think that having charisma is having a gift, but if you believe it and you did not receive that divine gift, I have good news for you: you can go and claim it. John Antonakis, Marika Fenley, and Sue Liechti demonstrated in this study that charisma is not innate.

I believe that charisma has to do with a person's capacity to attract, amaze and generate admiration in others. And unlike gifts, abilities can be acquired.

It's like public speaking, flirting, or listening. One is not born knowing, but they are qualities that one learns with practice. What happens is that we usually call the involuntary practice a gift, while we call voluntary effort and dedication.

The Charisma Is It Learned Or Born With It?

Imagine a ten-year-old boy who goes to school and who, in the yard, spends 30 minutes playing Minecraft alone. When he comes home, he spends two hours on the PlayStation and, while he dines, he is watching TV. He falls asleep in bed while watching a YouTube video on his smartphone in which another person narrates - with limited vocabulary - how he plays whatever the fashionable game is.

Now imagine another child of the same age, partner of the previous one. In the courtyard, he plays soccer with his friends, complains about a foul, and argues why he should be penalized. At lunchtime, he tells them that he is going to the circus next weekend and that he wants to see the most famous magician in the city. He tells them what he is capable of and how magic exists. Then he comes home and sits down with his parents to talk. He explains that the math teacher has a mania for him and that, furthermore, math is useless in the real world. They argue. They do it properly, and each one gives their opinion. They have dinner talking about the weekend circus and how good that magician is. Then, in bed, his eyelids close as he reads how orcs invade Middle-earth, according to Tolkien.

Which of the two children do you think will have more "Gift of people" or more facility with adult speech?

It is not so much a question of being born with it but of exercising throughout life.

Just because you haven't consciously practiced, it doesn't mean you haven't trained. And if not, ask Mr. Miyagi and Daniel San.

Be that as it may, charisma is one of the personal qualities that everyone would like to have. It is one of the characteristics of the world's most successful and influential leaders and people.

21

So can it be learned?

Definitely YES.

If you want to learn how to be charismatic, read on. If you want to learn how and hope to achieve it in the five minutes you have left of reading, be delusional.

It does not work like that. You have to work a bit.

How to have charisma: scientifically proven techniques

In their study, John A. and his collaborators determined that charisma is born from relating and, above all, communicating. They analyze various facets until they find the most relevant that can convert people into charismatic leaders.

They divide them into two parts. The first nine have to do with verbal language, and the last 3 with non-verbal language.

The goal is to get attention, maintain interest, generate emotional connection, and project credibility. Maybe it sounds familiar to you.

Here Are The Techniques That Will Grow Your Charm.

- Metaphors And Analogies

Explain what is complicated in a simple way. The key is to convey a new idea by relating it to another that your audience already knows. Remember that not everyone has the same level of knowledge on the subject you are talking about. Try to use metaphors with everyday concepts like home, food, or technology. In this way, the spectrum of people who can understand it will be greater.

- Stories and anecdotes

Stories are great for several reasons, but the biggest of all is that instead of giving the information head-on -which usually raises resistance- they help you show the lesson you want to convey more indirectly. That is the audience that draws its conclusions.

You don't lead them by the hand like a small child. You open the door for them, and they are the ones who walk through it. And that makes them feel competent.

- Contrasts

Contrasts help to see things more clearly. If everything is black, when you add something white, it will stand out. If everything is verbal, when you add something visual, it will make it look more. If you advertise what you offer and precede what they lack ... Do you know what will happen?

- Rhetorical

Questions Rhetorical questions work, in part, like stories. First, they direct their attention where you want it. It's hard to hear a question and not think about the answer. And then they actively participate in the conversation. They don't need to respond verbally; just by thinking about that answer, you are already making them participate.

- The rule of three

The rules of the three are magic. Here you can see its effects. When you list adjectives, adverbs, or qualities, three is the correct number. You can see it in hundreds of speeches, but this is one of my favorite examples. By the way, the one in the video is quite a charismatic person. Chance?

- Moral convictions

Integrity is one of the most appreciated qualities in people. We like those who help others, say what they think and who, besides, act according to those principles. Show your interest in being fair and doing the right thing but be careful to act accordingly. Otherwise, you will create a gap that will affect your credibility.

- Reflect the feelings of a group

Among the skills that will trigger your charisma highlights understanding others' feelings and having the ability to show and stir what you have in common. We have a preference for those who have our same passions and our same problems.

Talk to a mile vista about your son's problems in equestrian class or the cost of spare parts for your Porsche, and you will end up as far from him as the Poles.

Talk to him about how hard it is to make ends meet, and you will have his undivided attention.

- Establish demanding objectives

We do not value the easy. Nobody does it. You don't have to be special to keep it simple. What we like are those people who achieve what seemed unaffordable. Those who one day proposed something that seemed impossible and, later, they succeeded.

Who generates the most admiration for you, who runs 5km, or the one who completes an Iron-man?

- Show confidence self-confident

Charismatics are usually trustworthy people. People must perceive that you believe in what you tell them. That you are sure that it is true and that it can be achieved. Confidence is a basic attribute to give off charisma. If you don't believe in yourself, it will be more difficult for others to do so.

- Gesticulate naturally and energetically

Just as a person transmits more qualities and virtues dressed than in balls, a speech generates more positive attributes when accompanied by gestures that dress the message.

Don't hang your hands or speak with your shoulders slumped forward. Maintain an upright posture and gesture without fear. Notice how people talk on the terraces of the bars when they are not under any pressure. No one is an immovable trunk.

- Congruent facial expressions

One of the easiest ways to detect lies is to see that the person's facial expression does not correspond to what he says.

And the lie is an enemy of integrity and moral convictions. Perhaps that is why so many politicians lack that charisma they once dreamed of. Do you want to get it? Start by being congruent.

- The lively and varied tone of voice

Think of someone you want to hear. To which you go to Youtube to see their videos. The one that makes you activate the sound on Facebook. The one for which you would pay money to listen to it live. Most likely, it offers vocal variety in three dimensions: speed, pitch, and volume. Making yourself palatable is the first step to becoming charismatic. Or can you think of someone charismatic that you don't feel like listening to?

Besides, five other techniques also help to gain charisma and are:

- Invoke a sense of urgency
- Persuasion
- Use repetition
- Talk about sacrifice and effort.
- Appeal to the story to compare or motivate, include humor in your communications

The Scientific Basis For Charisma

We all know some of those who manage to be the center of attention in any social gathering, without great fanfare or fuss, simply through their mere presence. Many of them are movie or television stars (unfortunately, we find less and less of these characters in politics), but we will also have come across some of them in our working lives - the inspiring boss, the charming commercial - or their fascinating charm that will have interfered with our loving purposes.

But is it something innate, or is it the product of a long learning process and developing social skills? Is the charismatic person charismatic because he behaves specially or behaves however he wants because his spell has bewitched all his companions? Rather the latter, the researchers note.

Various studies have been aimed at finding out what traits define charismatic people, which should not be confused with unbearable egomaniacs who, all told, tend to cause more rejection than acceptance. As John T. Marcus pointed out half a century ago, the charismatic leader is not the one who belittles others, but the one who manages to inspire those around him to bring out the best in them, which explained the success they had known historical figures like Adolf Hitler, Winston Churchill or Charles DeGaulle. Although debatable, they all had something in common: a vision and the ability to identify with it for his followers. Leaders pay attention to others and do not criticize them. However, recent research has more clearly detailed what it is that defines a charismatic person. It is not just a question of being one, but also of behaving as such, as Jay A. Conger, one of the social scientists who has dedicated most to the subject, points out. In his book *The Charismatic Leader*, Conger adds that it is in the intensity of your actions that you find the deciding factor in being a leader, as well as bomb-proof credibility. But what are the actions that distinguish these irreproachable leaders? Here are some of the ones that Conger and other colleagues have defined over the years.

They listen. For those around you to feel appreciated, the charismatic leader needs to listen carefully to them, pause to reflect on their ideas, and not consider their ideas better than others. No person with charisma receives others' trust if they perceive that their superior continually ignores the proposals of others and considers their own wonderful. Besides, they are good communicators since they make others feel that their ideas are appreciated (even if they are ultimately rejected), and for this, communication skills are required.

Build confidence and inspire. It is achieved through experience and good action, mainly through the ability to recognize and amend one's own mistakes and make others understand their successes and mistakes in the right measure. A leader who has lost his credibility will hardly ever be considered a reference among his followers. Besides, through their colleagues' trust, they can serve as inspiration, enhancing their virtues and relativizing the defects that we all have.

They are not conformists. The most valued people perceive some error or injustice in their environment and are capable of starting the necessary process to solve such a problem. For a charismatic person, something can be improved, and that therefore requires their leadership. Their discontent leads to action and action to change. - They are visionaries. It is no longer simply a matter of being able to have a good idea, being skilled in certain fields, or being very productive, but developing a personal and non-transferable project that distinguishes them from their peers. If they can shape this vision in the right way, attract their followers without manipulating them, and gain their trust through the right means, the leader can take on any company, no matter how ambitious. After all, charisma is closely related to the height of your sights. Charismatic people lead by example and are willing to sacrifice - they

Take risks, and they sacrifice. To be able to achieve that personal vision, leaders must lead by example. And, therefore, they must act following the ideas they espouse. You cannot ask others for something you are unwilling to give and expect to continue trusting. Being the first to help, to recognize the possibility of failure, and to accept the consequences of a wrong decision is the difference between the leader who shows his face and the one who hides or the one who, worse still, always places the responsibility of the mistakes on their peers.

They are creative. Wit and the ability to abandon predetermined conceptions distinguish a charismatic person from a merely competent one. Their aspirations are different from those of other (conformist) mortals, requiring a different skill set to help them spearhead projects. If they are in permanent struggle with the *status quo* imposed, their tools for change cannot be the same. If they want to reach an audience accustomed to certain messages, they will have to use an alternative form of expression that distinguishes them from the conventional. You know: if you want different results, one must follow different methods. –They do not criticize others. Even if they have made mistakes, gossiping behind their colleagues' back only leads to a loss of confidence from their colleagues, who suspect that they may be the targets of malicious comments from the "smartass" on successive occasions. Deep down, the most charismatic people are so because they appear human. However, it may sound paradoxical: they recognize that anyone can make an error - even if they know how to hide it well - and they remember that the important thing is not to repeat it. Of course, it is important not to fall into the condescension of those who consider that others' mistakes are so frequent that it is better to get used to them.

They speak of "we", not of "me". Egocentricity is not exactly a common quality among charismatic people; yes, it involves others in the project that one has started. It is important that all company members feel part of the same boat, not that they are mere companions of the leader in realizing his company. The important thing is the common objective and that each one adopts the role that the company needs, not the personal fulfillment of the leader.

There are cases of men and women who have a special charisma for preaching, advising people, and knowing and transmitting God, but who have not necessarily founded a religious congregation.

At the beginning of the third millennium, it seems very normal to speak of charisms. And if our objective is to awaken the charism, it is convenient to know what this term means or wants to mean. We need to have clear notions about this concept if we are going to center life and the consecrated identity.

A Charismatic Person

"I attract people not because I am an extrovert, I am above average, or I exude charisma but because I care about these people."

I think that phrase encapsulates much of the reality about charisma.

If you try to apply these strategies like pushing a button, you may be more influential and even more persuasive. Still, you probably won't get into the area that charismatic people enjoy.

If what you want is to be charismatic, if you want to have that personal magnetism that seems reserved for a few, you don't have to use strategies as buttons but internalize them. They have to be part of your personality, your way of being.

And the best way to start including them is to show a sincere and genuine concern for others.

Does it matter to have the charisma to flirt and other aspects of our life, or can we do without it? How can you get it?

Recently an entry was written about the Pareto principle applied to the sex market or how many guys give you the bullshit that only 20% of the male population gets it hot and on top of it without the slightest run-in problem with females. Well, now it turns out that it's not even 20% anymore. Now according to some enlightened ones, it's only 5%.

It's not a joke.

I guess in three years, or so, we will be talking about 2%, and in ten, it will be negative numbers.

29

Flirting is not as easy as pulling out the torpedo and starting to pound it with the same force and claw as when you crush almonds. But it is not as difficult as sending a human-crewed mission to one of Jupiter's moons. Since we're here, I think the last chick I messed with was from that part of the Solar System.

Now I tell you. Do not be impatient. I freak out when a 35-year-old guy tells me he's starting to have trouble keeping his cock erect. When you investigate a little, you usually discover that they are men who have been with the same aunt for more than ten years, who is increasingly ugly and unbearable.

To understand us, I will give you an example. I met a guy from Barcelona who had a pretty cool painting of Dalí in his living room. When the four guys on duty meet at his house, we all look at him. It was impossible not to. However, the owner of the work did not even care. I was sick of seeing her every day. For him, they were seeing that Dalí was like seeing the toaster in the kitchen for me.

Something like this happens to many guys: just by fucking the same lady, they lose their sexual appetite. And it is a tragedy. However, since I am a convinced polygamist, I don't have those problems.

I'm getting more and more excited. To the point that if this does not stop like an older man.

Some friends with a girlfriend or wife do not suffer from Downed Soldier Syndrome either. I guess it goes with the person. The fact is that this weekend he had met a girl who seemed normal. I already saw some strange thing or other during the appointment, but nothing activated my anti-crazy arachnid sense.

Well, after kissing, and sucking, snitch, I took her home. I threw the jackfruit on the bed, and with all the heat, she took off my pants. The lady put her head close to my underwear, and I was convinced that she was going to suck it off. But instead, she was like analyzing it, and after a few seconds, she commented on its quality and design. I did not give it more importance and continued with my business. The thing went further, and I took out the condoms. The girl began to tell me the virtues of that brand of condoms and tell totally out of place stories in which she used them. I didn't pay much attention to her and started undressing her. She got on top of me, put my cock inside her in a quite mechanical way, and began, ATTENTION, to talk about the objects in my room.

For example, the wardrobe, a pouf to store clothes, or even a painting that I bought from a Basque friend. All this while moving her waist. I tried to attract her towards me and get on top, but the girl was following her ball, and it was grating me a lot. Like I weren't fucking nailing her or something. In the end, I couldn't help it, and the torpedo fell apart. That's right: I couldn't continue.

I tried without success to make it stony again, but there was no way. The most surreal thing is that the GIRL was OFFENDED. Like 'don't you like my tits? Don't I make you horny? 'As if her behavior had been impeccable, and I was as unpleasant as a bucket full of raccoon diarrhea. As far as I can remember, this has only happened to me three times.

The other two were because the stink from one of her cunt was not normal. It was so repulsive that I even seriously wondered if he kept a corpse in there. The other was because I pulled her panties down and saw that she had a fairly large scab from a wound between the hairs down there. It grossed me out.

This chick got mad at me too. It is what it is to be a gulf that sometimes you see yourself in bad situations.

But what I want to talk about today is fucking charisma. Why? Some of you have recently asked me how to work it and such.

Now, what exactly is charisma?

According to the Royal Spanish Academy, it is the ability that some people have to attract and fascinate.

31

Unfortunately, it is a recurring theme in those seduction books that fill your head with ineffective and fanciful bullshit so you can preserve your virginity. At the same time, you drop the tickets to the fucking guru on duty.

Let's be honest: we all want to be magnetic people capable of captivating others, Especially if it is about 'hot' ladies who want to jump off a cliff with their ass in pomp and wet pussy to land on our imposing 'column of Hercules.'

I believe that charisma is made consciously or unconsciously. But IT IS DONE.

The typical charismatic guy who everyone likes is at all parties and attracts the attention of girls who do not leave the house without their Hello Kitty panties, possibly someone who, from a very young age, has made a little effort to understand how human relationships work. For example, a typical trait associated with charisma and this prototype of males is smiling a lot when spoken to.

Possibly one of these noobs at a very young age discovered that showing his teeth generated a greater sense of harmony and good vibes among others, and he developed it to the point that it now comes naturally to him.

I say this because, for example, the Popular Party's image advisers tell their leaders that even if they are dealing with thorny issues or responding to brutal insults, they have to smile.

Logically they cause the opposite effect.

For example, Richard is always smiling. Far from looking charismatic, he is so forced that he looks like a psycho-killer. Another trait associated with charisma is leadership ability.

Come on, somehow influence other people's lives or their way of understanding reality. Again, for others to follow you first, you have to, somehow, have learned to give them reasons for it.

For example, in the underworld of the neighborhood youth, the typical douchebag which goes with the cigar and hides at the doors of the bars while smoking a joint and tells you about the last night of the wild party, knows that it is cool. He knows that he does and says things that others don't even dream of. He knows he is an idolized youthful rebellion figure.

He knows that blondes like bad boys who invite them to try the back seat of their car that smells new. He knows that in that context and in that age range, he is the fucking master and that, therefore, there will be others who will love him close and imitate him.

However, among older people or even in the Peppa Pig fan club, I don't think it goes down very well. By this, I mean that the charism is often also linked to a certain context.

For example, a scientific lecturer may be funnier and cooler than the others and still be a nerd, not very masculine and boring to the women who appear on Tele 5.

Maybe a guy who has a very special way of playing The saxophone, such as John Zorn, for many, is a visionary genius to emulate when for others little more than a madman who plays badly and, on top of that, senseless.

Sometimes, the charisma that a person generates does not arise from their personality but their work.

For example, in the gigs, the rock tends to shit on me and on the offspring that at the moment I do not have because I am very hard-pressed. I recognize it.

When they see the results or the rewards, they thank me, and there is more laughter and merriment than at the end of a Power Rangers episode. When you have people in your charge, the hell you force yourself not only to make yourself respected but also to make others trust you.

It is something you LEARN. You need to generate some charisma if you want others to pay you minimal attention. In fact, for a few years, a most curious phenomenon has been taking place. Many geeks go into engineering because they have poor social skills and think they will not have to deal too much with others.

However, the higher they get, the more presentations, talks, client meetings, and the like have to do. This is because companies increasingly depend on technology, and for certain purposes, they need supporters who know the subject and not graduates in Business Administration or economics.

It is much easier to teach an engineer the four basics of business than a clerk with certain technicalities. So much so that, for example, in the same City of London, most 'financial geniuses' come from careers such as Mathematics, Physics, or any engineering. In other words: they have to put on the suit, become visible faces, and of course, DEVELOP SOME CHARISMA.

It is true that many times some extreme geeks, the kind that has written on their faces that they like to play Fortnite and that from so much pounding it daily and every hour they have wounds on their dicks, have become true leaders highly appreciated by their peers.

Now, is it convenient to generate charisma with women?

OF COURSE.

Some guys flirt because they have excessive charisma. And although many of you have other qualities, such as a physique as appealing as a delicious bag of Goblins (hey, I am not saying that I miss them a lot, damn it), you should not neglect the charisma.

Why?

Because, for example, there may be others who are as good as you and who on top of it don't stink like boredom and the brain only gives me to lift dumbbells and not shit on myself".

As I have already shown you, you can develop your charisma even if you are as hypnotic as a croquet game and more closed than the typical Catalan who calls all Spaniards who cross Europe fascists.

It's not a joke. There are crazier and crazier of those. The radar is activated at the same time that the pot goes away. Like, 'Oh, look. Some random perfins, about which I do not know absolutely, which could be insulting sense motion gratuitously. Do not miss this opportunity! Wake up, Ferro! Feixistes! Feixistes! Feixistes!

That's right. But going back to the nitty-gritty, it would be interesting if you asked yourself some questions.

For example: How can I be more attractive in a certain environment? How can I like myself without becoming a clown or being tiresome? How can I stop being dull?

And so on.

You will be good not only for playing slimy cunts, but also for life. So, in general. Charismatic people make, for example, a simple flat blue sweater looks amazing and modern when they wear it. Why? Because they know how to put it on. They have been concerned with being suggestive with their outfits.

In any case, you don't have to obsess over the subject either. Just keep it in mind.

The more interesting your life and inner world and knowledge, the greater your charisma will be.

Suppose you know how to show it to others in a charming way. In that case, you are going to see how, without the slightest effort, uncles and aunts are going to count on you for everything, how no one will bother to do you a favor, or how sexual, job or other offers are rained on you—another type.

You should also bear in mind that, unlike what some sons of bitches say who want to fill your head with bullshit, there is no 'homogeneous type of charisma.'

Some people captivate because they are very strange and others precisely because they are so normal and hearty that they unwittingly like them and spread their joy.

Some are charismatic for having more balls than the rest, and others for knowing how to talk to magazine models without shaking their voices and without placing them on a golden pedestal.

You have to find what aspects of yourself you can enhance or expand to become a reference, on an axis around which several people rotate for one reason or another.

I recommend it because it is fucking incredible when a superior comes to you and recognizes that thanks to you, this or that has worked or a compromising situation has been avoided.

It's cool when a 25-year-old kid comes to you and tells you that he has learned more from you than in all the university courses.

Or when an aunt lets you know that she loves spending time by your side while kissing your neck.

Seduce with Charisma

Let's look for the meaning of seduction. It covers the area of relationships with the opposite sex and the persuasion of other people to your way of thinking, your perspective on life, and much more.

If you become a charismatic person, you will not only increase your attractiveness with the opposite sex, you will also have the possibility of moving up at work, you will have many more friends, and you can even do all kinds of projects because other people will want to help you or at least it will be. Easier to convince them.

Seducing with charisma is incredible. It is not like the classic seduction that is often indirect or direct; this seduction is more emotional, more spiritual.

Seducing with charisma does not necessarily mean that you will drive women (or men) crazy into wanting to have something sexual with you. No, that is secondary. What does happen is that they will feel an emotional connection with you.

Charisma, by nature, seduces the masses. One of the times I was able to verify this was when he used public speaking power. I know perfectly well that people get bored with boring monologues and meaningless stories; they want to feel something special and feel emotions.

Whenever I gave a speech or a presentation, I tried to be funny, magnifying my charisma. I began to tell anecdotes that moved me a lot. When I came down from the stage, several people approached me to congratulate me on the good message I had given them, and others hugged me. And a lady (I was very surprised by this) told me that she was a fan of my presentations; she loved my way of thinking and, above all, for seeing herself reflected in me.

On many occasions, I successfully seduced with charisma, and one of those was when I was in another city. I went out to meet people on the street and found out that I was there because I just wanted to meet people who liked the idea. Suddenly I said some things about myself, and I showed my personality with which, many times, they were enchanted despite being of the same sex.

This is what can be done when seducing with charisma. While it is true that it is not very sexy, it is deeper than everything you have already learned so far about seduction.

To seduce with charisma, you have to be in a state of great confidence and optimism. Many people are always in a very passive and monotonous state. They do not seduce easily, so they go to the discos to see if they have any luck trying alcoholic beverages; they believe that by drinking and leaning on the bar, the woman of their dreams will appear and invite them to go to her home. In life, you get results by acting and not waiting.

This type of behavior seems regrettable to me. If you want to seduce with charisma, learn to be optimistic and positive. Girls love being with upbeat and cheerful guys, and best of all, these types of girls will help you on your self-improvement path. It's worth it.

Of course, some women like the bad guys, the serious ones, the unattainable, the unhappy ones, those from the dark side ... Leave them with their tastes, and it is most likely that these types of girls will not bring anything good to your life, you better go for the ones that will. That is why seducing with charisma is advantageous when finding a partner, because it attracts positive people into your life.

This is always the case with actors. Because of their influence, they have become great Hollywood stars, and they do what they love; they are happy with their work, therefore when you see them speak, you realize that they exude success through their charisma, and they manage to seduce you for no apparent reason.

For example, an actor that I love to see talk about is George Clooney. With his humor and confidence, he makes the vast majority of people who know him want to be more by his side. And I admit it, and I also want to be next to a person like him no matter how stupid he does.

Take, for example, Jim Carrey. When you see him in the movies, and even in the interviews they do on television, he does not stop being silly, and the public loves him. He is extremely successful on the big screen because there is no one globally; he is unique and original.

And there are many examples like those in the film world. The same happens in the world of politics, religions, sports, business, and so on.

There is always someone who stands out for his personality and is not necessarily the one with the most money, the most physical attractiveness, but rather the one who manages to seduce other people with charisma.

Seducing with charisma is not smiling all the time; seducing with charisma is not talking non-stop, seducing with charisma makes other people feel good while giving details of your attractive personality.

For example, you can show your leadership when you are in a meeting of friends, and you are the one who proposes new things; you are the one who asks others to make the toast, and everyone acts on your ideas. Great self-confidence and a good sense of humor will help you a lot too.

If you see that there are people who love the way you think, you find out that someone has copied your famous phrases, if you know that there are people who want to be like you, you are on the right track.

Seducing with charisma is, then, seducing by showing attractive personality traits while making other people feel positive emotions, whether in relationships with the opposite sex or with the general public.

Charisma for introverts and shy people

If you feel that charismatic people always get away with it, while it may be difficult for you to connect with strangers, this video is for you because I will teach you the five phases of charisma for introverts and shy people.

So that your social skills improve and you can socialize more easily with anyone, without seeming forced.

The 5 phases of charisma for introverts and shy people

- Skill

Growing up with certain complexes, I produced rejection at the first impression during my adolescence because treating others was,

39

frequently, somewhat surly and arrogant. Although I have not quite overcome it, after a lot of work, I have removed a good part of this, discovering that social skills are learned.

And the same happens with charisma; it is a skill that develops.

It is important to question the prejudices we have in this regard.

Society has sold us on being charismatic, and you have to be born with a gift and be outgoing. Lie!

Those people who seem to have a natural gift probably grew up in a context that allowed them to develop social skills from a young age. Some extroverts are incapable of being liked because they are pedantic, self-centered, speak badly, or do other things that scare people.

Defining charisma objectively helps you understand that you can develop it.

Charisma is a kind of magnetism that allows you to attract people, make them feel good in your presence, listen to you carefully and pay attention to what you say. So it depends entirely on how you behave.

Think of a situation in which things went well for you, you felt safe, and others listened to you. Seen like this, it is likely that on some occasions, you have projected charisma.

When you realize that charisma is the consequence of your actions, it is easier to see the possibility of developing it and achieving results.

As with all skills, you need to follow a method. To attract people and make them enjoy your company, you will have to get used to practicing three specific behaviors:

Listen carefully so that the other person feels important. Convey warmth so that she feels comfortable. Speak confidently so that he trusts you. If you are shy or introverted, this information does not serve you now, especially if you feel like you have nothing to say.

And it is that to show yourself authentically and attract people to you, and you cannot just be a package, like an empty gift package inside; you need to have substance.

You have to work to become an interesting person.

Because to have a charismatic personality, you must have your ideas and values, convictions that are born from having professional experience, experiences that enrich your world, and an image of yourself that you feel proud of.

- Read books on multiple topics to expand your general culture and ability to converse.
- Have hobbies and develop skills as the skills will increase your self-confidence in specific areas.
- Learn to speak in public, so you know how to present your ideas effectively (I teach you how to do it in this video).
- Do sports; you will feel good and gain security.
- Do activities that lead you to meet people with common interests.

As Henry Ford wisely said:

If you think you can or can't, you are right.

So think of charisma as a project that develops in phases and get down to work looking, first, to grow as a person.

- Context

According to Susan Cain, author of the book "The Power of Introverts," extroverts feel great when they receive large amounts of stimulation, while introverts feel better when they are in quieter, more discreet settings. So the key to maximizing your talents is putting yourself in the right stimulation zone for you.

Or in other words, if you choose the context wisely, you will feel more comfortable and achieve better results. And, just as you can feel a high level of self-confidence at certain times, the same happens with charisma. It is easier to develop in the contexts in which we feel comfortable.

And what do I mean by context? Mainly where, when, and who.

Where:

As a young man, it was a lot of stress for me to flirt in clubs or bars, while I felt much more comfortable in places with less noise.

If you are shy or introverted, quiet places with few people, small social events or gatherings at friends' houses will be better for you.

When:

Choose times when you feel a high level of energy.

If you are a day person, choose to socialize during the day; you will enjoy it more than if you do it at night, at which time you will be more off.

Who (or with whom):

It has a lot to do with the time and place. When you choose the time and place where you feel best, you are more likely to run into people like you, which will make it much easier to connect.

Whenever you can, plan your social life, meetings, and everything that leads you to interact with other people within the context you feel best.

Because it is not about trying to become an extrovert, but about flourishing, reinforcing what you are already good at, within a context in which you feel good.

- Practice and preparation

Your willingness and ability to connect with strangers is like a muscle... it grows stronger with practice and warms up with preparation.

Without practice, it is impossible to progress consistently. Without prior preparation, it is more difficult to face situations that take you out of your comfort zone than if you arrive with greased machinery.

Imagine a 10-step ladder. Which is easier, go up one step at a time, or take momentum, run up to it and jump from the ground to the top? The answer is obvious.

Charisma is a ladder of more than ten steps. To climb it, you have to walk one step at a time.

Now, to achieve this, you have to be moderately fit, and this requires preparation, which, practically, means:

- Know what you want. Because when you have clear goals, it is easier to act with determination.
- Test in low-risk environments and increase the difficulty step by step. Example: If you want to speak in public in front of 100 people, start by toasting at the family meal in front of 10. With each attempt, you will feel the fulfillment associated with the achievement, and this will give you the strength to continue.
- Take care of your body, rest well, eat healthily and play sports to improve your energy, your self-confidence, and the image you transmit of yourself.
- Take care of your mind, surrounding yourself with people who bring you positivity and push you to achieve your goals.
- Just as athletes stretch and warm-up before competing, it will be useful to warm up to give your best before each match.

Practically, this means:

43

Dress for the occasion with an outfit that looks good on you and makes you feel good.

Start with easy conversations before entering a social event. For example: on the way to the place, ask ten strangers to explain how to get there.

Charge energy before and after. If social situations consume your energy, before going out to any event and once it is over, spends time alone to recharge.

Practice and get ready, so the charisma muscle is strong and ready.

- Intention

Charisma is an intention-based mind game because magnetism begins with what you project visually, depending entirely on what you feel.

Think of a time when you felt a lot of joy; what did you project? Surely positive energy, bright eyes, and a feeling of being bigger than usual.

But do you remember a sad moment? Sure your energy was low, your gesture showed you smaller than usual, and your gaze was lost anywhere.

To project an authentic, charismatic personality, always start your interactions with three mental tricks: curiosity, friendship, and conviction.

Curiosity leads you to be genuinely interested in people, showing yourself as someone who listens and pays attention. This leads you to seek eye contact, get closer, and show the other person that their presence is important.

Friendship unites us with other people with whom we feel an affinity. With friends, we feel good, and we are open. If you treat the people you just met as if they were your friends, the interaction will flow, and you will have a good time. You will smile more often and convey goodwill, making them feel comfortable.

Conviction, like faith, is an immense force. Being convinced means firmly believe, which helps others to believe. Speaking from conviction, your body language is expansive and your posture upright, showing a high self-confidence level.

By combining these three mind tricks, you will show a genuinely charismatic personality.

- Focus

A frequent concern that I have heard among students and clients is the following: "I don't know what to say." This produces insecurity, and many times prevents us from approaching strangers. We think that if we open our mouths, we will speak nonsense and make a fool of ourselves.

One of the reasons why curiosity is useful is that people usually like to talk about themselves.

This benefits you. Because if you don't know what to say, you have to get the other person to talk about themselves for both of you to be happy. And by putting the spotlight on the other person, you free yourself from making intelligent comments.

Two resources will help you: The question and the recognition.

By asking her questions, you show interest, you make her feel good about talking about herself, and she gives you useful information to connect with.

Keep in mind that everyone is passionate about something. Look for what he is passionate about, and you will see how his eyes will shine when talking about it. Besides, if you discover topics that both of you are passionate about, it will generate a very high connection because few things unite as shared passions.

In the process, you will discover qualities and experiences that you will find worthy of a compliment. Tell her. This will make her feel even better in your presence, as long as the compliment is sincere.

So ask, listen and acknowledge. It is all you need to connect.

Start developing your charisma right now.

Learning to be a charismatic person, being shy or introverted, is not an easy task. It will require you to do things that are uncomfortable for you and confront you with the fear of negative judgment associated with rejection, failure, or ridicule, especially at the beginning.

But as you challenge yourself and allow yourself to expand your comfort zone, you will realize that you really can do it.

- So get out there and start developing new skills that make you a complete person.
- Choose the context well to increase your chances of success.
- Practice frequently, starting small, and warm up your engines before each match.
- Start with the right intention to foster fulfilling interactions.
- And finally, focus on the other person so that you connect with them without carrying the weight of the conversation.

If you do this, you will be just one step away from becoming a charismatic person, and your shyness and introversion will be forgotten. You will no longer have to Google how to develop charisma for introverts and shy people.

CHAPTER TWO

ATTRACT WOMEN WITH THE PSYCHOLOGY OF ATTRACTION.

T he ability to attract sexually or generate erotic interest in other people is a skill. But you don't need to have an angel face or spectacular eyes to do it. Some other elements and factors are valued equally or even more.

The First Impression Is Decisive.

As much as we boast on numerous occasions that "what matters is the inside," the eyes cannot escape a physique. The first impression always matters. Let us think that once this first impression is formed, the person will confirm that impression. Something that can go in our favor if this first impression is good, but very against if it is bad.

Appearance is processed in the brain instantly before we even know it. Thus, in less than 2 seconds, we have already made a quick judgment of the person in front of us. His way of dressing, his complexion, his nose... Everything is cataloged and classified. He has already told us a lot without saying anything, or rather, we have interpreted a lot.

It takes us only a tenth of a second to determine how attractive it is when it comes to the face. With which, there is love at first sight. At least the love of the physical.

The psychologist and sexologist Antoni Bolinches assures that: "the woman looks first at intelligence; then, in sympathy, if you have fun with him: and finally, in personality, in his being a mature, magnetic man." He clarifies that the intelligence that attracts is "the constructive one, which makes a woman feel good, not the intelligence that overwhelms."

According to Bolinches, men "at first are hooked by female attractiveness, but over time, that attraction diminishes. And so they need that relationship to be more or less comfortable. They are looking for a travel companion who provides emotional support".

Hair And Smell, Key Elements

Hair is one of the attributes that we value the most. Specifically, women's preferences move between two poles. On the one hand, according to research, it is deduced that lustrous and dense hair is attractive to them. On the other hand, baldness is not as badly considered as some may believe. This is because hair loss is directly related to high levels of testosterone in the blood. Many studies consider that this hormone is responsible for the attractiveness that we find in the other. So if you are starting to bald, you have too much testosterone, which is also attractive. Otherwise, you can count on the physical preference of women and try to have your hair neat.

The smell is the second deciding factor. Unless we are fetishists about it, an unpleasant stench makes us do anything but want to mate with the other. In any case, it is preferable not to risk and opt for perfumes or deodorants with fresh and pleasant aromas, especially if we are looking to make an excellent first impression since the scents are those that also last as memories in women.

Beauty Is Not Everything.

Although they are not beautiful in most people's eyes, some people do have "something" special that makes them irresistible. It is an "I don't know what" that works as a magnet for them: their way of speaking, their gaze, their laugh, their humor. That "interesting" feature is also successful.

On the other hand, a few days a month, women are more attractive to men during their ovulation period.

At that time, men are attracted to a set of sweet and pleasant aromas that women give off. For example, pheromones make them feel attracted and raise blood testosterone more than 100% in just minutes. It is important to emphasize that men must let women know that they like their aroma to feel pleased and attracted.

Other Physical Factors That Arouse Sexual Attraction

Unconsciously, all humans tend to be attracted to symmetrical faces. This anthropometric trait is considered the greatest exponent of beauty. The eyes' color is not so determining. Still, the intensity of the limbal ring, the strip that exists around the iris, is. The darker it is, the more attractive we find it.

Good stature and well-built muscles also add to the appeal. If we go back to the first stages of human evolution, we observed how the strength of Homo sapiens was the key element for the survival of the whole family.

And this heritage has continued relatively to this day. Today, bigger and taller men give women a greater sense of security and protection. This explanation would be part of the evolutionary theory that explains the variables that make us more attractive. However, if these attributes are lacking, you can start working on them by exercising or practicing a sport. Height is not a complication since there are even

49

smaller women to whom a short man may seem tall, too. Some women prefer men of the same height or shorter. It is not an absolute requirement.

We Are Not So Different From Animals

We know that some of the elements that attract us most physically from other people are equally valued by certain animal species. For example, lionesses also look at males' fur, specifically in its quantity, density, and color. The more intense and dark it is, the more indicative it is of high testosterone levels and the more they like it.

Female red partridges prefer males whose colors are more intense. These shades are synonymous with a parasite-free immune system and a good diet. On the other hand, the horns, teeth, or crests have transmitted the females' protection and "symbolize" power.

The Wrinkle Is Also Beautiful

The signs of youth are not much better valued than their opposites. At least, not as much as what they want us to believe from some mass advertising and marketing media, Creams, tricks, treatments... The fight against age and the passage of time.

But a study carried out by the Autonomous University of Madrid refutes this propaganda effect. Their conclusions suggest that women feel more sexual attraction to facial features that distinguish a male from a female face than those that show youth.

That is, they value more, for example, the presence of facial hair, marked lips, or bushy eyebrows, than the fact that there is no mark or scar. Even the brands make some more attractive to women since it is a mystery to know the history that led to this consequence.

Love And Attraction Are Not The Same.

Very linked to sexual attraction is falling in love. But it is influenced by other factors, such as the circumstances and the time in which each person is, their receptivity, affinities, desires, values, or shared interests. Everything counts.

Therefore, sexual attraction is physical and chemical. Without a doubt, as we see, chemicals (substances and hormones) contribute to its emergence. Still, without a good first impression, there is a lot of ground to be traced. There is no doubt that sexual tastes and preferences vary from person to person. However, an assortment of good impressions that generate pleasurable sensations in each of our senses will help trigger that sex appeal.

The Five Definitive Laws Of Attraction:

How We Choose Our Partner

We meet thousands of people throughout our lives. Still, only a handful of them attract our attention, and only a few end up being our partners. Why do we choose some candidates and not others? What makes a person attract us? These are questions that have preoccupied philosophers throughout history and psychology since it was born as such. And although it seems as old a topic as humanity itself, new research is published every year about it. Studies on the matter are more or less framed around two main theories:

The evolutionary theory believes that our choice of mate is based on purely biological criteria: we look for a person with whom we have a better chance of surviving and reproducing. This is why men prefer the most fertile women (young and with better genes, prettier) and women to those men who guarantee the family's stability (the wealthiest and most committed).

The social theory believes that social, not biological, processes guide our mate choice. According to this, the laws of attraction are guided by men and women's roles in society. We, therefore, seek the partner that our social environment expects us to find. According to psychologist Alice Eagly, one of the main defenders of this theory, women are attracted to men with more money and power because society has limited their ability to have money and power, not because biology pushes them to do so evolutionists think.

Although there are fervent defenders of each theory among psychologists, most researchers accept that biological and social aspects influence our behavior. Therefore, both approaches are not exclusive but complementary. As Dr. Noam Shpancer, professor at Otterbein University, explains in Psychology Today, there are some laws of attraction that have been widely studied and accepted by most psychologists:

- The law of familiarity "Touch makes love," The saying goes, and that's what psychologists think. If we do not have frequent contact with a person, it is impossible for us to fall in love with them and, much less, to think about being their partner. The more time we spend with a person, the more chances there are that we like him. There is also a saying that "where there is trust is disgusting," and, indeed, some people fall apart as they spend more time together. Still, according to Spencer, this is only the exception that proves the rule.

- The law of physical attraction. No matter how long we go through a person, we will not like it if we do not find it attractive. The physical influences, of course, and in a decisive way. The harsh reality is that no one is willing to spend their days with a person they consider physically repellent. Otherwise, as Shpancer explains, physical attraction is governed by market laws: "The best merchandise is the most expensive, so buyers who cannot offer what they ask for have to choose what they can afford. Deep down, the rich ride in Mercedes, the middle-class ride in a Toyota, and the poor ride public transportation. The same thing happens with physical attractiveness. The most beautiful people end up with others who are very handsome, the mediocre with the mediocre, etc.".

- The law of personality. Research has identified two personality traits that make a person particularly attractive: a person's competence, or level of intelligence and social skills, and their "warmth," that is, their ability to be close and caring. If you are wise and affectionate, you will flirt more easily.

- The law of proximity. As anyone who has had a long-distance relationship knows, either the parties meet soon or the courtship will fail miserably. The usual thing is that we choose as a couple of someones that we have close, whom we can see but daily, almost, because it is the simplest for both parties.

- The law of similarity. The studies leave no room for doubt: we are attracted to people who are like us. Our partner does not have to be the same, but they have to share certain hobbies, values , and concerns. If we can choose between several people (as we all do), we prefer someone who has things common to a very different person. These five laws operate equally in men and women. They are decisive in choosing potential candidates, but how do we make the final decision? Why do some couples last us for months, years, and others a lifetime? According to Shpancer, "these laws serve to choose the candidates, but they do not work in the final selection." In his opinion, "biology and the environment push us to go to the right store, but it cannot determine what we are going to buy. We decide that ourselves. In the final selection, a subjective, dark and capricious internal process intervenes, which does not necessarily obey the dictates of reason, evolution, cultural pressure, and not even our plans and intentions".

As an alpha, you must be realistic with your limitations to consider attracting females, so you must know these laws. That way, you guide yourself with your search.

The attraction is one of the reasons that can lead us to establish a loving relationship.

Some authors consider that affiliation is the basic phenomenon on which the processes of attraction and love rest. Affiliation is a basic human tendency that leads to seeking other people's company and whose primary function is to ensure the survival of both the individual and the species. In this sense, it is considered that one of the objectives of the affiliation is to enter into relationships, express love and sexuality.

Attraction

Interpersonal attraction can be understood as the judgment that one person makes of another along an attitudinal dimension whose extremes are positive evaluation (love) and negative evaluation (hate). In addition to this cognitive-evaluative dimension, this judgment is associated with behaviors (e.g., trying to do things with the person that attracts us), feelings (e.g., feeling sad when we cannot be with that person), and other cognitions (e.g., attributing to that person many positive characteristics).

The Consequences Of Association And Reinforcement.

The effects of the association on interpersonal attraction, following classical conditioning principles, consist of being attracted to those who appear to be associated with good experiences. We will dislike those associated with bad experiences. In this sense, the MUM effect consists of people resist transmitting bad news to others, even if we have nothing to do with them. When transmitting them, we will appear associated with the negative event before the eyes of the receiver. We will therefore be unattractive to them.

Exchange and interdependence. According to the theory of social exchange, a person will be attractive to us if we believe that the rewards derived from such a relationship are greater than the costs involved. The judgment of the person's attractiveness involved in a said relationship depends on the comparisons we make using two criteria: a) the comparison level based on past experiences. Any current situation will only be judged as beneficial depending on this comparison, which previous love relationships can form, and, b) the level of comparison with alternatives. A somewhat good relationship can be the best evaluated if it is the only alternative we have.

In addition to these psychosocial explanations, a series of factors play a fundamental role in the appearance and maintenance of the attraction that we come to feel towards certain people. Next, we will review the most relevant ones.

Proximity

Proximity not only gets people to know each other, it often influences dating and marriages as well. Research by Festinger, Schachter, and Back showed that the three people with whom college students living in a dorm had the best relationships were the people who lived closest to each other. Likewise, authors such as Byrne and Buehler have verified that the students' relationships during the semester are a function of the distance between the seats. That is that physical proximity influences the fact that the students get to know each other. However, the correlations found between physical distance and attraction do not assure us that proximity causes relationships. It could be that people who share certain characteristics (e.g., religion, economic status, etc.) prefer to live close to each other.

There are several explanations about the influence of physical proximity when establishing relationships:

- The people who are closest physically are also, generally, the most accessible.

- With repeated exposure, feelings of anxiety about the unknown decrease, and that new person gradually becomes more familiar.
- Proximity can increase familiarity, and familiarity can, in turn, increase attraction. The effect of mere exposure is that the repeated perception of an initially neutral or positive stimulus leads to a greater attraction to the stimulus.
- Similarity can also increase this familiarity since people who share certain spaces tend to resemble each other in other aspects, such as ideology, aspirations, problems, etc. We will tend to get together either because we are similar or because we have become similar due to being together.
- Finally, according to theories of cognitive consistency, when we have to spend a lot of time with a person, and the relationship is unpleasant for us, we tend to restore balance, either by trying to get away from it or by discovering that that person was not as unpleasant as we assumed.

Proximity positively influences attraction as long as the person is initially positive or neutral, not negative.

Negative And Positive Affect

Experiments consistently show that positive feelings lead to positive evaluations of others, liking, and sympathy. In contrast, negative feelings lead to negative evaluations, dislike, and antipathy. Affection can influence the attraction of two forms:

First, someone else can do something that makes you feel good or bad; people who make you feel good will tend to like you, and if they make you feel bad, you will be disliked.

Second, suppose a person is present only when your positive and negative feelings are activated (for whatever reason) as a consequence. In that case, this person will also be nice or unpleasant to you. The general idea is based on classical conditioning. When an attitudinal object is associated with a stimulus that causes negative or positive feelings, the observer develops negative or positive attitudes towards the object. Numerous experimenters have shown that positive affect leads to liking others, while negative affect leads to dislike.

If positive reactions can be transferred from person to person, so can negative reactions. If negative emotions make other people unpleasant to us, and if affection is easily associated with anyone, then we transfer our negative feelings from one person to another if we see them together. Research on stigmata, negatively perceived characteristics (e.g., race, age, foreign accent, physical disability, etc.) indicates that this negative association occurs just as easily as positive associations. Even if a stigma is overcome, the previous stigma's effect will not necessarily dissipate.

Personality Traits

Anderson found that the five most valued traits were being sincere, honest, understanding, loyal, and trustworthy. Likewise, in Moya's research, the best-evaluated personality characteristics were understanding, loyalty, ability to capture others' feelings, sincerity, and joy. Other studies have shown that the most valued traits in people are grouped into two sets: a) affection (e.g., affectionate, friendly, happy, and considerate), non-verbal cues (e.g., smiling, looking attentively, expressing emotions), and dispositions attitudinal (e.g., showing a liking for people); and, b) competence, which includes social skills and intelligence (e.g., having an interesting conversation, etc.

Another series of attributes related to the power, prestige, or social position of the person we interact with is of considerable importance to qualify as attractive, especially for males. In fact, in press advertisements, women offer physical attractiveness and seek financial security. In contrast, men offer financial positions and request certain physical characteristics.

Similarity

The results of psychosocial research show that, in general, as the similarity between people increases, so does attraction. The two dimensions of similarity that have been studied the most by social psychologists are attitudinal and personality similarity.

The similarity of attitudes refers to how two individuals share the same attitudes about a range of topics. Byrne indicates that the greater the similarity, the greater the attraction. This result has been found in people of all ages, in very different groups, and different countries.

The study by Smeaton, Byrne, and Murnen confirmed the proportion hypothesis that predicted that attraction differed according to the proportion of similar attitudes shared. Despite these results, a series of investigations indicated a slightly greater effect of different attitudes than similar ones, in part because most people assume that a stranger, especially an attractive one, harbors attitudes similar to theirs. This assumption of general agreement with one's opinions is called the false consensus effect, and a consequence is that agreement is expected while disagreement is surprising. Suppose on some special issues. An individual believes that he or she has a minority opinion and that the majority of people disagree. In that case, the disagreement will be expected and will have less effect than an unexpected disagreement.

In the case of personality similarity, the research results are less consistent. Moya argues that the lack of relationship between personality similarity and attraction can be explained because personality characteristics are not usually publicly exhibited. Other times, the personality trait's very nature attracts both alike and those who are different. In general, it has been shown that similarity produces greater attraction than difference, at least in the following characteristics: sexual orientation (that is, if the person is male, female, or androgynous), depression, type A behavior, seeking sensation, and cognitive style.

The following explanations show how similarity can influence attraction, both positively and negatively:

- Similar attitudes activate positive affect, while different attitudes activate negative affect, affecting the attraction.
- According to cognitive consistency and balance theory theories, people naturally organize their likes and dislikes in a balanced way. In this way, balanced relationships occur when someone is similar, and we like them.
- The similarity is reinforcing. The most valuable proof that others approve of our ideas, customs, and tastes is the fact that they have them (Festinger, 1954) precisely. This formulation suggests that we are interested in other people's opinions not because we seek precision but solely because we want to verify what we already believe. However, when people resemble each other because they have some negative characteristic, then it is possible that the similarity, instead of leading to attraction, leads to rejection. Sometimes, the difference can be more reinforcing than the similarity since it allows us to learn new things.

Valuable. Also, feeling unique and special is highly valued.

- The choice of people similar to us in certain dimensions (e.g., educational level, social class, or physical attractiveness) can result from comparing and evaluating the various alternatives we have and their costs and benefits. This is because, generally, the most valued people are the hardest to get. According to expectation-value theories, in real life, we will feel attracted to the most valued people within the field of those who may reciprocate us. In this sense, the pairing hypothesis refers to the fact that married couples and couples in love tend to become couples based on their similar physical attractiveness.

Finally, when questioned directly, university students do not consider social, ideological, and religious similarity as a relevant attribute in a partner's choice. Two explanations would account for this result: a) people are not aware of the importance of situational determinants of behavior; and b) this attribute may be important at the beginning of the relationship, but not for the choice of an intimate partner. However, according to French data, couples' meeting spaces would be closed or reserved for people with a high socioeconomic level. For people with a low socioeconomic level, they would be public open places to all the world. This suggests that even though certain similarities are not relevant when choosing a partner, it is more likely that couples have certain similarities (social, ideological, religious) to the extent that the meeting spaces for couples differ according to the economic stratum.

Reciprocity

Once two individuals discover enough similarities to move toward friendship, an additional step is imperative. One of the factors that influence effective relationships' development is the existence or not reciprocity. We are also attractive to these people. Almost everyone is happy to receive such positive feedback, and it is quite unpleasant to be evaluated negatively. An exception is that individuals with negative self-concepts sometimes respond well to accurate negative evaluations, possibly because they are consistent with their self-schema.

Although mutual liking is often expressed in words, the first signs of attraction can be non-verbal indicators. Gold, Ryckman, and Mosley found that when a woman responded positively to a man by gazing at him, talking to him, and approaching him, he tended to be attracted to her, even when he knew their attitudes differed.

Someone who has a bad image of us is not rewarding. Besides, according to the cognitive consistency theories, a person likes me and dislikes me in an unstable situation. Aronson and Coe found that when two people shared the dislike of a third, the attraction between them was greater than when they did not share that feeling.

Physical Attractiveness

As Hatfield and Sprecher indicate, given the same characteristics, a person with a pleasant physical appearance is more attractive than another with less physical attractiveness. Physical attractiveness is especially decisive in the first encounters or when the contact is superficial. According to the process of cognitive ignorance, the person that we initially decide has no interest, is not paid attention to, and is forgotten. Research has shown that men often ignore unattractive women.

In various studies, both men and women and people of different races have agreed that an attractive female face is one with both a childlike appearance (large, wide-set eyes, small nose, wide smile, and small chin) and mature features (prominent cheekbones, cheeks narrow, high eyebrows and large pupils). Height has been valued positively in men's physical attractiveness but negatively in women. Another physical characteristic that seems to influence physical attractiveness is body build, the waist-to-hip ratio in women's cases. Alice found that attractiveness decreased notably when an unattractive body matched a very attractive face. Also, overweight people are generally perceived as less attractive.

The following explanations show why a pleasant physique is attractive to us:

- According to implicit theories of personality, there are numerous beliefs about which people's characteristics are associated with each other in our society. In this sense, the halo effect considers that whoever has a good quality will also have other good qualities. Some research has shown that people tend to believe that attractive men and women are more stable, interesting, sociable, independent, dominant, exciting,

61

sexy, balanced, socially skilled, and more successful than those who are not attractive. However, physical attractiveness can be associated with negative characteristics. For example, very attractive women may be judged as more materialistic and vain than less attractive women. They may be considered more guilty than the latter when they are tried for a crime involving deception.

- Attractive people also attract us because our public image is favored when associating with a person of these characteristics. Thus, various studies have confirmed that when a man appears accompanied by a very attractive woman, the impression he causes improves.

- Attractive people can behave in a way that increases their evaluation and makes them more attractive. Reis showed that attractive men had more relationships with women and developed a greater social competence in this field than less attractive men. However, the most attractive women did not establish more interactions with men, were less assertive and more fearful in their relationships with men than the less attractive women.

- According to the affect-centered model, good-looking individuals activate the positive effect, and affect, as already discussed, is an important determinant of attraction.

People are not entirely correct in estimating how others judge their attractiveness. Men (but not women) overestimate their good looks. Because many biases favor attractiveness, it is not surprising that many people care about their appearance. This preoccupation with one's attractiveness and fear of negative judgments by others is known as appearance anxiety.

Judgments about whether a person is attractive are not solely a matter of the person's physical details in question. Situational factors influencing the observer are also important. Kenrick found that if a person had previously seen several highly attractive individuals, the person in question is less attractive.

Behavioral indicators also affect perceptions. People react more positively to a person whose gait is youthful than someone with an elderly-like gait, regardless of gender or age. Furthermore, adults who seem very young are also judged as weak, naive, and incompetent, but loving and honest. Those who appear to be very mature are perceived as more dominant and attractive but less affectionate and friendly.

Attractiveness, Perception And Social Behavior

Contrary to the beliefs that beauty depends on who looks and that there are radically different beauty patterns, fifteen studies have confirmed that people of different nations and ethnic groups agree when they indicate what type of individuals are physically attractive and not. For example, people of different cultures (13 countries and four ethnic groups) judged a female face as more attractive if it showed the following characteristics: large eyes with dilated pupils, small nose, high cheekbones, narrow face with thin cheeks, wide smile, lips thick or full and small chin. However, other results show cultural variability: blacks in the United States evaluate heavier women as more attractive than whites in the United States. This suggests that although there is agreement on the body structure and attractive facial features, there are ethnic variations in the parameters of body weight and size that define an attractive person.

Studies allow the conclusion that people perceive and evaluate attractive people more favorably; it is the effect called 'what is beautiful is good.' The review by Langlois confirmed that the most attractive children were evaluated as more friendly, more competent, with a better fit and affective balance, and with greater interpersonal competence than less attractive children. The same was true of attractive adults: they were judged as more competent at work, more friendly, and better fit or mental health.

Consistently, attractive children and adults were also treated more positively. There were fewer negative interactions with the most

63

attractive children, more positive interactions, and more care for more. While attractive adults received more attention and were given more rewards. More positive interactions were established with them, fewer negative interactions, and more help and cooperation.

It has also been confirmed that attractive people act more positively (e.g., they are more popular, slightly more intelligent, have more adapted social skills and behaviors, have better physical health) and possess more positive characteristics (e.g., greater self-esteem, better mental health, more extraversion).

Finally, attractive people self-perceive or judge themselves slightly better than less attractive people (they perceive themselves as more competent and better mental health).

Attractiveness Factors

The above results confirm the explanation of attractiveness: a) cultural norms and values determine the behavior and judgments of the 'judges' and 'evaluated' through their learning; b) expectations and stereotypes are learned ('there is no lame or one-eyed person good') and are confirmed through behaviors and self-fulfilling prophecy (e.g., when faced with someone unattractive, I treat them worse, to which they respond more negatively).

Although the tendency to perceive that 'what is beautiful is good' is common in all the cultures studied, what differs are inferred positive traits. For example, in Korea, it is inferred that an attractive person cares more about others and is more integrated, consistent with that culture's collectivist values . While in the US, it is inferred that the greater the attractiveness, the greater the assertiveness, dominance, and strength, consistent with the dominant individualistic and competitive cultural values in those societies. Another study with Asians (Taiwan Chinese) confirmed that attractive people were evaluated positively on both socially desirable and undesirable traits. Still, there was no relationship between attractiveness and judgment on non-normative traits (of medium desirability). That is, physical attractiveness is associated with traits that are normative in a given culture.

Now, three facts question the sociocultural explanation about 'what is beautiful is good':

- The relationship between the attractiveness of a person and the judgments and behaviors attributed to him is not greater in adults than in children. However, according to social-cultural arguments, people learn beauty patterns and their correlations as they socialize in a given culture, so adults should show this effect with more intensity.
- Likewise, the relationship between attractiveness and the judgments and behaviors attributed to a person is similar for men and women. This fact questions the sociocultural idea that this effect is based on different gender roles that emphasize more female physical beauty than male.
- Lastly, the self-perceptions of attractive people are only slightly more positive. This fact questions the sociocultural perspective that indicates that perceptions and interactions are internalized in the self-concept.

Attractiveness And Evolutionary Explanations

The high cross-cultural agreement in the judgments about attractive features (infantile face, amphora body for women, regular face, and muscular triangular body for men) is consistent with an evolutionary explanation.

However, a series of facts also question the evolutionary hypotheses:

- Since attractive traits similarly influence men and women when it comes to inferring judgments and behaviors about people, the evolutionary hypothesis is questioned that states that when it comes to choosing a partner, attractiveness is more important for men since it indicates the greater reproductive capacity of women, while resources are for women, since it indicates the ability of men to ensure the survival of their offspring.

- Since the relationship between the person's attractiveness and the judgment and behavior attributed to it is similar for children and adults, the evolutionary hypothesis affirms that attractiveness must be important because it is related to reproduction is also questioned, that is, with adulthood.

The results are congruent with the evolutionary hypothesis that attractiveness is a general indicator of good health - the so-called good gene theory. The fact that it associates the attractiveness of a person with their better evaluation and quality of interaction in childhood is also consistent with the evolutionary theory of parental investment, which suggests that parents invest more in children with greater survivability and reproduction - healthier because they are more beautiful, regardless of whether they are boys or girls.

Love

Love is such a complex phenomenon that it has given rise to many definitions

broad and vague that can be applied to other intense emotional events such as bereavement or rape. Besides, love is a dynamic process that is constantly changing during the relationship, so its definition will vary depending on its state. The data provided by various investigations carried out from different disciplines clearly show that there is a progressive decrease in initial passion and that this, together with the gradual growth of commitment, gives rise to a cycle with an initial phase of passionate love strongly associated with sexual desire followed. of a phase of partner love that lasts for about two years in most cases.

Types of Love

One of the basic types is sexual or passionate love that would be characterized by:

- Strong uncontrollable feelings of attraction towards the desired person and of anxiety and discomfort in their absence;
- Strong physiological activation and sexual desire;
- Obsessive thoughts or rumination about the loved object; and,
- A certain pattern of behaviors, such as expressing affection for the desired person, supporting them physically and emotionally, and unconditional acceptance.

On the other hand, non-passionate romantic love would be composed of:

- Thoughts of need, of 'caring for' and of trust in the partner;
- Feeling of well-being, difficulty concentrating, and 'floating in the clouds'
- And, to a lesser extent, intense physical reactions; and
- Behaviors of intimacy, support, and tolerance of the other.

Of all the love typologies, Lee will be the first to try to empirically validate his proposal. Lee distinguished three basic love styles: Eros, Ludus, and Storge.

The combination, in different degrees, of these primary styles, would give us other three secondary styles independent of the first: Mania, Pragma, and Agape:

- **Eros or passionate love** is characterized by an irresistible passion, intense feelings, strong physical attraction, and sexual activity. The Eros lover values love highly but is not obsessed with it or pressure his partner to intensity but rather allows things to develop mutually. The characteristic of this type is self-confidence and high self-esteem.

- **Ludus or playful love**, with little emotional involvement and no future expectations. This style of love does not have a preferred physical style but rather likes all kinds of partners. Even though many people see this love as morally negative, Ludus does not try to hurt other people. He usually makes the game rules very clear before starting the relationship.

- **torge, or friendly love**, is characterized by a long-lasting commitment that develops slowly and prudently and is based on intimacy, friendship and affection. The similarity in terms of values and attitudes is much more important to Storge than physical appearance or sexual satisfaction. The orientation of this love is more to seek a long-term commitment than a short-term passion.

- **Mania is obsessive love**, with a strong dependence on the partner, intense jealousy, possessiveness, mistrust, and ambivalence. This lover tries to force the couple into commitment without waiting for it to evolve naturally.

- **Pragma refers to pragmatic love**, love based on the rational search for the ideal partner. The pragmatic lover considers age, education, social status, religion, or the ability to be a good father or mother. Unlike Storage, in which love can grow without being particularly concerned about the partner's future projections or the partner's family background, the pragmatic lover is likely to establish conditions before developing a relationship.

- **Agape or altruistic love**, of absolute renunciation and totally selfless surrender. It is a rather romantic love in which sexuality and sensuality are not relevant.

The Hendrick and Hendrick scale of attitudes towards love is the one that evaluates this typology from an individual approach to love relationships. With this scale, Hendrick and Hendrick classified the romantic stories described by university students in these six different styles:

*(34%), Storage (66%), Ludus (2%), mania (2 %), pragma (17%)
and agape (2%).*

More than three-quarters of the stories described corresponded to partner love, followed by a third of them framed in passionate love.

From the point of view of gender differences, Hendrick and Hendrick found that men, compared with women, attach more importance to passionate love (eros) and playful or entertaining (Ludus). Women, compared with men, are more inclined towards friendly love (Storge), logical (pragma), and possessive (mania). These results have been interpreted from the perspective of the functions that these forms of love have had for each sex in the species' evolution.

Functions Of Love And Evolution

The evolutionary conception provides us with arguments about the biological functionality of loving behavior for the individual as a member of a species. This approach sees love as a natural part of the human condition and, perhaps, natural to other species. Love is biologically relevant if it helps promote species' survival, a central theme of evolution theory. Five million years ago, the survival of species depended on reproductive success. Sexual desire and commitment, respectively related to previous aspects of reproductive success, were reinforced in higher primates whose biochemistry led them to seek pleasure from sexual activity and female-male bonding and parents-descendants. Ancestors who acted this way were more likely to pass on their genes than those who were not motivated to sexual activity and/or establish stable emotional bonds. As a result of this evolutionary process, humans are genetically pre-programmed to have sexual activity, to fall in love (stable emotional relationships with a partner), and to care for descendants (parental love). The evolutionary perspective admits that current environmental factors, social influences, and non-genetic aspects of the organism determine sexual activity. Although, the historical influence or the ten thousand years of civilization established as in which we currently live, has acted only during 5% of the existence of the species or over 400 of the 100,000 generations of humanity.

This theory socio-biological, we can explain sex differences in sexual behavior and love from two core processes that have to do with the differential parental investment and sexual selection:

- The sexual selection consists of two different processes: a) Intra-sexual selection refers to the pressure that members of one sex exert on the other through competition. In a species in which males compete for females through their hunting ability and strength, the strongest and best hunting individuals are more likely to dominate the competition and survive; and, b) Epigamic selection is the other part of sexual selection. If one sex selects its partners of the other sex-based on certain attributes such as physical strength and aggressiveness, these attributes must be more characteristic of one sex than the other.
- Is defined Parental investment as the expenditure of time, energy, and risk of the parent in the offspring that increases the probabilities of survival of the latter (and therefore reproductive success) at the cost of the father's ability to invest in another offspring. While the typical parental investment may have been highly variable throughout our evolutionary history, the minimum possible parental investment of females, due to nine months of gestation and subsequent months of lactation, has been much greater than that of males in our species. A woman can have a maximum of 25 children, and the average number of children in simple hunter-gatherer societies is five. Ancestral males might have benefited reproductively from copulating with any fertile female if the risk was low. Therefore, it is reasonable to hypothesize that natural selection favored males who had low thresholds for sexual arousal and reactive to new sexually attractive females.

On the other hand, our female ancestors had little to gain reproductively and much to lose if they copulated randomly with new males. Selection is unlikely to have favored females who were sexually attracted to a wide variety of males or solely because of their presence.

According to the socio-biological theory predictions, in the case of the human species, since women must be fertile, they will be better sexual objects when they have a youthful and maternal appearance. For example, the narrower the waist is relative to the hip, the more men will prefer them and value them as more attractive, healthy, and reproductively valuable. It can also be assumed that women would be more selective in selecting their mates since they have a greater parental investment in their offspring than men and can father a few boys in a limited period.

Therefore, women are going to look for attached men with resources to protect themselves and their children. In particular, when choosing potential sexual partners, they will pay more attention to the attributes of status, dominance, and aggressiveness. They will select those with the greatest capacity to obtain resources.

Predictions from socio-biological theory regarding gender differences in behaviors are common with role theories that emphasize that women are assigned and socialized in passive, lower status, and communal roles while men do so. They are inactive roles of higher status and agentic; therefore, women should be less approving of casual relationships. They should have fewer different partners. Sociobiologists argue that although men may be somewhat more permissive than women in extramarital affairs, men especially disapprove of women having such relationships since they must guarantee paternity with the utmost certainty.

From this perspective, it is predicted that men will value playful love more, consistent with their lower parental investment and their positive orientation towards casual sex and obtaining the maximum number of possible partners. Women, given the greater parental investment and the effort necessary to raise a few descendants, will tend to value more pragmatic and friendly love, as well as the criteria of social power and status to choose their partner. Therefore, men's playful love and the pragmatic love of women would favor the species' reproduction.

According to these predictions, cross-cultural research has consistently confirmed socio-biological hypotheses that women prefer older sexual partners and evaluate them based on their resources. In contrast, men prefer younger and physically attractive partners. In this sense, Buss's cross-cultural research confirmed in 37 different countries that women tend to evaluate their male partners based on their economic capacity, ambition, and perseverance. In contrast, the attributes positively evaluated by men to choose a female partner are health, beauty, and youth, and they will choose those with the greatest signs of reproductive capacity. Likewise, in Oliver and Hyde's meta-analysis, men presented more permissive attitudes towards sexual relations, earlier initiation of coital sexual relations, a higher frequency of Intercourse, and a greater number of sexual partners than women. This greater male centrality in sexuality is supported by anthropological research. Of the 849 societies examined in Murdock's Ethnographic Atlas, 708 are polygamic (one husband for several wives). Only 4 are polyandrous (a woman can have two or more husbands). In addition to the four polyandrous, they are all polygamic, the reverse not being true.

According to the socio-biological augmentation, the differences between genders will be reinforced, especially in cultures that impose fewer social constraints. These allow the entire behavioral repertoire to be explored and allow innate differences to manifest more strongly.

Universal Character Of Love And Cultural Influence

From a cultural perspective, some authors have postulated the transcultural existence of romantic or passionate love. Thus, Jankowiak and Fischer, in a review of 186 cultures, have found that

88.5% of them have indicators of passionate love. Other authors, particularly social constructionists and relativists such as Averill, postulate that passionate love is a phenomenon constructed by social discourse at a given historical and cultural moment. Thus, Hendrick and Hendrick, among others, argue that it is exclusive to Western culture and emerged around the 12th century. However, some authors such as Berscheid point out that in much earlier documents, such as the Bible, Hindu, and classical Chinese texts, there are descriptions of desire and passionate love.

More and more psychologists, anthropologists, and other scholars believe that love is a universal phenomenon. However, its specific meaning can vary markedly from one culture to another at different times. Before the modern age, it was not a prerequisite for marriage. Hence, in many societies, it was arranged by parents or relatives, perhaps hoping that love would arise in the couple in the future. Still, there were no great expectations of romantic love. Studies carried out in Western cultures have found that the relationship between marriage and love has changed over the last thirty years. A generation ago, especially women wanted to marry even in the absence of romantic love. Still, since then, men and women have agreed on the idea of romantic love as the basis of marriage. It seems that in the 20th century, in Western societies, romantic love has become a fundamental reason for maintaining long-term marital relationships.

The belief that one should marry only for love becomes an ideology when it is widely shared by a society. Since people today share this belief, it is difficult to understand how marriages in previous centuries could have been happy. Perhaps the people of other times shared another ideology. Perhaps there was often early anticipation of sharing life with a partner, sexual fulfillment or coming to love the partner more deeply over the years. However, some of these anticipations sound a lot like today's anticipations except for 'falling in love.' It is possible that the bond between love and marriage has not changed as much. What may have changed is the ideology of love from 'marriages must Be arranged' to 'marriages must be based on love.' To some extent, this depends on how love is defined (Hendrick and Hendrick, 1986).

Socio-Structural Factors And Intimate Relationships

Some authors have insisted on the influence of social structure factors in beliefs and loving behaviors.

Guttentag and Secord stated that the demographic ratio between men and women is an important variable to explain the dominant type of love. When there are more men than women in the population, the few women are valued. An idealized vision of women, of the family, and a non-passionate romantic vision of love prevails. In this context, a more partner style of love would probably dominate. When there is an excess of women, the family and marriage will be devalued. Extra and pre-marital sex, singleness, and separations would be frequent, committed love would not be dominant, and a playful and erotic love style would predominate. These authors reviewed demographic data from different countries and historical periods, such as ancient Greece, medieval Europe, and the United States, that confirmed these hypotheses during different centuries.

On the other hand, Eagly and Wood argued that sex differences in the criteria for choosing an intimate partner should be smoothed out in societies characterized by greater gender equality, since men's preferences for younger women, capable of being good attractive housewives, as well as the importance given by women to men's social resources reflect the differences in status and roles between men and women. Reanalyzing the partner selection criteria, it was confirmed that the greater equality between the genders, evaluated by a UN indicator on the degree of labor and institutional insertion of women, as well as salary parity with men, there were fewer differences between the sexes in the importance assigned to financial resources and being a good householder as criteria for choosing a partner.

From this socio-structural perspective, the differences in beliefs about the love between nations and between genders depend on social resources, demographics, and distribution of power and status among gender roles. Socio Economic development will directly reinforce the importance of passionate love, love as a criterion and prerequisite for choosing an intimate partner and marrying. It allows the person to value subjective rather than practical aspects. Social and economic development, which is associated with a lower difference in status and power concerning gender roles, will cause more similarities in men's and women's responses about love. Levine concluded that economic development would reinforce individualism, the relative equality of opportunities between men and women (higher education, greater female labor participation, and legal equality), would increase the importance of subjective feelings and personal decisions in the formation of couples, which would be associated with an increase in divorces and a decrease in birth rates (greater control by the woman of contraception and greater planning of the offspring, not experienced as an obligation). Therefore, the differential distribution of resources and roles would explain the differences between men and women and between nations.

Cultural Factors And Intimate Relationships

Other studies have shown the influence of cultural values on beliefs about love.

Dion and Dion suggest that different cultural orientations strongly influence how people conceptualize love and intimacy.

The more individualistic cultures, in which intimate relationships are established face to face and more or less symmetrically, value the passionate romantic component of love more. In contrast, in collectivist societies, intimate relationships are organized through the extended family's intervention. The pragmatic and friendly aspects of love are valued more.

Thus, romantic love is a more important basis for marriage in individualism than in collectivist cultures. In the former, two people's love and individual decisions seem natural to form a stable couple. In the latter, in general, the formation of the couple is a decision of the elderly. It is based on arrangements that respond to the families' wishes, and it is a duty for the individuals. Most of humanity lives in collectivist cultures, and in general, the family has a great influence on marriages. Most of the brides are adolescents. In two-thirds of the societies, a dowry is paid for them. Marriage is conceived as a socioeconomic contract between the families. In 1980, in China, only a third of marriages were free from family influence. In 1989, in Korea, 40% of marriages were arranged, as 72% of Turkish women interviewed in the 1970s. Parental arranged marriage was very common among Indian and Pakistani immigrants.

From this sociocultural and normative perspective, the evaluative norms would explain the differences between genders and between nations more than the differences in resources and roles. Even controlling the level of economic development, cultures whose values emphasize autonomy and individual decisions, and value internal attributes and feelings (individualistic), will reinforce the importance of passionate love, love as a criterion and prerequisite for choosing a partner. And marriage. Collectivist cultures, which are characterized by greater differences in status and emphasize family decisions and normative duties, will give less importance to love as a criterion and prerequisite for forming a stable couple and will value more the practical and friendly aspects of the relationship. Love. It can also be assumed that normative cultures, which emphasize the need to obey rules, will reject playful and pragmatic love and emphasize criteria such as chastity and social status.

These cultures that do not tolerate uncertainty and emotions should also emphasize the style of love mania - strong emotional and possessive activation. Hierarchical cultures, which emphasize the legitimacy of status asymmetries and obedience (from children to fathers and from wives to husbands among others), and masculine, competitive cultures that emphasize gender differences, will also reinforce differences in response between men and women, in particular by reinforcing people's support for traditional gender criteria (e.g., women will value more social status and men will value chastity and feminine characteristics such as being a good housewife). Let us remember that according to a sociocultural argument, cultures that impose more constraints will reduce gender differences in normative responses (e.g., there will be fewer differences between men and women in the valuation of pragmatic love if it is normative in collectivist cultures).

In summary, the phenomenon of love presents an inter and intra-individual variability and a cultural and historical one. Therefore, based on these.

Theoretical and empirical approaches, the cultural and gender differences are described below in two different ways of conceptualizing love: the types of love and the consideration of love as a prerequisite for getting married.

Types of Love And Social-Cultural Factors

A study on the importance of people from 15 countries and regions of the world to Hendrick and Hendrick different love styles has confirmed the influence that economic, social, and cultural factors exert on the valuation of these types of love.

Considering that the lower the score, the better the type of love and that scores above three indicate disapproval, using the national averages, it is confirmed that the erotic style is the most valued, followed by the storge mania style. Ludus and pragma are the least valued styles (see table below).

Besides, cultures that emphasize the friendly and partner style (Storge) also value practicalities (pragma) and place less importance on possession, jealousy, and strong emotional arousal (mania). In this sense, cultures that emphasize passionate love also value manic loveless.

Erotic love is more valued in female cultures, in uncompetitive societies, which value the quality of life. Countries with high social development and cultures with a low rejection of uncertainty are less normative anxious.

The storge and pragma love styles, which do not have such passionate overtones, are more valued in collectivist cultures where intimate relationships are based more on family obligations and duties and cultures with a low aversion to love.

The uncertainty that is, intolerant societies that are less emotional and value gradual and calm love. Countries with less socioeconomic development and greater hierarchical distance attach more importance to love's social and practical aspects. Therefore, these results corroborate what has been found in previous studies, that is, the higher prevalence of the pragmatic and partner love style among African countries and collectivist eastern and less developed nations.

In individualistic cultures that value the individual more and with high avoidance of uncertainty that is more normative and emotional, the manic style related to possession and high affective activation occurs more intensely.

Finally, the playful love style is more valued in collectivist cultures, with low socioeconomic development and low uncertainty avoidance. For example, in these cultures, African countries, due to both the absence of resourceful male partners and a certain greater tolerance and acceptance of casual sex, extramarital sexuality is more frequent.

All this information allows you to make an analysis about which is the preference in your region and to start the hunt based on these references.

Types of Love And Gender Differences

Regarding gender differences, the results show that women, compared to men, are significantly more in agreement with pragmatic love and storge love. At the same time, they value Ludus's love and love more negatively.

It is in feminine (vs. masculine) cultures where there are more differences between women and men in the valuation they make of the playful love style. Therefore, men value playful love more. In particular, it is men from feminine cultures who value play love more than women.

It has also been found that collectivist countries with less social development show a greater difference between women and men in the valuation they make of storge love. Although women show more agreement with the style of friendly love in all cultures than men, this type of love was more emphasized by women from collectivist and less developed societies, probably to compensate for lower resources and autonomy.

The results also indicate that men and women in individualistic countries show a greater difference in their pragma style valuation. Women show more agreement with the practical aspect of love than men in individualistic cultures. However, it is in collectivist countries where both men and women value it more importantly. Likewise, the differences between men and women in their valuation of the pragma style were greater in masculine cultures than in feminine cultures. Therefore, pragmatic love was emphasized more by women than by men in individualistic and competitive cultures, probably as a way of adapting to their environment.

Love and physical attractiveness are more valued as criteria for choosing a partner in individualistic cultures, emphasizing feelings and personal decisions when establishing intimate relationships and in cultures characterized by establishing more egalitarian or less social relationships, hierarchical and greater social development. On the contrary, the valuation of innocence, social status, and good health is more important in societies with fewer resources, less social development, and highly hierarchical. The higher valuation of the more material and realistic aspects of love seems consistent with the sociocultural context. The components of survival and social adaptation of intimate relationships are more relevant in these contexts.

Marriage And Social-Cultural Factors

50% of people from collectivist cultures respond that they would be willing to marry a person even if they were not in love. Studies have confirmed that most people refuse to marry someone who has all the requirements without being in love with him/her, and only a minority accepts it. But, especially, the individuals from individualistic and masculine countries claim to be less in agreement with marrying a person who has all the qualities. Still, with whom they are not in love. Besides, the countries with greater social development and less hierarchy give more importance to love as a prerequisite for establishing intimate and couple relationships. Therefore, these results confirm the studies that indicate that love tended to be more important in westernized, more developed, and individualistic countries, such as the USA, followed by Brazil, England, and Australia, and less important in less developed nations. More hierarchical and collectivist from the East like India, Pakistan, Thailand, and the Philippines. The two least collectivist and most economically developed countries of the Asian countries, Japan and Hong Kong, gave love greater importance. These studies suggest that basic needs' satisfaction allows for the development of more personal fulfillment and expression needs, such as romantic love. Individualism and egalitarian cultural relationships increase the importance of internal attributes and personal decisions regarding marriage and marriage. Couple.

A Basic Principle of Human Psychology Successful Men Deploy to Get Women Like people tend to want to keep their thoughts consistent with their actions. Psychologists call this the Principle of Commitment and Consistency.

Once a person has behaved differently, they adjust their thoughts to be consistent with their behavior.

In the 2004 American election, the Bush-Cheney campaign used this brilliantly by having campaign goers sign a statement stating that they would vote for Bush. Having performed the loyalty action, most of the attendees then adjusted their thoughts somewhat favorable to Bush.

The Signatures are just one way that market experts use the Principle of Commitment and Consistency to their advantage. Once a person commits to an action, they feel a strong need to justify that action to themselves.

Hence, they behave consistently with the commitment they have made. No matter his political vision, the Bush campaign did a good job of getting favorably committed supporters who were a force to be considered and counted, and those supporters flocked on Election Day.

In most cases, the Principle of Commitment and Consistency helps us as individuals. Life is so complex that we don't have time to process all the complex information in one situation if we have already done the same kind of processing in a previous situation. Instead, we remember what decision we made first and stick to it. We think, "Oh, this is just like when so-and-so happened, and I did such a thing then." Then we proceed to do said thing.

For example, if you need to drive to a place that is in the same area of the city where you work, you will get in your car and take the same route that you normally take to get to work, instead of getting a map to see if you will save time by taking another route or street.

81

Usually, this is beneficial since you would probably spend more time looking at the map than it would take to drive a slightly longer route. When it comes to interpersonal relationships, people tend to project qualities onto us according to how they have treated us. If they do us a favor, their reason must have been that we deserved it because we must have some positive qualities.

Yes, you should never stop a woman from

performing acts of generosity towards you.

When she does you a favor, she increases the good impression because she thinks you are worthy of that attention.

To put it differently, always allow women to do things for you. If she offers to pay for something, let her. Never say, "Oh no, I'll pay." If she offers to cook for you, great. Don't say, "Give it up, I'll buy us a good dinner."

Be grateful, stop in, and get into the mindset

that you deserve to have things done for you.

Great Behaviors That Instantly Lead To Low Status

Avoid the three behaviors below, and you will immediately differentiate yourself above 95% from the other guys out there. This, by itself, when women notice it, immediately makes them feel wetter around you.

- Show off

"You should see my amazing house."

"I'm about to get a six-figure raise a year!"

"I have a big PENIS."

The irony of showing off is that it communicates — that you are a needy guy crying out for approval. Why then would you have to talk about yourself this way?

Avoid putting your good qualities directly into words and allow the woman to discover them for herself. This shows his self-confidence while making him a bit "mysterious" in her eyes.

Be an endless source of fascinating discoveries for her.

- Step Down or Drop

Low-status men tend to be modest out of fear of offending others and because they want to be seen as courteous. Alpha males avoid claiming modesty except when it's an obvious joke.

Having high self-esteem is attractive to women. Think favorably of yourself, and the woman will think favorably of you. It may be okay to make an obvious joke about lowering yourself, as in the following examples (say it with a playful tone of voice):

- "I'm so weak, I'm not sure I can lift that heavy thing." - Spoken by a bodybuilder physique
- "I wear a leather jacket to compensate because my penis is so small. It's not even half an inch long!" - Spoken by a confident man who obviously has no sexual insecurities. (That is why he can joke about the size of his penis.)
- "I'm unemployed, and I live in my parents' basement!" - Spoken by a well-dressed man who obviously has tons of money.
- Lower other People

"Haha, Look at that bum and the rags you saw!"

When you put others down, it reveals its own insecurities. The bum on the sidewalk is no threat to you, so why does he act like he is?

And since women are sensitive creatures and have compassion for the less fortunate, all you'll do is make her stand up for those you downgrade.

Likewise, don't demean the guys who are your sexual competition, which also reveals your insecurity. Instead, just don't pay attention to them, as they are not worthy of your attention.

The Most Important Attitude Of Power You Can Have

If you're like most guys, who think that women are like a prize in life for working hard and living right. It is a tradition that goes back in history. In the Middle Ages, the beautiful maiden was the prize for the gallant knight at the end of his long and arduous mission.

I thought so, too. And it led me to believe that I would have to get the finest car, have the highest paying job, and spend tons of money on women to get them to like me. All my friends thought that too. The bad thing is, looking back, neither of us had much luck with the girls.

"Geez, if I keep working hard and I'm a nice guy who knows the right kind of flowers to buy," I thought, "women will like me." After all, whenever you ask a woman for advice, that's what they will tell you to do. Later, I discovered that women give terrible and bad advice! They provide you with the map to become relationship material only. Take their advice, and you'll be an easily controlled beta who has to wait months before sex, as opposed to an arousing alpha with whom women have sex right away.

Being a sophomore in college, I was very much in love with my roommate. I did all the right things that I thought I had to do to like him. He left the toilet seat downstairs. I would buy their CDs. I fixed things for her in our apartment. He even cleaned the place when she messed Everything up.

She told me it was so cute. But we never had sex. She never felt any attraction whatsoever to me. I was too… good. And good means beta.

Later, I became friends with a guy who seemed to be the opposite of what I thought of what a guy should be like. He wasn't spending money on women, he wasn't excited about shopping with girls, and he wasn't trying to impress women with his car or career ambitions.

But this man constantly had women who admired him, swirling around him, flirted with him, and had sex with him. He did, and I later realized that he displayed alpha male qualities that made women attracted to him on a primitive level.

Everything about him and how he conducted himself reflected her sincere belief that he was a good match. It was the attitude of power from which all his success flowed.

Due to his belief in being a good match, he:

- He would have sex only with women who had earned that honor.
- I would only feel affection towards women who had earned that privilege
- He would only be interested in women if they said something interesting and not just babbled.

Once you've fully embraced this mindset that you're a good match (and not her), you'll be more attractive. It is a fundamental part of human psychology that we tend to assign a higher value to what is not readily available. It is the basic concept of supply and demand: anything that is less in supply demands a higher demand price than usual.

From rare baseball cards to stamps, there are examples of the scarcity principle everywhere. Traders take advantage of it and abuse it all the time.

As an alpha, you can take advantage of this too, and you can increase your value through the following three secrets:

- Being Unavailable for a woman is the advantage you gain, and it is rewarding for Everything you have to invest. (If you take this attitude, how much patience do you think he will have for those women who put him in the "relationship" category and make him wait months for sex ?! Not much!)
- Don't jump in to return phone calls so quickly. As an alpha, you are a busy man, and women need to gain your attention. And when you're on the phone, you'll be the first to hang up, not because some dating book told him to, but because you really are a busy man.
- Not being available for appointments if you have other things to do on your agenda. (And by the way, to be attractive, you must be doing things with your life besides chasing skirts.)

Let me say this again because it is important — by not always being available, you will raise your value. When you adopt the mindset that you are a man of high value deciding for yourself if a woman is worth making time, you will also have certain tolerance rules for her behaviors. When she is not within your expectations, you withdraw your attention.

As an alpha, you live the life you want, free from others' need for approval. (Unfortunately, most people don't live the life they want for precisely this reason, that is, they are afraid of being disapproved.)

Consequently, you move towards the things you want and away from the things you don't want. You are a man of high value, and you are worthy of being treated as such by others.

Creating Your Own Reality

Your world is what you perceive it to be. On the Internet, you can find an immense range of beliefs and ideas, and all of those beliefs are supported by people's own observations.

For example, many religious sites talk about God as if it is obvious that He exists, while atheists say that does not make sense. Read in-depth, and you will find interesting arguments for both views. How can that be that both sides are right? It is because each person has their own vision of reality.

What if a leg is broken? That's bad? You're probably thinking, "Of course it's bad, damn it." But suppose you were a British soldier in 1914 and that broken leg luckily prevented you from being cannon fodder on the Western Front. Then you would thank heaven for his broken leg and his crutches!

Here's the detail: reality is what you perceive it to be. There is no objective reality. Everything is open to interpretation. What would you think of a rainy day? You will have a completely different perspective depending on whether you want to go on a picnic or a farmer suffering through a drought.

Therefore, you have the power to see the world the way you want. You can have your own reality, your own framework of things.

A person with a weak reality is consumed by the perceptions of the world of others.

A person with a strong reality is unaffected by others' perceptions and instead drags them into his world.

Let's say you go to a nightclub and have trouble finding a place to park. A beta that allows external factors to control it will be disturbed by this. But you can come up with a way to keep yourself from being disturbed. Not finding a place to park means there will be many people in the clubs, which means many more women.

Have you ever got caught in traffic? That's not so bad, because it's an opportunity to take a break, relax, meditate, and maybe listen to some music. You don't have to join the rest of the pack by getting upset. You have the power to have a positive perception of events.

87

Now let's look at what kind of frame you have when talking about yourself. You want to have the framework in which you are an award that women want to win.

CHAPTER THREE

THE ART OF CONFIDENCE AND TRUST

How To Appear Confident To Women

Confidence is being confident in your actions and your appearance. Being around a woman that you think is attractive can cause many men's confidence to drop. You might think of yourself as a confident person, but when confronted with a beautiful and intimidating woman, that confidence disappears. Seeming to be confident with women is something that men need to balance. Showing a lot of confidence could be considered arrogance, which could put women off. Consider the steps below as tips to appear confident.

Dress Properly And Groom Your Face And Body

Wear clothes that are comfortable and stylish. Pick a method and hold with it, from your tie to your shoes. Add attitude to your outfit by including a personal touch. This can be an eccentric tie, a unique watch, or an interesting strap. Presenting your personality shows the confidence you have in yourself.

Shave your beard, mustache, goatee, etc., so that you look neat. Having a clean face free of facial hair can make you feel refreshed and give you more assurance than you did when you got out of bed.

Cut your nails, the hair in your ears, and your nose, and wash your hair. If you usually comb your hair, do it. Avoid trying new and radical hairstyles when trying to impress a woman. The uncertainty of a new style could cause you to lose your confidence.

Speak slowly and avoid hesitating

Try to slow down your speech by at least 50%. When you are nervous, your voice tends to rise an eighth, and you begin to speak faster.

Focus on being calm when you speak. If you think about each word before saying it, you will automatically slow down. Similarly, this can prevent you from making a mistake when speaking and regretting it.

Stay on the topic of the conversation. Speak as much as required in conversation. When you answer a question, do not continue speaking to fill the silence.

Smile often

Practice a genuine smile in the mirror. A genuine smile is not very cheesy. Plus, it feels comfortable when you do it, and it doesn't come off as unpleasant to other people. A genuine smile shows confidence and is even better.

Maintain eye contact

Stare at the woman you are talking to or listening to during the time you are talking to or talking to you. Men who are not confident tend to wander with their eyes or look away. When a woman speaks directly to a man with little confidence, it is often very difficult for the man to return a sharp look, which indicates that he is nervous.

Try not to think too much about your actions

Understand your words' meaning, but don't analyze every conversation in your mind during and after you have them. Try not to overthink an action. This can be anything from serving a drink or placing a glass in your mouth. By overthinking these very basic actions, you make them emphasized. Likewise, the added pressure you put on the situation can cause you to mess up, which would not have happened if you hadn't.

Remember to breathe

Speak at a natural pace and breathe frequently. When people get nervous, they sometimes forget to breathe. When they finally do, they blurt out their words.

Take a look at your posture

Stand tall. Rotate your shoulders back and raise your head. If there is one thing you need to do when trying to appear confident, maintain perfect posture.

People who slouch look sloppy, sloppy, and shy. You will immediately feel more secure when your posture is upright.

Ten Keys To Project Safety

A self-confident person draws more opportunities than someone who is not. Those who are confident in themselves know their abilities and expose them, while those who do not will have so many concerns that they will prevent them from demonstrating their virtues.

Being confident people can open many doors for us, from getting a job to undertaking a project without fear of failure. Even in the most difficult moments, safety will help us get up and move out successful projects.

I know from experience that when things seem to be not going very well, thinking positively about our abilities helps us understand that if something fails, it is not because of lack of ability, but because that is what life is about: undertaking, failing, getting up and gaining. All entrepreneurs miss at some period. Not being frightened to fail is a characteristic of confident people.

How To Be A Confident Person?

Although it is not a simple task for many, we can become confident people by following simple steps. According to the French psychologist Émile Coué, if we repeatedly say "I am a confident person," we end up understanding it and acting as such because the mind can produce a preconditioned command when required. If we are sure, we will transmit that feeling to others, believing it.

However, it is not enough to believe that we are safe; we must also work with our image to transmit that security to others. According to various studies, people who know how to project a correct image are hired more quickly than those who do not care about that issue and even tend to receive better salaries.

These are some keys to projecting security through your posture and image:

Tone of voice. In the business world, a proper tone of voice is the key to conveying confidence. It's important to be heard, but speaking too loudly could convey arrogance. Conversely, speaking very quietly could make you lose credibility.

Diction. When it comes to engaging in conversations with others, it is best to speak slowly. Not pronouncing words correctly can be an indicator of insecurity; It gives the impression that we do not believe in what we say, and the listener will notice it causing the message to be lost.

Gestures. Gestures are an essential part of body language, as they lead to endless misinterpretations. When we do not understand a topic, we can make it known with gestures: opening our eyes a lot is a sign that we are not understanding, closing our lips with force transmits tension, or maintaining control of ourselves.

Smile. This is entirely one of the most critical components of non-verbal communication. Smiling naturally projects calmness, self-confidence, and the ability to socialize. Be careful: do not smile all the time, or you will run the risk of transmitting falsehood.

Greeting. When you arrive at a place, it is essential to greet everyone present, whether you know them or not. Come over, introduce yourself, and offer them your hand.

Posture. Sitting upright will convey confidence. On the contrary, looking towards the ground or bending your shoulders will make you look like a person who does not believe in yourself.

Walking. Moderate your step. A person who walks very fast may appear desperate, scared, or stressed. A confident person walks straight and at a good pace.

Way of sitting. Sit up straight and avoid moving every two seconds. Moving your feet, hands, or changing constantly transmits insecurity and nervousness.

Clothes. Make sure to wear clean clothes that are well-matched and appropriate for the occasion. Avoid flashy accessories: you don't want them to steal the attention of your interlocutors.

Look. When addressing someone, always look them in the eye—the same when someone else addresses you. Avoid looking at the ground or, at some point, lost in space.

Always remember to look for congruence between what you are and what you transmit. The image must go hand in hand with the abilities that are possessed, hence the need to learn to show that to others through the correct handling of the image.

Acting And How To Show Confidence Or Security

How to be a person showing security and self-confidence. If you can show confidence and certainty in your character, the other characters with whom you surround yourself, and even the viewers, observers of your work will trust and believe in you more easily. However, if the character seems uncertain or does not convey confidence, how do you expect others to accept that what you show is true?

Signs That Show Confidence And Others That Denote Insecurity

Quiet People, when they are anxious, are tense, and it shows. Their bodies are in constant motion, generally making sudden, jerky, and erratic movements due to their muscles' tension.

Standing Attitude

When an anxious person is standing, they usually have what is called "Happy Feet" (happy feet), that is, the little feet are dancing, taking little steps everywhere. A confident person is comfortable standing in a fixed place without moving his feet.

Balance your weight evenly, with your feet about the width of your hips apart. When the weight rests on one leg, it indicates the willingness to move. When they are more or less central, balanced, firmly planted on the ground, it indicates the intention to stay and not be afraid of a threat or attack.

Notice how in the entry image, you can notice that the confident character maintains a distance from his feet according to approximately the width of his hips, with a balanced weight distribution between his two legs. In contrast, the character is anxious. Her legs are dancing, and wide apart, her weight leans more on her right leg, and she stands on tiptoe, just planting her feet on the ground.

Sitting

When the person is sitting, position comfortably, leaning back on the seat and not anxiously forward. When you are confident, you may place your hands on your lap or behind your head as you relax or put them together in a bell shape when making and evaluating decisions.

Draw the lower portion of the body as if standing still, with both feet fixed on the ground or loosely crossed for comfort. Intertwined or spasming legs show signs of anxiety.

Head

One of the clearest ways to show confidence is to keep your head still. Anxious people are always looking for threats, looking from side to side, or avoiding the person they are talking to if they get nervous. Stare straight ahead as if you are observing a specific point to keep your head in one place.

Keep your head up at chin level, as if suspended by a rope attached to a point on the ceiling. Anxious people tend to keep their chin down, originally to protect the vulnerable neck from attack.

A self-confident character keeps his head still with his gaze on a fixed point; it seems as if he is not going to move it from there in a while, while the other character seems that he is going to move it from one moment to another, staring blankly for possible threats from outside.

Arms and Hands

We often wave our arms a lot when we speak or close and clasp if we are worried. You can minimize these movements, and you can even keep them still, resting on your lap or leaving them hanging next to you. A fairly common pose that conveys confidence with the hands is holding them slightly in front or behind the back, a typical posture seen in royalty and presidents. Holding your own hands can be considered a sign of anxiety, so be careful with this.

In ourselves, the one that transmits security keeps the hands relaxed behind the back, a posture also induced by the stretch that occurs when pushing the torso forward, relaxing the navel. This produces a slight tension in the rear part by supporting the upper part of the body on the pelvis, giving rise to a curvature where the hands are precisely supported. The anxious character holds his hands at chest level near the head, causing tension in the hands when brought together and a
95

certain stiffness in the arms. You may also notice that this posture will not remain immobile but perhaps agitated.

Restlessness is a clear symptom of anxiety. Overconfident people can hold their hands still without having to move or hide them. Showing your hands is a way to build confidence as it indicates that you are not nervous, have no weapons, or are not clenching your fists. To this end, it is a great idea to keep your hands out of your pockets, and although that said, if you keep your hands resting on the pockets of the pants, hanging through the thumbs that are inside, it can indicate a sign of confidence. Casual.

Unhurried

A general effect of anxiety is that people speed up, tend to speak, and move more quickly. A person does not need to act in a rush and shows this by acting steadily.

Speed

When you move, do it consistently. This is not to say that you move at an unnaturally slow pace or like a robot, even if it seems like it. The key is natural unhurried movement, such as how you act when you feel relaxed or relaxed.

Slow down your speech. We think much quicker than we speak, and it is easy to speak so fast that others do not understand us. Others may assume that our faster speech is related more to our anxiety than to our speed of thought.

When you are on the move, try to step with a distance between your feet, following a natural and relaxed pace, rather than taking shy and hurried steps.

Pauses

In addition to slowing down in general, add some pauses, both in your speech and in your movements. For example, when you get up, you can first move to the edge of the seat, pause, and then get up. In the same way, when you walk, point towards the place you are going, then start walking.

By pausing, you send a signal to the other person, allowing them to process what you are about to do, thus reducing the possibility that they might be surprised or worried. This is one of the ways that confident people inspire confidence in others.

Silences

Periods of silence and inactivity can be comfortable for a person who transmits security and confidence. Silence is very uncomfortable for many, and for this reason, it can be very useful as a weapon of persuasion that also enhances your image of tranquility and confidence.

Uncovered

When we feel anxious, we tend to cover ourselves with our hands and body, protecting vulnerable areas from possible attacks. People who feel confident do not feel the need to defend themselves and show it with a clear openness towards others. Notice how our safe character's posture remains straight as if exposing himself to others, while the second is curved in a closed posture.

Openness

When people feel defensive, they use closed body language. When they feel confident, they show open body language, exposing vulnerable areas of the body and stay relaxed.

Express Confidence

People feel capable of expressing emotions, including movements with the body. They tend not to over-excite as overly expressive people are seeking sympathy or trying to coerce others. Confident people don't need this. They tend to smile more, a smile that includes the eyes. You can notice the smile on the confident character, spreading to the eyebrows.

Naturalness

Above all, a confident person appears natural. He doesn't act like he's trying to control his body, nor that he needs it. For this reason, confident body language is generally evidence of true confidence rather than all acting. There is a fine line between what it is to appear confident, which shows signs of insecurity, and to express yourself with confidence and confidence in a natural way. Drawing this is difficult, but your character creates an almost instant connection with others if you do it.

Directness

Anxious people hedge their bets, preparing to escape. If your character feels confident, he can be direct, without the need to send signals that he is uncomfortable and ready to go out at any moment. Instead, you can participate confidently by interacting with the other person, showing that you feel safe.

Greeting

Assertively greeting another person, looking into the eyes, and smiling shows confidence. Keep your character with a relaxed body. If you shake hands, do so with a firm gesture without becoming too strong or aggressive.

Face to face with another person

When one person is confident and interacts with another, they may find themselves face-to-face, perhaps slightly leaning towards the other person. But beware! He does not do it dominantly, getting too close and too soon. The dominant person usually has insecurities and uses aggression to cover up a lack of confidence.

The confident person looks at others. You don't need to scan the environment for threats. They hook people with their gaze, which is relaxed without squinting, narrowing, or opening their eyes too wide. Observe our character's relaxed gaze, keeping his gaze and showing himself slightly inclined towards the other character, which is more in the background. You can see that his body, especially his head, is slightly displaced to his right, a little closer to his right foot than his left. Although curved in the form of an inverse C, his line of action remains inclined to the right, although only touch and barely perceptible to the naked eye, but enough to transmit self-confidence and confidence towards the other character.

Listen

Anxious or dominant people usually feel the need to talk. Confident people don't need to verify their beliefs or boost their egos, so they are comfortable just listening, which is a great way to get closer to other people.

Gestures

A confident person makes limited, firm, and gentle gestures, usually as a complement to amplify what he is saying. They do not perch defensively or make large, energetic movements to take up space. They normally use their hands with the palms open and relaxed.

At its core, trust is the lack (or effective control) of fear. A confident person does not seem threatened by others. But beware, this can lead to false confidence and naivety in the face of a real threat. This is why a confident person has a realistic threat assessment and contingency plan in place, so they know they can deal with the dangers that may arise.

There is a nice line among others interpreting your body language as a sign of confidence or arrogance, so you have to be careful with this. A calm and confident person is likable and admired. An arrogant person, on the other hand, does not usually like and despises himself.

99

The distinction is that the proud person uses his confidence to gain position or status since he feels or wants to feel superior to others. The calm and confident person, on the other hand, feels the same with others.

Tips To Promote Trust In Your Partner

Trust is not always a choice. As much as you love a person, if they have not been able to show their concern and love for you, you may simply not be able to put (part of) your destiny in their hands. Various causes justify the lack of trust, but this is usually the plague of couples affected by infidelity. How to believe him again, give him confidence or even love him? Doubts assail the mind, like an eternal hum that makes us unable to sleep peacefully when we know that he is partying or even with his friends. Although it seems that all is lost, be clear: there is a way out of this situation. You just have to propose it.

Trust is also a mutual effort. You will not give all your trust to a person if he does not get involved. Like a flower garden, trust works. It cannot arrive suddenly and above all it needs tests. Evidence that we can open ourselves fully to this person. But remember that trusting does not mean letting go or closing your eyes to any problem or doubt. To avoid potential future dramas, be aware that things may not turn out well and that the person you love may, like anyone else, fail you. If you can anticipate negative feelings, value the confidence you can give a person, and communicate with respect and sincerity, you will have saved yourself many troubles. Or at least you can wear them better.

Whether you have just started a new relationship, are trying to overcome infidelity, or simply want to boost your current confidence, we give you 15 tips to save your relationship. It may take the time or cost you to apply them, be patient and see how you can modify each of them to your situation. Remember that each person is different, and those appearances are often deceptive. Trust takes time (don't be blinded by promises that may not be kept) and commitment. And most importantly, if you care about this person, don't lose hope of having the same relationship as in your beginnings.

Identify the reason.

Do you no longer trust him/her? The first thing is, without a doubt, to find out why. Sometimes the reason is obvious, but sometimes not so much. If you understand the reason for this weakness, you can advance better and strengthen your relationship.

Learn to trust yourself

After infidelity, it seems difficult to trust the person again. And it makes us rethink a series of things: How come I haven't seen anything? Could I have prevented it? These doubts reflect an absence of confidence in yourself. Keep this in mind in your next relationships and talk to your partner to convey mutual trust and confidence.

Recognize the patterns

You may not have earned it, but some patterns (and relationships) repeat themselves. Why? Because you always end up looking at the same type of people. If your previous relationships have not worked, it may be because you choose precisely people who do not correspond to you. Learn to recognize these patterns, so you don't stumble over the same stone again.

Community with respect

It seems obvious, and yet it is the most difficult thing to do: listen to the needs and fears of the other, on the one hand, and express your perception, on the other. Healthy communication requires respect and honesty. Everyone must have their space.

Anticipate negative feelings

Feeling angry or jealous about a situation is the most normal thing globally, especially after infidelity. These feelings will occasionally arise, learn to control them, and above all, identify them so that they do not harm you in your relationship.

Clarify your expectations

If you have just started a relationship, it is good to tell your partner what your expectations are for the future and what you do not want to live again. It will allow you to know if you want the same and above all, it will save you from very complicated situations due to lack of communication. Make clear what you think, so we will also boost confidence.

Try to see your partner objectively

Doesn't that suit you? Well, it is the greatest way to boost confidence. This is born of knowledge by what you try to see with eyes outside your environment, skills, and attitudes in different contexts. Also, do your introspection. It will help you see if this person reciprocates you.

Assess whether it deserves your trust

Love often blinds us, and it is good to have an outside perspective to analyze the situation. As much as you like this person, try to find out from your family and friends if they deserve a vote of confidence. If you are deeply in love with him, give him a chance, cautiously.

Apply the "shared screen" technique

If your ex-partners continue to condition you when it comes to trusting today, apply the "shared screen" mental technique: on the one hand, place your ex-boyfriend, and on the other hand, to your current partner. It will help you match and contrast your trust in each person and value your new relationship.

Do not carry your past

In a general way, do not speak of your past as "baggage." These lived experiences make you what you are, but they do not affect you in your new relationships. Learn from history without obsessing over it. And remember that each person is different.

Accept Risk Taking

If your companion has been unfaithful to you, they will naturally get defensive with a new person. Although some questions such as Is it worth it to be with a person knowing that he can also deceive me? Arise logically in your mind, do not reject love and all the opportunities it offers you. Accept the risks but don't limit yourself when it comes to trusting.

Accept your differences

You may not agree with everything and that some issues (such as children) separate you, but if you choose to get involved in this relationship, you accept the other as they are. Don't seek to change it or make it adapt to your own will. Trust is born out of mutual understanding and respect.

Spend more time together

Yes, it also seems obvious but physical contact unites. You will know the saying, "The touch makes the affection." The extra time you spend together, the more you should feel collaboration and trust.

Say goodbye to surveillance.

If you have been unfaithful, surely you feel the need to control at all costs everything your partner does precisely because of this loss of trust. You have two alternatives: either you give him a new chance, and you propose to trust him again little by little, or you do not see yourself able to trust him again in any way, and you leave him for your good. Controlling all their activities and relationships will not unite you anymore.

Go to therapy

If you feel that you cannot solve your problems alone, do not hesitate to go to a professional. It will guide you to learn to trust yourself and create a healthy relationship.

How To Project More Confidence

Projecting confidence is key to take advantage of the opportunities presented to you in the workplace. When a professional demonstrates that they have confidence in themselves, they can recognize their abilities and direct their efforts towards achieving their goals. On the contrary, lack of confidence will make fear prevent you from achieving your goals.

In this sense, security is the engine that will allow you to achieve your goals. Whether it is getting a new business, getting a promotion, or starting your project, the trust will help you overcome obstacles and make the best of each experience as an opportunity. Growth.

Working on their safety can be a complicated task, so it is important to create habits to boost your image; Consistency will help you improve certain aspects and convey greater confidence to your team. Here are some tips to achieve this:

Improve your speech: You must learn to communicate clearly and concisely, consider factors such as: speak slowly, practice your breathing, use an appropriate tone of voice, and take care of your body language since your movements should reinforce your arguments, not distract your interlocutor.

- **Recognize your areas for improvement:** A confident professional is aware of his or her abilities; however, working on your weaknesses to turn them into strengths will allow you to inspire confidence in your collaborators.
- **Take care of your image:** Choose the right clothing for the position you aspire to; a correct professional image not only projects security but also shows your interest in what you do.

- **Do not improvise:** It is normal to feel nervous before a meeting or conference; preparing yourself will help you overcome this situation since you will demonstrate confidence when presenting your arguments, and you will be able to share your ideas more easily with your interlocutor.
- **Smile:** Is one of the most critical components of non-verbal communication; it not only reflects confidence but also speaks of your ability to socialize.
- **Greeting**: When introducing yourself, a firm greeting is essential to show security and interest in our interlocutor; on the other hand, you must maintain eye contact and an upright posture.

The first time you interact with someone, pay attention to your body language, each of the aspects mentioned above influences your collaborators' perception. Showing security will help you join your team more easily; simultaneously, you will contribute to developing a work environment that promotes cooperation, facilitates communication, and stimulates productivity.

Are You Insecure? How To Gain Self-confidence

No one is 100% sure. We all have small vulnerabilities. The important thing is to understand yourself to overcome uncertainties. There are no completely safe people, although there are those who may pretend otherwise. We all know uncertainty, either because we would like to control the future or not appreciate ourselves enough.

But if we determine to live with our doubts and limitations and are aware that there are things in life beyond our control, we will gain security because we know how to deal with our anxieties. "I will only do it when I feel convinced of myself," we say many times when faced with a great challenge of work, affective, social, family, or economic nature. If they ask us when we will be safe, we will usually reply, "I don't know." We are not sure of the answer either.

Self-Confidence

What is it like to be sure of oneself? If we ask a question to a wide variety of people, we will find so many different answers that we may be surprised.

To be sure, I will say that I have no doubts about what to do and how to do it. Others said that being safe is about acting despite doubts and trusting the results of action.

For some, it is about being immune from criticism. For others, are these same criticisms listening without falling into self-devaluation? Perhaps this last option allows us to understand better the dynamics of insecurity to overcome it.

If we value p or what we are, that is, because we are here, for the easy and pleasant fact of living if that appreciation is transmitted to us through gestures, attitudes, and words if our achievements are recognized. Our aptitudes are used, we will understand soon, we are related to others.

From our early practices, we will feel that we are not required to justify our existence, that we are not loved in exchange for what we do or do not do, but because we are deemed worthy of love, thus, without compensation. Genuine love and appreciation, given to us because we exist, are basic security construction pillars.

False Ideas About Self-confidence

When we have not learned to feel valuable for ourselves, we are likely to search for models. An internal voice tells us: "Just as I am, I am not worth too much, my resources are scarce or weak; Being who I am, I will achieve nothing, so I must be like "That guy," they do feel sure of themselves."

We commit to these standards all the conditions that, as we imagine, make up the safety of a person. That is, we place in them everything that we do not recognize in ourselves.

Thus, we will see them as beings who do not doubt, who feel strong, who do not admit objections, who travel the highways of life like huge and powerful trucks before all other vehicles turn away. We create an ideal of security that, like all ideals of the self forged from deficiencies, becomes an unattainable goal and, by its very presence, painful.

It is worth saying that to compensate for our feeling of insecurity, we propose a security model so far removed from true human emotional constructions that it ends up being impossible and, in the end, creates even more insecurity for us. It must be said soon: there are no people who do not doubt, who do not fear, who are unaware of uncertainty. Those who claim to be on the fringes of these human experiences hide, in truth, great insecurity.

When the possibility of defeat, of mistake, of doubt, of not having control over something or someone is not admitted, when criticism is feared, when one lives under the overwhelming pressure of demands, it is often appealed to compensation mechanisms created to hide all that.

Doubts Away

The greater the doubt, I will try to demonstrate greater conviction; the greater fear, I will try to show greater recklessness; the more hesitation, the more momentum. I can convince others that I am a safe person, but I will never convince myself; I will live all my actions with a great inner tension load, pending that I am not seen as doubtful, uncertain, fearful. And that will have huge present and future emotional costs.

To sustain that image, I will have to close every door that leads to the interior of myself, and I will have to censor all questions about myself, my feelings, my searches, and my needs. Denying insecurity does not make us feel safe. It turns us into beings that block areas of their psychic and emotional world and, therefore, are left in a situation of greater vulnerability. On the contrary, accepting doubts, fears and uncertainties allow us to ask ourselves what we need to face each situation in our life.

And it leads us to explore what resources we need are in us and what stage of development. What do we need to strengthen them? What help should we ask and, from whom, how to achieve it in an equanimous and functional way. In other words, it helps us transform and grow. Those who build an image of unshakable security and present themselves to the world clinging to it are prisoners of that facade.

Those who admit their deficiencies, their imperfections, are more whole and free. The great psychotherapist Viktor Frankl pointed out that when a person discovers and accepts their values and aptitudes, they stop configuring themselves by pursuing external models, so often illusory and false, and gain the freedom to be in your way.

This is, in my opinion, the most powerful antidote to insecurity. The more we know ourselves in our possibilities and our limitations, the more we value ourselves with what we have and with what we don't, the better we are in a position to assume our existence in the here and now.

The Fear Of The Future

It is definitely in the here and now where our life takes place. Insecurity, like fear or anxiety, is related to what has not yet happened, and we do not know if it will happen. It is not in what happens at this moment but in what will come.

What will happen if I am wrong? How do they react if I can't? What will convert me if I don't? Review the main verbs in these sentences, and you will see that they are formulated in the future tense. Add other phrases taken from your harvest and referring to insecurity, and you will see that the same thing happens. Insecurity uproots us from the present, takes away our axis of living.

In his beautiful book The Wisdom of Insecurity (Ed. Kairós), the philosopher Alan Watts points out how we cling to the illusion of controlling the future. We believe that if we could look at it with certainty, we would know what to do and avoid where not to go. Where not to look out? What to choose?

The dream of establishing the future leads us to believe that, if it were possible, we would live a completely safe life. And through there, we come to the other large source of self-doubt. The beginning, as we saw, is not having been adequately valued and accepted with our idiosyncrasies. The second is the non-acceptance of change as an indispensable component of life. Life is a succession of uncertainties. Instability is, therefore, inherent in it. Accepting it will make us live safer.

The Pillars Of Self-safety

Let us analyze this paradox when I know that not everything depends on me when I recognize that there were factors beyond my decision, my will, and my control when I verified that my possibilities have limits, freedom, and ability to choose to improve.

By allowing everything that does not depend on me and I can not assure myself, I can concentrate on what does concern me, on my resources and possibilities. When I know that I cannot do everything, I will do better than I can.

The safest person is not the one who knows and can do everything but the one who knows what things he ignores and applies in what he knows. Thus, we can arrange the pillars on which security is built:

Sincerely explore the inner world to know your resources and accept your limitations.

Believe who we are and value what we are, rather than aspiring to be another, to be an ideal of illusion. Assume that, in life, many events are out of our control. We cannot give assurances about them, nor can we ask for them.

Focus on those actions that depend on us and utilize our available resources to them. Include doubt, uncertainty, perplexity as possible companions for our actions and decisions, knowing that they are part of human passions and sensations, and without struggling with them. It is not the absence of doubts, fears, and questions that will make you a confident person, but your ability to act with them and your satisfaction with the processes rather than the results. What gives us security is having been faithful to our thoughts and feelings and honest in using our resources.

Do your thing with your heart and detach from the results; it would be the slogan that leads to safety. When you stick to the result and how others will value it, you incubate the germ of insecurity.

Thus, we will see them as beings who do not doubt, who feel strong, who do not admit objections, who travel the highways of life like huge and powerful trucks before all other vehicles turn away. We create an ideal of security that, like all ideals of the self forged from deficiencies, becomes an unattainable goal and, by its very presence, painful.

It is worth saying that to compensate for our feeling of insecurity, we propose a security model so far removed from true human emotional constructions that it ends up being impossible and, in the end, creates even more insecurity for us.

It must be said soon: there are no people who do not doubt, who do not fear, who are unaware of uncertainty. Those who claim to be on the fringes of these human experiences hide, in truth, great insecurity.

When the possibility of defeat, of mistake, of doubt, of not having control over something or someone is not admitted, when criticism is feared, when one lives under the overwhelming pressure of demands, it is often appealed to compensation mechanisms created to hide all that.

Starting from this meaning, we find a series of terms that also use the concept we are now analyzing. This would be the predicament, for example, of the expression "breach of trust." With it, what is meant is that someone to whom another person has supported and given credit at all times has taken advantage of that circumstance, consciously or unconsciously, to harm or make fun of her.

Similarly, we cannot ignore another term that similarly uses the word we are dealing with now. It is a "vote of confidence." With this expression, you want to show that someone authorizes another person to carry out a certain action.

However, the same expression is used in the political arena. And it is that with it, it is established that, within legislative chambers, the members of the same give their support and acceptance to the actions that the reigning government is carrying out in a specific area or situation. Similarly, it is also used to refer to when those give authorization to the government entity to undertake certain tasks.

Precisely within the aforementioned political sector, there is also the expression "question of trust." With it, it comes to refer to a process by which the head of state or government is analyzed by the rest of the legislative chamber members in order, through a corresponding vote, to choose whether or not they should continue to carry out their functions.

Resolution refers, on the other hand, to familiarity in dealing: "You don't have to comb your hair every time I go to your house, we already have enough confidence," "How dare you talk to me like that? I never gave you such confidence. "

For social psychology and sociology, trust is a hypothesis made about others' future behavior. It is a belief that estimates that a person will be able to act distinctly when faced with a certain situation: "I am going to tell my father everything, I am confident that he will understand me and help me."

In this sense, trust can be strengthened or weakened according to the actions of the other person. In the example above, if the father helps his son, the trust will be strengthened; otherwise, the trust will be betrayed, and, in the future, the child will most likely not act in the same way.

Trust supposes a suspension, at least temporarily, of the uncertainty regarding the actions of others. When someone trusts the other, they believe that they can predict their actions and behaviors. Trust, therefore, simplifies social relationships.

The Art Of Flirting Based On Confidence And Good Self-esteem

Self-confidence and self-esteem are concepts of a psychological nature that greatly influence when meeting new people.

When what we are also looking for is to have an entertaining conversation with someone but to flirt, these two aspects' relevance is even greater. Here we will see some key ideas to know how to comment on them in this area of life.

Self-confidence and self-esteem in its expression when seducing

It would be a disagreement to think that people who have problems acting with confidence when flirting suffer this problem because they have low self-esteem or because they do not believe in themselves in a global sense. It is very common to meet people who generally trust their abilities in contexts that they face almost every day, such as studies or work, but who at the same time falter when they show self-confidence in specific situations they face. They confront each other in less systematic ways, such as when trying to flirt on weekends.

And it is that self-esteem and self-confidence are not completely homogeneous elements. Still, they have several facets and can change depending on the situation to which we are exposed. Many shy people are confident when speaking in front of an audience about a topic that fascinates them and they know well. Simultaneously, those who are usually popular can become insecure and vulnerable if they have to speak in front of the public about something they do not know well.

This means that to enhance our fluency in one area of social life, we must work in that area and not in any other.

Thus, the fundamental thing is to develop self-confidence and behavior patterns that promote self-esteem, specifically in seduction for the present case. Of course, working on self-esteem in a global sense, in the face of life as a whole, is important and contributes to making social interactions normally more fluid and enjoyable.

However, we should not stop at that, which can be used as an excuse for not having to "leave the comfort zone" and start developing communication skills based on meeting people and, why not, also seduction. Given that these types of challenges occur specifically in social interaction overcoming them must also focus on this type of social experience and not on others. In other words, the keys to developing self-confidence and self-esteem should be linked to the act of breaking the ice, showing interest, asserting yourself to people we don't know, and, in general, flirting. Let's see several ideas about it.

Four communicative keys to express seductive self-confidence when flirting

113

These are several fundamental psychological keys that you must consider to gain ease and confidence when flirting.

Boost Your Self-confidence From Improvisation

Memorizing "pre-made" phrases when flirting is a mistake. At most, you can use one from time to time to break the ice and start a conversation, but once you are in the dialogue proper, what matters is the fluency and social skills applied at the moment, not the witty phrases read in a book or on the Internet. Seducing is, among other things, knowing how to adapt, responding to the focuses of interest that unite them both, and creating a comfortable climate that is comfortable.

Of course, improvising in this way is more complex than applying a sequence of guidelines that we can follow step by step. However, although this fact complicates things, at the same time, it provides another element that contributes to making everything easier, and that we will see in the next point.

Self-confidence is demonstrated by assuming the imperfection of communication.

In the end, the ability to create technically perfect conversations is much less seductive than the attitude of self-confidence that is present by assuming that the conversation will have expendable or outright absurd moments. Self-esteem and charisma are shown in accepting that the important thing is not the technical correction but the stimulating sensations and emotions in the dialogue.

Obsessing not making mistakes keeps our mind divided on several fronts (and therefore more vulnerable to going blank) and denotes fragility. In this way, it seems that we hide in that succession of words and gestures.

People with more ability to flirt take it for granted that sometimes there will be misunderstandings or exchanges of ideas that are not very informative. Still, they can turn this into a display of attitude and even fun experiences that lend themselves to the joke. Due to this, it is usual that when seducing, the act of trying to perform ridiculous actions works: the very intention of doing that and showing that we do it while being aware of how absurd it is makes it, paradoxically, not ridiculous.

The Fear Of Rejection Is Based On An Illusion

This does not mean that the fear of rejection does not exist; On the contrary, it is a very real phenomenon and whose appearance (to a greater or lesser degree of intensity) is not rare, even in people who are better at flirting. The point is that on the one hand, as we have seen, we must not fight to eliminate the fear of rejection from our mind, and on the other, it must be clear that it is not based on facts that can reveal very unvarnished truths. Uncomfortable about who we are.

The fear of rejection has to do with anticipating the distressing implications of someone showing disinterest in us. This can very well happen: there are no reasons to assume that everyone finds us fascinating. But does this say something very bad about our identity? If they reject us, we seek to bring positions closer because they don't know us well in the vast preponderance of cases.

On the other hand, hardly a single interaction or series of a few interactions with someone will give us a realistic reflection on who we are. Self-concept, our idea of "I," is built over time and through hundreds of experiences. Having someone say "yes" or "no" at a point in the conversation is not going to break the schemes from which we analyze who we are, as frustrating as it can sometimes be.

115

Without Practice, There Is No Progress

Finally, knowing all of the above is of little use if it is not put into practice. To develop the social and emotional management skills necessary to flirt, you have to apply them to reality. For this reason, many people go to the psychologist to obtain the theory and a series of guidelines to commit to this process of change and use it effectively and avoid unnecessary frustrations, starting with what works for "beginners" and ending for the most ambitious challenges.

Trust Is The Key To Attracting Women

Have you ever tried to begin a dialogue with a wonderful woman, only to find yourself drowning in your own words and stuttering like a maniac?

There is something about the image of meeting an attractive woman that turns men into jellyfish, but if you can overcome this fear and learn to be confident with women, you will look much more attractive.

If you're not feeling confident, show confidence anyway. In other words, pretend until you do.

It's not simple, but if you work hard to maintain strong body language and to keep your words in check, you will gradually begin to feel the confidence that you only intended to have at first. Remember, practice makes perfect.

And while we're on the point of practice, you must put yourself in place to be around attractive women as much as possible.

If you find it challenging to stay calm with pretty girls, visit strip clubs, hostess bars, modeling events, and anywhere you know, attractive women will be in abundance.

Don't try to get involved with some of these women; hang out and have fun joking around. By regularly placing yourself in these settings and forcing yourself to interact with them, beautiful women will lose their charisma. It will be much more relaxed for you to communicate with them in any setting.

Also, sign up for dance or yoga classes. You will meet many women on these sites, and you can have fun just interacting and having fun with them.

And as a bonus, women associate sexuality with men who can dance, so it's a situation you have nowhere to lose.

Last, and perhaps most important, erase the thought of outcome dependency from your mind. By not worrying about the result, you relieve yourself of the pressure, and it becomes easier to have fun and do your best.

Treat beautiful women exactly as you would any other girl, and stick to your original game plan, no matter how much you are tempted to revert to your old habits.

I always have a positive attitude, and it is the first step to achieve success with women. Therefore you must make an internal change in yourself.

If you thought you would get a girl's attention by playing the victim, you would only achieve her pity. Therefore, it is recommended that you show yourself happy, positive and show that being by your side is the greatest thing to happen to her.

It shows security, and it happens to many men that they feel a little intimidated by women since they are afraid of failure or making a fool of themselves.

Therefore, to achieve success, you must put aside fears, anxieties, and nerves and just be yourself.

There is no magic secret to being confident with women. Like everything, it's just a matter of changing your mindset.

Confidence Attracts Women, Discover How To Show Confidence

Showing confidence is easy for many men when they are with other men, but the game changes when they are in front of a girl they like, sadly. So don't be surprised if you feel nervous or insecure when talking to a girl you like. Nevertheless, you should know that trust is the first thing you should develop if you are interested in seducing her. While gaining confidence can be difficult, you can at least pretend you have it and get it to notice you.

Go straight to the point

Some men fail to express themselves well when in front of a woman they like. As a consequence of this, they end up over-explaining to you. If you want the female of your dreams to be attracted to you, you must not allow nerves and fear to eat you up. Instead of hinting that she knows you want to ask her out, tell her that you want to ask her out. Instead of asking indirect questions in the hope of getting the answer to the question currently in your head, ask the question. In this way, you will avoid looking like a lost child, and you will finally have the necessary answer.

Show your softer side

Don't be scared to show a little emotion. Women respond well to men who can express some emotion. To work, you need to show your true feelings and share with her things that you are genuinely passionate about. Once she discovers that you can value the things that excite you, she will appreciate you much more. However, avoid losing your appeal easily when it starts to lead to the wrong things. If you start to get emotional in negative terms, she will think that there is something wrong with you and immediately walk away.

Do not ask for their approval

Nothing shows less confidence in a man than feeling the need for constant compliments. Allow yourself to earn the compliments and handle your reactions correctly. If she offers you a compliment, politely thank her and tell her that you appreciate her for noticing. This will make her see that you are a man who has confidence in himself and does not need anyone's approval. Which by itself will help you appear much more attractive and will make him fall head over heels in love with you.

The truth is, if you show enough confidence, you won't even need to try too hard to attract any woman you want. So start practicing these tips right now and make her feel attracted to you almost instantly.

CHAPTER FOUR

HYPNOSIS AND SELF HYPNOSIS

Terminology

Self-concept

Vrey defines the self-concept as the configuration of convictions concerning the self and attitudes towards the self that is dynamic and what the self normally is aware of or can become aware of. This is an organized configuration of perceptions and conceptions of the self. Elements of this configuration include the following.

- A perception of one's characteristics and abilities.
- Evaluation of one's abilities in comparison to that of others.
- Experiences that are perceived as being either positive or negative.

Self-esteem

Self-esteem can be defined as the value a person attaches to himself. A synonym for self-esteem is self-worth. This implies attaching a value to the core of a person's being, namely the self. Self-esteem is the valuing of a person's perceived self, in the sense that a person does not always perceive himself as others do or as he/she is. Self-esteem, therefore, refers to the self-evaluation of one's qualities.

A man with low self-esteem can be described as follows:

- He feels worthless.
- He is often pessimistic, negative, and has no self-respect.
- He often lacks self-confidence.
- He is often unwilling to venture or take risks.
- He already sees himself as a failure before any task has been attempted.
- He is easily discouraged.
- He tends to become withdrawn.
- He may be easily intimidated.
- He may feel incapable and inferior.
- He thinks that reward and praise are "incidental"- they happen by chance or by pure luck and are not a result of any action of his/her.
- He may constantly put himself down - using adjectives such as "bad," "stupid," "helpless," and "pathetic" to describe himself.

The following traits are also common among men with low self-esteem:

- Projection of blame onto others.
- An over-response to flattery.
- A lack of interest in competition.
- A sensitivity to criticism.
- A hyper-critical attitude (rather emphasize the faults of others to cover up their shortcomings).

Hypnosis and the self-concept

This chapter will focus on the development of the self-concept. Hypnosis will be looked at to determine its effectiveness as a technique for building a high self-concept and positive self-esteem.

The Self-concept

A definition of self-concept

Burns defined the self-concept as the total of the views that a person has of himself and entails his beliefs, evaluations, and behavioral tendencies. According to Vrey, the self is: the Gestalt of what the individual can refer to as being his own". Therefore, the self-concept involves everything that concerns the self, such as how a person sees himself, his values, his goals, his strengths, and his weaknesses. It includes how he thinks and feels. The individual's behavior and actions are all part of his sense of self.

It can be assumed that the sense of self consists essentially due to the individual's answer to the question, "Who am I?" The child learns to know himself through interacting with others and the environment. The child's information from his environment and others will influence his thoughts about himself. This implies that the individual is not born with a self-concept but gradually acquires a self-concept in his interaction with others and his environment. This interaction consists of the individual's consciousness of his particular environment in a set of social relations. The self-concept is thus the reflection of the way others see you.

This self-consciousness that results through the individual's interaction with his environment stems from a covert reflective process in which the individual views personal or potential actions from others' standpoint with whom he is involved. In other words, the individual becomes an object to himself by taking others' position and assessing his behavior as they would. This assessment involves an effort to predict the responses of others and an evaluation of these responses in terms of their implications for the individual's identity.

Cooley substantiated the idea that the self develops due to the process of interpersonal communication within a social milieu. According to Cooley, each social relationship in which the individual is involved reflects the self incorporated into the individual's identity. Since most people are involved in an assortment of social relations, each providing a particular reflection, it can be said that people live in a world of mirrors. Each mirror reflects a certain picture of the self to the individual. The likelihood arises that some of these mirrors will provide a more accurate picture than others. Regardless of the reflected picture, the individual can't escape these definitions of his identity that he sees reflected in others. Cooley refers to this as the looking glass theory. When seeking to define the concept of the looking glass theory, Cooley puts it as follows:

Each to each a looking glass.

Follows the other that doth pass.

As we see our appearance, figure, and dress in the glass and are involved in them because they are ours so in our imagination, we perceive in another person's mind some thought of our appearance, manners, aims, deeds, character and friends, and are differently influenced by it. A self-idea of this sort appears to have three main elements: the thought of our appearance to the other body, the imagination of his judgment of that appearance, and some self-feeling, such as pride or mortification.

The images reflected by the individual, through the different mirrors, will be interpreted in terms of each individual's uniqueness. The reason for this is that people differ in terms of their degree of sensitivity to others' opinions and the degree of stability with which they maintain a particular kind of self-feeling. Besides, people differ in the amount of social reinforcement frequency that· they seek to maintain their self-feelings. People vary in their particular mix of positive and negative feelings associated with their self-concept. They also vary in terms of which aspect of their lives is most closely connected with self-feeling.

The Looking-Glass Theory formulated by Cooley shows the importance of significant others in the development of the self-

123

concept. These are the most influential persons in the child's life because of the different images. Depending on the surrounding circumstances, the image reflected in the child will be seen by the child as either a negative or positive one. The child incorporates these images into his/her developing self-concept. A prerequisite for the assimilation of images into the developing self-concept is that the image is constantly being reflected over time.

The formulations of the individual's self-concept are not limited to positive perceptions or reactions and definitions of others. On the contrary, individuals are also seen as acting subjects. This can be explained by the "I" and "Me" dimensions of the self-concept, as explained by Mead. The self as object refers to the "me" while the self is subject to the "I." The "me" dimension refers to the attitude, feelings, and perceptions that the person has of himself as objects (Ferns 1988:13). Raimy refers to the self as the object as encompassing the individual as known to the individual. The "me" is all that the person can call his own. The "me" is the objective self and comprises four components: the spiritual self, the material self, the social self, and the physical self.

On the other hand, the "I" aspect of the self encompasses all the psychological processes that control and influence the person's behavior. As a subject, the self is thus seen as a doer in that the self is involved in active processes such as thinking, remembering, doing, and experiencing. Therefore, the self is far more than only that which the individual sees that he/she has or does not have or that which he/she learns about himself through the different images that are reflected back to him. The self is thus not merely what we are but also what we do.

The self as the subject of "I" and the self as an object or "me" implies "I as the knower" and "I as the known." Even though a distinction can be made between the self as an object and the self as a subject, these two aspects are related and cannot exist independently. The self cannot exist apart from the person who experiences himself and is an executor of behavior. Mead explained a reciprocal interplay between the self as an object and the self as a subject.

To sum up, the self is the center of being that the individual becomes aware of and includes all aspects of being human. It is the individual's total personal life-world and the center of experience and meaning. Each individual interacts with his life-world. Because of this interaction, the personality comes into being since every person will give meaning to his environment.

When the learner's self-concept is referred to, it applies to the group of ideas that the learner is likely to have about himself at any given time. Self-concept is the private interpretation that the learner has about his abilities, talents, potential, and behavior.

Characteristics Of The Self-concept

The formulated self-concept is "steadfast."

Hamachek explained this characteristic in terms of a person known to himself and became predictable. There is, therefore, a connecting thread between the way a person is today, what he/she was like yesterday, and what he/she will be like tomorrow.

Comb and Snygg stated that the perceived self's maintenance is the motive behind all behavior. The person strives to come to terms with, defend, and improve the self he/she is aware of. New experiences are interpreted and understood in terms of the existing self. Whatever the self is, it becomes a center, an anchorage point, and a standard of comparison.

It could be that the learner's experiences in the classroom are in opposition to the image that he/she has of himself. The learner may initially resist any changes or experiences that are in opposition to the existing self. Jerslid referred to this as the learner's efforts to safeguard his picture of himself. This is the picture of the core beliefs of self-concept formed in the early stages of the life-span. The self's endeavor

125

to protect himself and interpret new experiences in light of these perceptions does not imply that changes will not occur but indicates that changes will come slowly. It is possible to make changes, but these changes will involve long consecutive reinforcement.

The implications of this are that the core beliefs formulated in the early stages of the learner's development may be resistant to change because of steadfastness. The immutable characteristic of the self-concept that makes it resistant to change shows the necessity of making certain that quality interaction occurs during the early stages of the learner's life-span. During this time, factors such as the family, friends, society, and the school should interact so that they make a positive contribution towards the formation of the self-concept. If this does not occur, then these factors interacting with the self-concept will ultimately contribute to developing a negative self-concept.

Resistance to change is not necessarily a negative process. At times resistance could also be seen as positive. It is through resistance to change that the self becomes a constant personality. According to Purkey, it does not matter how negative the self is, but the fact that the ·self remains constant is necessary because even if it is a negative one, it will be better than having no self-concept at all.

Hypnosis is not in itself a treatment but a therapeutic tool. In other words, hypnosis comprises a set of techniques that, in combination with other therapeutic approaches, can enhance them and provide excellent results. Hypnosis usually helps the therapy be shorter in duration and its results more stable.

Another erroneous belief is the one that affirms that hypnosis breaks or weakens the subject's will. Regardless of what we want to understand by will (later, we will see in more depth the relationship between hypnosis, consciousness, and will). For now, answer it to say that both hypnosis and self-hypnosis help strengthen the person's determination to pursue their goals.

Another false belief that people often have is that hypnosis makes you lose control of your actions. The myths associated with hypnosis and television shows also contribute to this harmful belief.

The reality is that it is unlikely to hypnotize someone against their will or force them to perform extravagant acts that go against their sense of ridicule or moral criteria; If you perform them under hypnosis, we can be sure that you can also perform them in a waking state.

Hypnosis is a completely natural process, not "static" but dynamic, to improve the patient and a special relationship with the hypnotist.

Another false belief is that in the hypnotic trance, you lose consciousness of what is happening. In a trance, both medium intensity and deep, various total or partial amnesia phenomena can occur. Besides, it usually leaves the person in a state of drowsiness, but this does not imply that they are at the compassion of the hypnotist's orders. However, the various hypnotic dissociation states can produce opposite consciousness phenomena, such as states of hyperlucency and sensory sharpening.

Another important issue is the assumption that everything happens automatically and unconsciously in hypnosis, without the person having to strain. The need for active collaboration should be made clear (this is especially important in self-hypnosis, as we will see later).

Finally, it is essential to establish appropriate limits and realistic expectations.

Frequently Asked Questions About Hypnosis

Who produces hypnosis?

It should be clear that hypnosis occurs, in general, after a series of linked suggestions. The therapist produces it with the collaboration of the subject.

Are they all hypnotizable or just certain types of people?

The ability to be hypnotized is, like any other ability, a matter of degree.

Does being hypnotizable respond to a personality type?

Absolutely. Responds to an aptitude.

Who has been hypnotized is already subject to the hypnotist's power, unable to resist new trances?

The answer is negative.

Can the subject be hypnotized to do or say something against his will? Can someone be forced to perform acts contrary to their ethical or moral principles?

No one loses their volitional attitude or ability to make decisions and respond freely, consciously, and responsibly to hypnotic suggestions.

Can hypnosis harm health? In what cases and conditions?

In general and as a therapeutic technique controlled by a specialist, no.

Does hypnosis create dependence on the hypnotist?

Absolutely.

Could there be a risk of not being able to get out of the hypnotic state?

Under no condition

Are you asleep in the hypnotic trance? Unconscious?

In the hypnotic trance, you are hypnotized, neither asleep nor unconscious.

Is hypnosis always a monotonous induction ritual?

Do not

Does the subject have to be relaxed to enter hypnosis?

Relaxation helps but is not strictly necessary.

Hypnosis, Will, And Conscience

First, if the subject is inducted objects actively, the hypnotic trance will be impossible. Second, hypnosis is impossible to induce behavior contrary to the hypnotized subject's ethical and moral beliefs.

On the other hand, the intervention of cognitive resources in behavior carried out under hypnosis is proven.

However, when subjects are questioned after a session, they perceive their

involuntary behavior. Reasons:

- There are certain hypnosis preconceptions, such as the hypnotist's control, the involuntary execution of the behavior, and the hypnotizable people's special characteristics.

- Subjects internalize the need for involuntariness and behave based on that belief.

The hypnotist messages involve relaxation, mental abandonment, inner concentration, and serenity, which is the inhibition of logical reasoning.

- The speech is suggestive; in fact, the ability to form suggested images is closely related to hypnotic susceptibility.

Regarding the relationship between hypnosis and consciousness, state theorists define it as an altered state of consciousness characterized by the loss of planning behavior, alteration of attention, the selectivity of perception, tolerance to distortion of reality, or alteration of memory.

To study this statement, one should start by clarifying the term "altered state of consciousness" and, in a more general sense, the very concept of "consciousness." For these investigations, subjective measures have been used, extracted from the subject when comparing consciousness with memory about the process, registered cognitive resources, or the will shown by the subject.

However, it seems that more appropriate than these measures would be the psychophysiological ones, whose results would allow us to distinguish between hypnotized and unhypnotized individuals. Although, in this sense, we find important contradictions between the data provided by the different authors, it is clear that there are psychophysiological differences between individuals in a trance state and a normal state.

Hypnosis And Self-hypnosis

Almost everyone has experienced everyday situations in their life that are similar to a "hypnotic trance" (e.g., when daydreaming, when losing track of time, etc.). It should be remarked that the main difference between these types of "trance" and self-hypnosis is that the latter requires motivation and is aimed at achieving a specific goal (e.g., pain relief, relaxation, etc.).

In the hypnotic state, the power of "conscious criticism" is eliminated; that is, the suggestions enter directly into the unconscious.

The question we ask ourselves in this section is, "How is hypnosis related to self-hypnosis?" Well, the answer is that many experts agree that all hypnosis is self-hypnosis. That is, a hypnotherapist can help guide or induce the trance, but it is always you who is in control. The person cannot do anything while undergoing a threat or a clash with their most fundamental interests.

At this point, another problem may be asked: "Are there limitations to self-hypnosis?" By practicing self-hypnosis, one is both the "operator-guide" and the "subject" (it is like being both the director and the protagonist of a movie). This involves some limitations, such as, for example, that some techniques will require more practice (as in regression). However, hypnotic effects can be achieved with self-hypnosis alone (e.g., surgical interventions have been performed only with pain prevention-oriented self-hypnosis such as anesthesia) (V. Rausch, 1980). Regarding self-hypnosis, whether or not it can be used and being useful depends largely on the person's own desire to change.

Varieties Of Auto Hypnotic Techniques:

This section will apply the different methods that can be used to induce a hypnotic trance. These techniques can be adapted and modified to be useful to the characteristics of each person.

A useful recommendation is that all the techniques described below are preceded by some general relaxation instructions applied by the subject before starting the technique in question. This goes to

favor the appearance of the trance state.

The techniques we refer to are the following:

1. Recording Of Cassettes:

This technique has the advantage that the person can practice self-hypnosis without feeling that they want to find the right words and suggestions at the optimal time. As the person gains self-hypnosis, he can include suggestions that respond to increasingly specific objectives and specific post-hypnotic supports. In many scripts, the subject may also include his suggestions. For this technique to be more effective, special attention must be paid to the following guidelines:

- Make a detailed and specific list of objectives (what we will work on, why we will work on it, and for how long).
- Write down everything the person wants to say to himself (including guidelines for relaxation, stress management, etc.).
- Write several suggestions for each objective.
- Try to make the trance as deep as possible (imagine that as you go down a ladder, you enter more and more into the trance, etc.).
- Find and produce material to visualize mentally.
- Work with only one or two specific objectives in each session.
- Use background music if desired.
- At the end of the trance, I will add some suggestion to re-enter a self-hypnotic trance the next time I practice it (I thought that when I breathe deeply… and imagine that blue color… I will feel relaxed and well again…")
- Begin the recording with a normal tone of voice and then decrease as the session progresses.
- Do the session in a quiet place without interruptions.

2. Indirect Language Method:

This technique uses indirect and permissive requests and suggestions using flexible language. It is suggested that the person "could" do something or that "maybe" he/she will notice a change when taking such action. An example of a suggestion to start a session using this technique could be: "Now I would like to see how good it could feel to breathe in a relaxed and deep way."

3. Direct Language Method:

What distinguishes this method from the previous one is that the suggestions are formulated more forcefully and authoritatively. An example of suggestion: "... I will start to feel heavy ... I felt my feet sink into the sand ..."

4. Visual Fixation Method:

This technique consists of fixing visual attention and concentration on some point or object in front of them; that is, the person concentrates on a point, and as they do so, they gradually enter a trance. An example of starting a session using this technique could be: "... as I look at the blue color I will relax more and more ...".

5. Technique Of Guided Images:

In this method, the mind is encouraged to form mental images, sensations, etc., about various scenes. An example of suggestion: "... each exhalation frees me from stress ... I can imagine a kettle from which all the steam escapes, ... releasing it from pressure ...".

6. Use Of Dreams For Self-hypnosis:

The main objective is to reach a self-hypnotic state and obtain some dreamlike information to create positive suggestions. Example: "... I know that this state of relaxation ... is similar to the dream state ..."

7. Ericksonian Technique Of The "Handshake":

It is selected for the state of the hand at the beginning of the practice session. It is a matter of starting the session by extending either of the arms forward to shake someone's hand. Once at this point, it is a matter of inducing sensations in this arm (from "... an indicator that my trance has begun, maybe that I begin to feel the arm lighter ..."

8. Self Hypnosis With Music:

It consists of using music as a vehicle through which the person will enter the trance state. This music can be relaxing or active; the important thing is that the person experiences an absorption of attention. Start with relaxation without music and then introduce music as you go into a trance. This method has the benefit that it can

133

be used at any time since the subject can call up the music in his mind whenever he wishes.

9. Deepening In Self-hypnosis:

This technique can be used in combination with other techniques. It consists of leaving and re-entering the trance abruptly, which will favor each time you enter a trance. It is deeper. An example of suggestions with this technique would be: "... recognize the feeling that I am relaxed ... (= trance) ... and now I begin to wake up to a state of greater alertness ... (= awakening from the trance) ..."

Self-hypnosis is an excellent tool that you can use to program your mind. It operates on the principle that your brain becomes extremely receptive to suggestions when you relax and stop thinking. These suggestions then take root in your mind and leave their mark on your life.

Your brain is a very complex organ. You are constantly thinking, rationalizing, and reasoning. You often resist taking new thoughts and attitudes that you need to create a better life for yourself.

Like affirmations, self-hypnosis is a gradual process. Every time you do it, you program your mind towards what you want, but that programming usually fades. Thus you need to repeat your self-hypnosis sessions from time to time until your mind becomes fully convinced of the new ideas you are acquiring.

You don't need any fine equipment or software for this. Just use a cassette tape. To create and use your self-hypnosis tape effectively, follow these instructions.

- Make sure there are no distractions. Turn off your cell phone and disconnect your phone line. You don't want to record for 20 minutes and be interrupted!
- Don't worry about making a mistake in the words while you are reading the writing. Just keep your poise. When you listen

to the tape later, any speaking mistakes you made will seem so trivial that you will hardly bother to notice.

- Make sure there is no environmental noise, such as air conditioning or road traffic.
- When you start to read the writing, use your regular voice. Speak at a moderate pace, neither too high energy nor too slow. So when the recording is talking about "relaxing oxygen," go down slowly and use a more relaxed voice. When you listen to the tape, you will move into a deep state of tranquility, so you need the tape to have a calm voice.
- When you listen to the tape, again turn off phones or other potential distractions. You don't want to be in a deep sleep only to get violently interrupted.
- Get comfortable, with your body lying down and relaxed when you listen to your tape. I like to lie down on a sofa.
- Listen with an open mind. Follow the instructions you have given yourself.

Engraved Rite

Close your eyes. Take a deep breath. Allow yourself to feel relaxed.

I want you to feel all your tensions today, all your worries producing tension, gathered into a tight little ball on your forehead. Feel the tension of how you worried

about being rejected by girls in the past.

Feel the stresses of work, your career, your ambitions, and everything else on your forehead. Now I want you to imagine all those tensions draining out. Let them drain out of your forehead, down your face, down your chin and neck, down your chest, your stomach, your waist, and then down your legs and through your toes until they exit your body.

All the tension is leaving your body as you relax more and more. As you inhale, I want you to imagine that you breathe warm air, and it relaxes you. Feel the relaxing oxygen that gives you a warm, soft sensation, feeling all this in the chest cavity. Feel then how relaxation radiates throughout your chest and through your body.

Let your breath go deeper and deeper, giving you more and more relaxing oxygen. With each breath, you will enter more and more into that great state of relaxation.

(Pause 15 seconds)

Since you feel relaxed and focused, as in my voice, I would like you to repeat these affirmations mentally to yourself as I say them. I feel very good about myself. (After each of these statements, pause, and repeat). Being an optimistic person makes it possible to achieve anything I want in my life.I am constantly in continuous improvement. There are no limits to something I can accomplish, so I will program my mind to become fabulously successful beyond my wildest dreams.

I know this will work this way because I am adopting the same mindset as those truly successful men.

Now that you have said your affirmations, I will count to 10, and with each number that I say, you will be more and more relaxed, one more relaxed, 2, 3, 4, deeper relaxation, 5, 6, 7, more relaxed, 8, 9, 10.

You are now at the deepest level of relaxation that can be reached while awake. Now you will use this opportunity to program your mind to its maximum benefit.

You are a sexy man. You can make a woman happy as any man can. You want to have sex with sexy and attractive girls.

You are in charge of your own time. Nobody else has it. You choose how successful you can be in what you do, and you enjoy that power. Because you have a power of outreach, being positive, you radiate an aura of balance, of brilliance, and stillness, of constant confidence.

You have an impressive mind, and the power you have is making you stronger and stronger. It determines you achieve your goals. Now take another breath and continue to enjoy the feeling of deep relaxation. Say the following affirmations to yourself with me:

I throw away the need to allow other people to control my life. (again, pause after each of these, and repeat.

I just need my approval.

I cannot be aware of what other people are thinking about me, and I am the only one in charge of my own life.

I'm a dynamite alpha male. I walk like I am, and I think incredibly big about myself.

I love women because they are a source of fun and pleasure in my life. When I have sex with a woman, I do it with enthusiasm and for myself and my beautiful accomplice's total satisfaction.

I have lusted after making love to women. I love to make love. I love to give love.

Now is the time you just listen and don't feel the need to repeat anything. Continue enjoying the way you feel so relaxed. Just let your mind be in simple totality while letting all these thoughts flow.

When you are with a woman, you remain calm and relaxed, no matter what happens, because you are managing your own life. You don't worry or concentrate too much on what she is thinking about you, because you know well that you are a fun, interesting man, and she is lucky to be with someone like you.

You are the most important character in the universe. You are completely amazing, and any woman would be lucky to be with you—everything you want you to get because you radiate warmth and optimism. You are never going to be someone else's servant, anyone else - be it male or female. You are a natural leader, not a follower.

Things

You have an active life. You have fun, and you are looking for emotions every day, even in the details. You take care of your health, because you want to be a strong and attractive person, and live a good time. Your life is interesting. You enjoy telling stories to women about the fascinating things that happen in your life. You have an intense desire for financial success, and you know that you can achieve anything you dream of, and you enjoy getting closer to that dream.

You have ambition and want to be successful with women, your health, good friends, financial abundance, and the hobbies and passions you want. Now take a deep breath and relax. Stop for a moment and enjoy the feeling of being in full control of your life. You can be successful if you want to, you will love every minute of that success. You love that your dreams come true, as they will.

Soon you will come out of the relaxed state and begin to be more awake. As I count to five, you will be more and more awake, one, two, more awake, three.

As you wake up, you feel restored, full of energy and vigor, massive confidence. Four, your eyes open. You are an ALPHA MALE—five, fully awake. You feel restored and in a great mood!

Erotic Hypnosis And Seduction

Eroticism has been a long practice in seduction. Various well-known seductresses have to use eroticism in seduction, which involves eye, voice, body movement, chant, enchantment, incense, oil and wax, paraffin, gel, petroleum jelly, perfume, acts, letters, images, and symbols.

As these are parameters in seduction. To begin explaining erotic hypnosis and seduction, we would look at Sigmund Freud's psychosexual development analysis. He categorizes the Anal, Phallic, Libido, Genital, and Oral, which play an essential part in our sexual development. To duly define eroticism in a centered context, it is not necessarily the BDSM, Social deviance, fetish, or Lolita as most sociologists and sexologists drafted from Lolita's novel is more intense passion in the seduction of sexic and sexiness of feeling and being sexy. See it as using your mind's passionate will to please, persuade, and appeal to an individual for desires. In holistic healing, psychotherapy (psychoanalysis), neurolinguistics programming (NLP), Sex Therapy, etc., erotic seduction and hypnosis are alternative therapies for healing the mind, neurosis, psychosis, sexual repression, disorders, and sexual abuse victim. It is also useful in resolving karma, regrets, and unaccomplished wishes/dream projection and strengthening and empowering the mind, self-concept, business concept, and mana.

Erotic hypnosis is an alternative technique in self-discipline, pleasure, and cultural practices; erotic hypnosis has also been used for pleasure, discipline in self-development, and institutionalization. Most social deviance groups, personality development, and cultural groups carry out intense and extreme erotic seduction practices. In this context, erotic hypnosis and hypnotics are for pleasure, play, leisure, therapy, and discipline.

These techniques have been used only, and thereby any practices and pleasure have been verified and derived, and consciously thought out before practicing.

To begin, I will digress into shame and guilt, psychosis, and neurosis a little. This is because our belief system, values, and norms are rounded around ID, Ego, and SuperEgo. ID explains our inner desire,

139

drives, wills, and Ego explains what society expects from us. And SuperEgo is the decision and negotiation that occurs within the Id and Ego. In erotic Hypnosis, Shame and guilt are the motivators for drive and will. Therefore, as you begin exploring erotic seduction and a sense and feeling of shame and guilt, that is to open the door to better erotic hypnosis. However, at the initial stage, you might begin with that shameful paranoia which discourages thoughts, imagination, and mockery, or that guilt and gut feeling called psychosis which gives you this high of I am becoming this individual practicing this practices, that gut feeling of realization might bring intense guilt, but this is the beginning and entrance to erotic hypnosis. The instant one begins exploiting erotic hypnosis (hypnotics) and seduction. There is an increase in self-confidence, heightened self-esteem, better social relations in friendship, romantic relationships, and your sex life, and strengthened mana.

Erotic hypnosis helps to accept the world from a different perspective, build your emotional intelligence, endurance skills, and tolerance. It is almost the same principle of self-discipline in yoga, holistic healing, and wellness therapy. Most individuals with sexual disorders such as attraction disorders, arousals disorder, and sexual anxiety, et cetera, use erotic hypnosis and seduction as an alternative therapy. Let dive into my practice of erotic hypnosis and seduction.

The general term erotic does not imply intense passion, lust, fiery desire, or red and black magic/magick. It means using your mind, imagination, and visualization to desire, persuade and appeal. You can control your thoughts, imagination, fantasy, and dreams. Practicing erotic hypnosis makes an expert and applying erotic hypnosis and seduction anywhere.

A simple practice to achieve is a still and clear mind; to begin with a breathing exercise. Breathing exercises are essential in calming your mind, relaxing tension and muscles. It also aids in accessing your emotional, mental and subjective world.

First, sit in a calm place, or the environment; ventilated, where you won't be disturbed. Relax your arms, legs, and eyes/gaze have an object of concentration, then begin with an inhale and exhale from the stomach through the lung to your nostril, repeat this as much as you can, once you commence feeling the presence of cool/warm or goose-bumps sensation around you then you have access into your subjective world.

The second is self-hypnosis. Self-hypnotics practice is good because it helps in visualization and aids clear thinking and imagination. With self-hypnosis is just a step to create a subjective, emotional, and mental world with your mind. Self-hypnosis is very good to combat stress, anxiety. It is mostly called psychoanalysis in psychology and psychotherapy as this helps you understand your thoughts, imagination, dreams, and fantasy. Why is this important in seduction and eroticism? This is because you need to know how your mind works, as we control the imagination, fantasy, and dream.

Erotic Hypnosis deals with the actualization of your subjective dreams fantasy in the real world. Like, I have a nudist fantasy, and I wish to have a massage on a nudist beach with a nude masseur; this has been created in my mind through my ability to imagine and the fact that I love the idea. I accept the idea without guilt and shame is what hypnosis is as my mind has been hypnotized by imagination to have a nudist masseur for my massage session, which is done with my mind. In psychotherapy, where the therapist and the client become co-subject, to share your dream and imagination at this phase, you begin to realize that once I being the narrating fantasy of a nude beach with a nude masseur, the therapist and the client exist in the same psychical environment, for the therapist listening, it might not necessarily be the same experience.

Still, in his psychic environment, the therapist begins to create the replication of the same dream. That is why most therapists like to be more detailed in objectivity and co-subjectivity. In the dream analysis of the nudist fantasy of the nude beach, nude masseur, detailed description of the nudist fantasy visualized; I am a nudist, an African descent, chocolate complexion, 5 ft. tall.

Athletic/Muscular body, stocky legs, bubble butt, I walk into a beach. My beach description is an island with palm trees, blues, oceans, white sand, lots of corals, flowers, seaweeds, crabs, eels. The beach has a dock and tent facing the beach; close to the tents are massage table, adorned in a white robe; standing next to the massage table is a nude masseuse with a raw pineapple fruit drink, waiting for the next client, in the tents, there is a table with drinks, the waiters are all nude, walking in and out waiting and attending to guests, the atmosphere is hot, windy and chilly, the trees, leaves are in swift motion with the wind, and its sounds create the natural mythopoetic ambient that welcomes and transcends you into this heaven on earth where everyone is free in self and nature as I quickly arrive; I received, ate and drank my pineapple fruit from a masseuse and began my massage session under the beautiful palm trees with chilly wind and sea breeze. As you read or listen to my description, I and the heard ostensible of your mind exist in the same physical environment to fully understand the fantasy world created and exist in different physical environments/surroundings.

This is called inter-psychical and intra-psychical. Inter-psychical is the world of the nude beach, the ocean, waves, breeze, trees, infrastructure, the tent, people, etc. Intra-psychical is the subjective feeling, the perception I try to persuade inside the environment. Inter-psychical is also very phenomenal, as it can also exist in the physical space you exist in and in the objective and subjective world.

The next step is to use this mind-ability, breathing exercises, and visualization to create effective erotic hypnosis and seduction.

Body

The body is in the physique of anatomy in ambient consciousness in an expressive artistic and aesthetic manner in a balanced interaction and elasticity with the psyche and body (psycho-somatic), and in the

142

theory of deep social mind of the theatrical mind, thy self and self-concept and business concept, which Include; The use of the five senses; Seeing, Hearing, Touch, Smell and Taste is a composite of the body, physiology, mana, and mind, also is the heat exchange, (energy), temperature, electro-magnetic bond field, electro-chemical contact reaction in the aura of aether body and exchange in the etheric world, the light of reflection and refraction (seeing). Holistically this stimulation is done by arousing the moon center of the body: sensitive and pleasure spots in the body; Ajna (third eye (intuition or instincts) or mind's eye and heart chakra or opening chakras), eyes, neck, upper and lower back, lips, earlobes, nipples, breast, vulva, vagina, penis and scrotum, anal orifice (anus), anal sphincter, G-spot, Play pleasure spots, perineum, perineal- raphe, phallic of the navel, the calf of the legs, feet and toes, arm, hand and fingers, touch, feeling, movement and dummy trail, piercing, massage, dance BDSM, others include, aura scents, influence, sexual intelligence (sapio sexuality), wishes and dream fantasy, reasoning, character and behavior, psychic arousal of flirts, tease, erotic hypnotics of mental illusion.

Eyes

The most important and essential organ for hypnosis is your eyes, and your eyes are the door to your soul. The pupil and the iris of the eyes allow light to pass through into the retina as accommodation which helps in sighting and vision for dim, dark, bright reflection and minds eyes and vision or visualization. It tells your emotions, feelings, shows desires. When in erotic seduction and hypnotics hypnosis, the eyes can tell shame, guilt, pain, and pleasure.

The ability to read the eyes and their emotions helps understand how to persuade, please, be an object of desire and subject for lust. The pupils and iris are the main part of the eyes, which aid in hypnotics; once you begin to touch someone, the iris moves its dilator muscles to dilate the pupil. Most circus magicians use this to take away your attention for a few seconds and change a reaction for you to see; master the art of seducing with the eyes will begin to persuade and

143

appeal to someone. In eyes techniques, use the general spiral hypnosis, clockwise and anticlockwise, for dilating pupils in hypnotizing and seduction. The winking blink of erecting eyelid and lashes: the eyelid and lashes signal lust, desire, and enchantment. Erecting your eyelashes and Dilating eye is done in this manner; use chi energy and transfer chi energy to the eyes, allow this flow through the eyelid, use chi energy to create lust, desire, passion, rejection, intimacy, the chi energy erects eyelashes and therefore letting you begin hypnosis. This is effective and useful for people with attraction disorder and in the awakening of the mind, eyes and opening the awareness of heart chakra and chakras, visualization or Ajna.

Lips

Lips are part of the oral and also display erotic. In this instance, you don't need to kiss, pout or lick the lips to hypnotize, although this works quite well for some individuals. Lips are very seductive. It is very arousing. For my erotic techniques, the lips function like a vulva which expands and contract. But in this manner it grows bigger. This is easier by letting the blood flow into your lower lips first and upper lips. This is seen with people with voluptuous lips. For women who apply lipsticks, you can expand your lips, thereby creating this seductive shape of your lips shaded by lipstick. This is useful in attraction and in seducing as when with your partner, you direct their gaze to your lips and quickly give expansion and contraction, most times like a lip-sync, a small movement of the lower lips and afterward the upper lips. Be cautious not to portray a pout, kiss which might be desperate or repulsive to the viewer and ruin your hypnosis.

The ear

Is also a sensitive part of the human body. It is sensitive to sound and touch. The ear is also very useful in erotic hypnosis and hypnotizing and seduction as you use breath, air, and lick to dangle in a show of desire, lust, and intensity. In auditory hypnosis and hypnotizing, the ear conveys your voice/sound into the brain and decodes these sounds into feeling as heard ostensibly. Therefore, having a whisper is always enchanting and hypnotizing; a whisper with a dangle of the earlobes and loops will get the subject for desire into pleasure.

Body Movement

The body movement is also a technique in erotic hypnosis, as this involves using your mind (psyche), muscles, body in depicting an act of your intended imagination in expectation and reception of the desired pleasure. This visualization of the mind has to be balanced in the psyche-somatic mind and body balance and stimulation, done by arousing the body's moon center. Most movements include hypnotizing seductive appeal; belly dancing, strip dancing, nipple jiggling, navel plays, tiptoes walk, swirl walk, slow dance, wheelbarrow, butterfly whirl, Spiral swirl walk, and dummy trails. Dummy trails represent seductive acting using yoga techniques/positions, Kamasutra, or general Hide and Seek pattern. Most of Kamasutra are slow-acting to seduce and enchant. When using yoga positions, this is more seen in Tantra and sexual yoga, which are more in healing, recovery, disciplines, institutional, rehab, Sex therapy, Neuro-Linguistic programming. Dummy trailing is very intense and requires experts. When used in institutional, make sure you understand the terms and agree to not lead to sexual abuse and assault.

Piercing

Is intense for social deviance groups, such as BDSM, body modification, etc. To piercing in erotic hypnosis is not to intend bleeding, tear but to transfer deep erotic pleasure to the skin, just like using acupuncture, dummy needles. The use of erotic needles, pins, or other tools can help intensify seduction. When ready for piercing, apply oil on the skin and apply touches on the sensitive area. You can also use your fingernails in piercing, as this helps you radiate heat in sensitive areas.

Massage

145

Is another body technique in erotic hypnosis; a pat by your friend, lover, and the boss can signify hypnosis. A warm wax or candle wax on your skin also implies the erotic sensation of a massage, But be careful about the misinterpretation of intent to be seen as sexual harassment. That is why emotional intelligence is needed. Massage helps to relieve stress, anxiety, tension, relaxation, and reward. Therefore using massage is very vital. Whichever massage technique you use, this is implied in erotic hypnosis and seduction.

Mental

The second category includes storytelling, narration, psyching, visualization and imagination. As explained earlier in my nudist fantasy description, you can see how I have used my imagination to create the fantastical world as my environment for desire. Most times, we create the world, people, objects, and things to heighten our desires. Psychically, in hypnosis, eroticism also visualizes in god and goddess worship. In the real sense, you are creating an archetype for your erotic pleasure and birth into the mental or psychical world of the heavenly, as in the myth of the sex worship found in these gods and goddess worship of Golem, Erzuli, Ayizan, and Aphrodite, Guédé, Dambalo-Wedo, and Aida-Wedo, in which your self-hypnotics is invocation and ascension into a realm or sphere in honor of your favorite gods and goddess for your worship and to fulfill that will for the work.

In self-hypnotics, your imagination is the creation of a world of realism that fits your reality. As you begin practicing self-hypnotics, you can enchant someone with your fantasy, dreams, imagination. Just like creating an invisible scriptwriter or a narrator, as writers call, "third person or writer's voice." These are useful in understanding how your subjective world and inter-subjectivity relate to you and using this in persuading and appealing. Tantra and tantric are also useful in mind. You are using both your mental or subjective abilities with your body to create a sensual and seductive movement using the mind to center. To sync with the world around you, Tantra requires deep discipline and constant training to apply Tantra in erotic hypnosis successfully.

Telepathy is also another technique in erotic hypnosis, using your mental abilities to communicate to the other person close to you or interpret the mind eyes or visual/vision as intuition or as instincts or awakening of heart chakra and heartbeat. It is transferring of energies, thoughts, and visuals in the form of congratulatory or validation. In a relationship, marriages, and twins, communication is usually telepathically without using words or symbols but using emotions, feelings, and thoughts. Therefore, I can send you my desires, feelings, and thoughts using my eyes, visual, memory, and vision. Mind etc. requires practices and discipline to achieve higher communication and used in erotic hypnosis. Understand social psychology of the deep mind, deep social mind of an ostensive and inferential representation in inter-subjectivity of mind as a social psyche/mind in relationships and interactions of social mind/psyche of person/people in the group and within groups, and understanding mental states of others.

Reiki is another mental technique, and I have used this severally and received various mental and physical feedback, thereby creating sync between mind and physical (psyche-somatic). Reiki is like telepathy but at a farther distance. These energies can help heal stress, anxiety, depression, etc. I have used Reiki with Tantra to send sexual energies within my body and mind.

Auditory

Auditory hypnosis involves using words, sound, or accent (phonetics) and intonation, speech, linguistic style, talking, and listening to generate sound and imagination for visualization and an ambient environment of influence and perception for realism. This involves the ambient environment, music, erotic moaning, breath, silence, and auditory schizophrenic enchantment.

Auditory works well with mental representation as you use the word to influence perception. The receiver creates an image of your hypnotizing perceived representation.

Tone, speech, and using emotions such as in the case of hypnotic schizophrenic emotive empathy, in my technique, the intonation, vocal pitch, and tone are in a range of crossfading, traveling on a wavelength between normal, slow, sensual, and moaning or heartbeat and inner voice for erotic hypnosis and hypnotizing. I have also used breath, silent breath (silence), and loud breath; this works well in rhythmic wavelength, which helps relaxation, congratulatory, orgasm, happiness, eroticism, and hypnotics of hysteria.

Music is also important in auditory hypnosis; sound effects and ambient effects, like, wind, rainfall, etc., are also effective in auditory hypnotics.

Having considered my techniques, why not try a few of these? Remember to use your imagination and have a safe word, limit as these can be compulsive and dangerous—happy Wellbeing and Wellness.

CHAPTER FIVE

THE ART OF BODY LANGUAGE

What Is Communication?

It is worth questioning what it is about communication? There are many definitions of this word, but if we look at the Royal Spanish Academy, we will see that we mean "Transmission of signals through a common code to the sender and receiver" by communication. That is, in general terms that two or more people get to understand each other. It is simple, and we are talking about the elements that intervene in every communication process: Sender, message, channel, receiver, and code. Often it seems that the common code par excellence (which allows the sender to spread a message and the receiver to interpret it) is the word, the language, but it is not always the safest.

Once it has been defined that verbal communication is not the only method used to communicate, it is important to make clear, on the one hand, the relationship of interdependence that exists between the verbal and non-verbal channels (since they are not independent of each other, rather they complement each other); and secondly, the contradictory nature of this relationship, since words can say something and gestures deny it.

Non-verbal Communication

When we talk about non-verbal communication, we refer to all those messages that we send without speaking. We talk about gestures, expressions, body movements, eye contact ... a whole series of signals that are very important in the relationship between people. Therefore, studying non-verbal communication means knowing how to interpret everything that words do not say.

If there are three important points to highlight about non-verbal communication, it is an unconscious type of communication that we cannot act on. Second, each gesture has meaning within the same context. Therefore, isolated gestures should not be analyzed but rather should be analyzed as a whole. And thirdly ... that human communication is very complex.

It should be remarked that non-verbal communication studies are relatively new. Although Darwin already pointed out some aspects of this science, until the beginning of the 20th century, there was no significant interest in communication through facial expressions. Moreover, it took the 1950s for some authors to decide to channel the issue.

As Flora Davis points out, "Words are beautiful, fascinating and important, but we have overestimated them excessively" since, in communication, not all the merit of the message goes to the words. Still, there are a whole series of elements that also are present. Psychologist Albert Mehrabian decomposed the impact of a message in percentages, giving a first and important place to body language with 55%, a 38% to voice, and the last place to words with only 7%. These numbers, known as the 7% -38% -55% rule, do not apply to any communicative situation, they vary according to the circumstances, and on numerous occasions, the author denies their universal nature. As can be read on their website: "Total result = 7 Verbal + 38% Vocal + 55% Facial: Please note that this and other equations concerning the relative importance of verbal and non-verbal messages were derived from experiments related to communication of emotions and attitudes (i.e., like-dislike). Unless a communicator is speaking about their feelings or attitudes, these equations are not applicable. "

Once non-verbal communication is well defined, it is important to know how to distinguish the three typologies: Paralinguistic, Proxemic, and Kinesic.

Paralanguage is the set of non-verbal elements of the voice. We refer to its intensity or volume, speed, rhythm, intonation, laughter, and crying to understand each other better. For example, a deep voice will give us more respect and authority than a voice with low dominance.

Proxemics refers to the use of space by two or more people in the communication process. That is the distance between the emitter and the receiver. Edward T. Hall was a pioneer in researching the use of space. They speak of different types of distance:

- Public distance (more than 360 cm). Distance to speak in a group.
- Social distance (between 120 and 360 cm). Social gatherings and parties.
- Personal distance (between 46 and 120 cm). It is the distance that separates us from strangers.
- Close distance (between 15 and 45 cm). It is the most important and is what a person has as their own space. Only people with a very effective relationship are allowed to join.

Finally, Kinesic or Kinesis studies the meaning of body movements and gestures in a communicative situation ... It is essential to highlight that the body movements carried out may or may not have the intention and that eye movement is also included in Kinesic. Since this type of non-verbal communication is the one that can be seen represented in the short film, we will try to define it in greater detail.

Kinesis types:

151

Posture: It expresses the attitude of people concerning their environment. A distinction is made between an open posture, when a person opens up to communication without putting up physical barriers such as crossing arms or legs, and a closed position, when we cross arms and legs, separating ourselves from our interlocutor.

Gestures: These are movements of any part of the body that can express a multitude of sensations and emotions. For example, showing the fist with the thumb raised will mean the familiar "OK."

Face expressions: Through the face, we express countless states of mind; we can express up to 1000 possible emotions. In his book Emotion in the human Faces, Paul Ekman shows that facial gestures reflect our emotions. After many years of study, he established seven facial expressions on the human face: happiness, sadness, anger, disgust, surprise, fear, contempt.

The gaze: Eye contact is very important since in the communicative act it plays a series of roles: it regulates communication (it is an indicator of the turn to speak or act), it is a source of information (a sustained gaze is not the same threatening than an affective look), expresses emotions and communicates the nature of the interpersonal relationship.

The smile: It expresses joy, sympathy, or happiness. In his work Social Intelligence, Daniel Goleman writes, "Ekman has identified eighteen different types of smiles based on different combinations of the fifteen facial muscles involved." Among them, it is worth mentioning, to name just a few, the fake smile that seems attached to an unhappy face and transmits an attitude of the type "smile and cheer," which seems the very reflection of resignation; the cruel smile displayed by the wicked person who enjoys hurting others and the distant smile characteristic of Charles Chaplin, which mobilizes a muscle that most people cannot voluntarily move and seems, laugh out loud.

Touch and smell: Human beings also communicate through smell and touch. Both the skin and the nose are receptors for messages.

Seduction

The cinema, television, literature, and theater have been in charge during all this time to remind us of great seducers who have marked history. Cleopatra, Casanova, Kenedy are just some of them.

Now let's take as a reference the meanings that the Royal Spanish Academy offers us about the word "seduction": Deceive with art and skill; Gently persuade for something bad. Physically attracting someone to obtain sexual intercourse from them and Seizing or captivating the mood.

It should be remarked that although most of the time we use this term to refer to sensual relationships, it is true that this is not the case since we can feel seduced by objects such as clothes or shoes, by the speech of a politician ... It is important to distinguish between affective, social and professional Seduction among others. For this reason, seducing is attracting or pleasing by physical appearance or an opinion. It is about offering something pleasant to the eye of our interlocutor. Argues the Psychologist Vallejo-Nájera, "We love that they seduce us because they are mainly offering us pleasure."

The psychologist affirms that "Seduction is related to love success, but it is not only that. We seduce each time we communicate, and we make the person in front of us feel attracted to us. There is a genetic load because more people are extroverts, who have it easier, and others less. But it also influences how we were the first relationships with parents, friends, teachers. "Therefore, Seduction does not only exist outside the love field, but we also seduce since we are little.

Vallejo-Nájera in Psychology of Seduction offers a classification of the existing seductive prototypes according to roles. He maintains that the first step is to discover which typology suits our characteristics.

153

- **Aphrodite:** Gives off sensuality, which offers serious, protective men. You want security and to feel pampered. His emotionality fluctuates between laughing and crying. The seductress feels that his image of a sexually powerful man is strengthened. To seduce her, you must offer her loyalty, security, and optimism.

- **The low life:** He seeks adventure and offers an overflowing passion to women who are a little insecure and maternal. For this, he entertains them with ardor. He is narcissistic but with self-esteem problems; therefore, he needs admiration. To win him over, you have to admire him and help him channel his emotions.

- **The rescuer:** It is the angel who solves all problems, offering help and generosity. They look for chaotic, clueless people with low self-esteem. He is motivated by feeling indispensable. To seduce them, you have to admire their help and help you to spend time with yourself.

- **The artist:** Creative and romantic, he looks for people who are sensitive to beauty, who are struck by his genius. They want to feel special, and therefore their idealism must be respected, valuing their authenticity.

- **The captivator:** Cheerful and agile verb, he is the king of empathy who looks for rigid and self-demanding people who need positivism. Enjoy life and to conquer him, you have to avoid being unhappy and not criticize anyone.

- **The intellectual:** Offers wisdom to anyone who wants intellectual stimulation. They are very selective and imply that they do not need the other. To conquer them, you have to respect their space and solitude and not overwhelm them with emotional demands.

- **The charming:** The oasis of tranquility and friendliness, support, and lack of pretense, especially with stress problems. The charmer does not argue and nurtures the opponent's self-esteem. It motivates you to feel comfortable.

● **The divo:** It is the style, the 'glamor' without apparent effort, with which he catches people overwhelmed by routine. The divo is ethereal, insinuating, and distant and seeks perfection. To attract him, you have to encourage him not to treat himself so harshly, to make him enjoy the small pleasures of an imperfect life.

The language of seduction

"To be seductive. We all secretly dream of it, and we all defend ourselves well from its attacks; it is the nature of Seduction (...) The truth is that everyone wants to seduce, and Seduction is at the center of all human relationships" Philippe Turchet, The language of Seduction.

We will start from a premise: The most seductive people, beyond their physical appearance, are those who know how to communicate. There may be beautiful people who do not have Seduction's art among their gifts, who do not have that charm that captivates their interlocutors. Thus the words communication and Seduction are two processes that go hand in hand.

Logically before a good communicator, we are captivated, but not by the message sent, but by how it is transmitted. The seducing art is based on sending imperceptible messages (some messages only last hundreds of milliseconds) to make our listener interested. However, these messages are not indistinguishable to the brain, which is in charge of processing and adapting to them. Thus, it can be said that gestures act as subliminal messages.

Philippe Turchet, who in his book The Language of Seduction advises fleeing from words to seduce, is the father of Synology. This science was born in the 1980s after several years of study. This discipline tries to decipher the meaning of small gestural details, facial micro-expressions, gestures, and body movements that we perform unconsciously (such as why we support our head on one of our hands or why we cross our legs).

We have already commented that words should not be as important as gestures in the communication process; that is why we must give a vote of confidence to gestures in the event of a contradiction between gestures and words. Many studies show that words are unable to convey emotions.

A very decisive stage in Seduction is childhood. Although it may not appear similar to it, this process does not develop when we reach a certain age, but since we are small and we make contact with social relationships, we learn to use it. We have always seen how there are children at school who are more charismatic than others.

Head and face

When it comes to representing emotions on the face, various elements act the mouth, the eyebrows, the eyes, and the gaze.

It should be noted that the left part of the face is the part of the emotions, controlled by the right hemisphere. However, the right part is the control part and is directed by the left hemisphere. Very contrary to what we think, our face is not symmetrical.

The eyes and the gaze

If we observe our interlocutor's gaze, we can answer some questions, such as if they pay attention to us or simply if we attract them. In this sense, the eyelids play a fundamental role, since when people are listening, we weblink to accept the information that comes from outside. A person who stops blinking does not pay attention. Like when we use the expression "Being in Babia" to describe someone clueless. The more I blink, the more immersed you are in the conversation.

Another detail to highlight is the brightness of the eyes or the size of the pupils. When we are in the appearance of someone we love, our eyes become moist, and the pupils tend to increase in size. Simultaneously, if our interlocutor looks at us, and the desire is mutual, his pupils will also enlarge.

The eyebrows

When we worry that our interlocutor does not open up to communication, our eyebrows immediately take a "V" shape. This gesture will show on your face that something is not right for many words that say otherwise.

The mouth

This part of the face is considered a very desirable area. Logically, the actions we perform with our mouths are different from what we can perform with our eyes. If we realize, when we are interested in a person, our gaze goes directly to his mouth. It is a form of approximation. Besides, we also use our mouth to moisten our lower lip, thus expressing our desire. If this movement is made from left to right, the desire is sexual.

The smile

To know if a smile has been sincere, it is enough to analyze if the eyebrows have descended, wrinkles have been created on the crow's feet, and if the teeth are visible. If this does not happen, the smile is fake.

The hand on the face

When our hands go to the face, it is not by chance; they also intend to transmit messages. A well-known sign covers your mouth with your hands, which is nothing more than an expression of shame derived from childhood when we hide our faces behind our palms.

Another well-known sign that creates a lot of controversies is that of stroking your hair with your hands. It is thought that this act is a sign of Seduction, but it is not like that; not all hand gestures with hair have that intention. Some are only self-contact, while others are looking for an approximation. To know how to distinguish, it is important to look at how high the hand is, if it is close to the listener or if, on the contrary, it is as far away as possible. Besides, the palm state also comes into play; if it is uncovered, it expresses opening, while if the person making the gesture is hidden, it closes.

Another very common gesture is to support the head; on the one hand, this gesture is nothing more than the desire to attract attention, to seek that our interlocutor looks at us.

Micro-itches

A distinction must be made between itching that appears because we are uncomfortable and itching that is sexual. When we talk about the former, we refer to situations in which we are with someone we like, but for some reason, we are uncomfortable, and our body reacts through itching in the ear, nose, chin, or cheek. Regarding the latter, the most important is the one that appears in the "Cupid's Bow," the space between the higher lip and the nose.

The gestures

Gestures in conversations are more than important. Rather than complement the word, they provide the true meaning of the message. Some studies show that Italians are the most seductive people in Europe. Coincidentally they are the ones who have the most gestures in their culture.

The hands

The hands say a lot about our emotions. If we present the open palm when we speak, this translates into an opening to communication; the opposite occurs when the palms are not shown. If we hide them, for example, behind our back, we are hiding our emotions. Also, when we decide not to participate in communication, our hands lower their temperature.

The shoulders

This area is very special since next to the neck, we reserve it for very effective relationships. By caressing some part of the body, we unconsciously take our interlocutor to the area where the caresses fall. If a man and a woman are attracted at high levels, they make small movements with the left shoulder as a call.

The trunk

The trunk is faithfully linked to our ego, to our person. If you think about it, when we refer to ourselves, we touch the trunk. In this area, a series of trunks may appear, especially in the left breast. This action represents contradictory wishes. When, for example, we want to get close to someone, but something holds us back.

Arms and forearms

Together with the hands, the arms and the forearms are an extension of what we say; they also symbolize people's relationships. When we caress our arms on the outside, we are expressing the desire to be caressed. It is very important to see how the fists are because if they are not supinated, we want to be caressed, but we do not open ourselves, especially to the person close to us. This gesture is deepened if a slight tilt of the head accompanies it. Another common gesture is crossing your arms and stroking your shoulder with one hand. If we caress the right shoulder, our feelings are closed; however, our emotions are externalized if we caress the left shoulder.

If what is caressed is the forearm, this gesture indicates a desire to be closer to the interlocutor. We offer ourselves to them; we are more distant from the trunk, from our person. Besides, the caresses in the inner part of this area indicate a relational desire.

When there are contradictory thoughts about a couple's desire, our body also reacts with slight itching in these areas as repression. These micropores represent a contradiction between what is said and what is thought, between words and emotions.

Fingers

The heart and the ring finger are two fingers that play an important role in the seductive process. The middle finger represents a physical desire, while the ring finger is the symbol of union. If a person wears a ring between their fingers and slides it all over their finger, it means they want to get closer. It does not have to be a sexual desire since, between friends, it can happen.

Elbows and wrists

Elbows are very present in desire; we use them to give hugs. Micro-itches may appear on the elbow; this gesture denotes a large opening.

On the other hand, when we talk and gesture, our wrists' state is of special importance. If we open them, presenting them, we offer ourselves to communication. However, if we hide them, we are expressing a rejection.

The legs

Just as the upper part of the body expresses affective desires, the lower part symbolizes physical desires, so both parts' messages are different. It should be noted that with the legs, we have much greater freedom of movement than with the arms. Besides, there are situations in which the legs are subject to being hidden (when we are sitting at a table), but this does not mean that they do not express their desire but rather express themselves with greater autonomy. Leg crosses serve to exclude and include people in a specific situation. Just look at which leg we cross and where the leg is pointing to know who we are leaning towards.

Another difference between the two parts of the body is that men do not use the lower part in the same way as women to express openness. First, the females open their ankles or, if they are sitting, make slight movements with the ankle that will point the interlocutor. However, males slightly spread their legs. Also, if they scratch their knee, they express the desire to get close to a woman. If what they scratch is the thigh, they manifest sexual desire.

What Is Body Language?

The communication that we carry out through our body greatly influences social relationships and is the perfect mirror of emotions.

It has happened to everyone that they have met a person, but this person did not convey confidence. This is frequently because there is a contradiction between what they are communicating verbally and their body language.

Body language: It is a kind of non-verbal communication based on the gestures, poses, and movements of the body and face. It is usually done automatically, so it is a good indicator of the person's emotional state.

On other occasions, the opposite may happen, that we meet someone who has coordinated body language and verbal communication and gives us good feelings. There are many moments in the business world when you have to speak in public and generally under pressure, so you must have good control over non-verbal language. This way, you will be closer to achieving your goal. The examples that you can see in this post will be great for:

- Presentations
- Talks.
- Network.

Of course, you must mind that non-verbal communication can be influenced by environmental circumstances, and, therefore, it is not an arbitrary truth. To be able to do an inspection and be sure of it, you must find periodic signals.

161

Body Language Clues To Watch Out For

Your gestures and postures say more about you than words. To be prosperous in business, you must know how to make an excellent impression.

Body language and non-verbal interaction can have a huge impact on your professional life, as well as creating or breaking a deal, a business relationship, and even your financial success. "In business, one of the most significant things is the impression you make on people," says Eliot Hoppe, author and body language expert.

Body language includes body movements, facial expressions, gestures, and tone of voice. Take note of Hoppe's tips to optimize your probability of success:

- **Posture:** People make assumptions about others in the first four seconds, says Hoppe. "In business, you have to remember that when you walk into a room, people have already decided for you before you sit down."
- **Handshake:** Physical contact is an essential part of body language, so doing it wrong could lead to rejection while doing it right can be the first step to a successful business transaction. "In most parts of the world, a business handshake is a norm, and from there, you can get a concept of whether the person is dominant and aggressive or passive," says Hoppe.
- **An important caveat:** Watch the "power play." Observations like weak or firm grips can be easy. But you should also check when greeting someone if the other person tries to move the grip so that their hand is up. "This is a power game," says Hoppe. Although most of these reactions are unconscious, sometimes they sign what the person wants from you.

You should also observe what the freehand does during the salute. Does the opposite person use the second hand to squeeze your hand or to press the other arm? The higher the free hand is, the greater the power play, according to Hoppe.

George Bush and Tony Blair were a typical case of a power-play touch. "Who put their hand up or walked into a room first was always a topic,"

Another tip: Don't hold a drink in hand you use to greet people. "All the other person will feel is a cold, wet hand," says Hoppe. "And you don't want to give that hypothesis."

Touching your face: Never touch your face. This shows a lack of trust and dishonesty while touching your lips can sign a lack of understanding. "When you see someone reach their face, you instantly distrust them," says Hoppe.

The tone of voice: Plays a very crucial role in communication. "If you are trying to persuade someone of something, pay attention to your tone of voice. If you are making a statement or giving an order, your voice should reduce its pitch at the end of each sentence. So if you're trying to convince someone, make sure you do it. "

Also, be careful: A person trying to disappoint someone tends to raise his voice at the end of each sentence.

Clothing: Red and yellow are colors of power. Be careful when wearing them, as they can show confidence or make you look arrogant in front of people.

Appear vulnerable: Look at your colleagues' items such as pens and glasses; do they have chewed edges? How do they hold their books or portfolios? These behaviors indicate how a person conducts negotiations, as well as their business trust. "When we feel helpless, we protect our neck area. When someone feels vulnerable, they try to protect themselves (holding books or papers in front of their chest or touching their neck), which is a technique to show self-confidence".

163

Standing posture: If you want to make the best impression face-to-face with someone, take a small step to the left so that your right eye is directed directly into the colleague's right eye.

How To Improve Your Body Language

Body language is ancient and innate to us; it is even more so than the language itself and facial expressions. That is why blind people make the same body language expressions as people who can see. It comes as pre-programmed in our brain.

I have always been fascinated with this and how it helps us achieve our goals in life. The power of body language is described very well by Amy Cuddy in her famous phrase:

"Our non-verbal language governs

the way other people think and feel about us."

If you're anything like me, then you've had a healthy obsession with this for some time. Some studies at Harvard, Princeton, and other major universities have shared something new on this topic and how to use it at work in recent years. Although the power of communication is very important in delivering the right message, the power of body language can be a determining factor in how someone makes us feel.

Here is a sampling of some of the studies on how to use non-verbal language to your advantage every day:

Your body expressions express more emotion than your face. We all turn up discovering how to deal with others based on facial expressions. Nevertheless, that may not be the best way to judge someone else's emotions. Researchers at Princeton did a simple experiment. They asked study participants to judge a photograph if they felt happiness, loss, victory, or pain. Some photos simply showed facial expressions, some body language, and some both.

164

In four experiments, participants guessed emotion based on body language - alone or combined with facial expressions - rather than easy expression alone. Extremely negative or extremely positive emotions are especially difficult to distinguish.

Body language is not something we have to learn. Most of the emotional expressions already come into our system. For example, scientists in British Columbia observed people with congenital blindness at the Paralympic Games. So if body language is so ancient and so powerful in expressing our true emotions, how can we best use it in our lives to achieve what we want?

Body Language Changes Us.

Amy Cuddy describes some of the most peculiar events of body language. It focuses on the business world and how non-verbal language is good for this, and the possibilities seem limitless. Cuddy chooses between two different types of body postures. One is the pose of power, and the other is the one that has no power.

Cuddy's research reveals a lot of interesting things. The first tells us that expressing more power poses helps us get jobs, makes us feel better and more successful.

You don't have to do much, just improve the position of your arms or legs. Cuddy explains that there will also be changes in our body when there are changes in our body language. These changes have to do with hormones:

- Testosterone. The "power" hormone, where among other things, it helps us to be better leaders, have more focus and attention.
- Cortisone. The "stress" hormone, which, among other things, makes us less reactive to stress, distresses us, and we feel powerless.

The key is to fake it until you believe it. Here are five poses to work on today to answer the question, "How can I improve my body language?"

Focus on the status of your feet.

Carol Kinsey Goman has examined the importance of body language in the workplace for many years. One of his best tips is to pay attention to your feet.

Many times we focus on the top, but the feet reveal more about our emotions than we would like to think:

"When you approach two people talking, you can be perceived in one of two styles. If your two colleagues' feet stay in place and twist only their upper torso in your direction, they don't want to join your conversation. But if their feet open to including, you know you are invited to participate. "

To find out if the conversations are over, she advises us this: "When you're talking to a co-worker who appears to be paying attention and whose top is tilted toward you, but their legs and feet are facing the door, the conversation is over. His feet are telling you that he wants to leave. The position of the feet can be revealed even if the legs are crossed. "

Smile; it will make you happier.

We smile because we are right, but does it work the other way?

Researchers at Cardiff University think so. Without actually feeling happy, people who laugh can make them even happier, says Michael Lewis, a co-author of the study.

"It seems that the way we feel about our emotions does not depend only on our brain; there are parts of our body that help reinforce the feelings we are having."

Being able to smile well is another story. For now, try smiling in the bathroom or another quiet place before a difficult conversation, job interview, or meeting. It will make you feel more triumphant.

Practice Amy Cuddy's "power poses" before critical meetings.

Practice three different power poses for 2 - 3 minutes before having an extensive interview.

Try them next time in a peaceful place and see if you get the same results.

Realign your body when you have a conversation.

Another tip of Goma is that if you try to change your position when having a chat, you will reduce the tension in conversations and develop faster solutions.

"If you physically align yourself with these people (standing, sitting shoulder to shoulder in the same direction), you can defuse the situation."

Lower your voice by breathing deeply.

Although this is not a specific type for body posture, it is one of my favorites. Men and women with more deep voices are more likely to rise to leadership positions and are perceived as an authority.

To lower your voice, especially before an interview, try taking a few deep breaths. It will relax your throat, which generally contracts and raises the pitch of your voice.

Body language is much more important than we often think. It is so important that, according to multiple studies, about 93% of what we transmit in a conversation is non-verbal communication.

What Should You Look For In Your Partner's Body Language?

Below you will see different non-verbal language techniques and what their meanings may be:

non-verbal language Meaning of facial gestures in non-verbal language

When we speak, we see the person in front of us, so eye contact with the other person's face is almost obligatory and continuous. Many elements such as eyes, smiles, or hands brought to the face have much more meaning than we think.

Pupil size

It is one of the great acquaintances within body language. The decrease can mean dislike for what is being seen, while the increase means pleasure. This effect is often invisible because the pupils also adapt to changes in the environment.

Eye contact

To a considerable extent, this factor depends on the person who receives it and, therefore, within non-verbal communication, and it can have a positive or negative interpretation. It depends on the awareness that the reaction is produced in the person.

Prolonged eye contact

Staring into a person's eyes for a long period can mean that you lie to that person. In this way, he keeps his gaze, sometimes without blinking, to dodge being discovered in the deception.

Look sideways

It is an action that can have an unenthusiastic meaning since, in non-verbal language, it means indifference and that you are looking for escape routes to distract yourself.

Touch your nose

It is different from the great acquaintances in body language. The main meaning is that the person making the gesture is lying, but sometimes it can mean that the person is offended or shocked.

Voice tone and volume

Are one of the essential elements in non-verbal language.

As a clarification, it must be said that the tone is the timbre of the voice, while the volume is the power of it.

Thanks to the union of these two elements, within the non-verbal language, we can find several meanings:

- **Sadness**: It occurs when there is a moderate volume and a solemn tone in the voice.
- **Joy**: It occurs when there is a great volume and a harsh tone in the voice.
- **Disinterest:** It occurs when there is a moderate volume and tone in the sound.
- **Nervousness:** It happens when there is a medium-high volume, and you speak fast.
- **Surprise:** This happens when there is a high pitch, fast speed, and accentuated pronunciation in the voice.
- **Confidence:** This happens when there is a high volume, a determined tone, and you speak at a medium speed.

Non-verbal language is the mirror of emotions. Know their meanings!

Take care of the mouth.

It is a careless action, and the person performs it because they are insecure or need to calm down. This gesture of keeping the mouth is because it tries to return to the protection of the mother.

Fake smiles

Another of the great acquaintances of body language consists of detecting when someone is forcing a smile. A genuine smile is one in which wrinkles appear in the fields near the eyes. For this purpose, fake smiles are those that do not have those ridges.

Laugh with you

When you have a conversation with a person, and a joint laugh occurs, it means that the person is interested in the conversation. If it occurs in a group, it has the same meaning.

Rest your chin on your hands

It is a movement that within a non-verbal language can have different readings depending on the position of the palm:

- **Open palm:** It can have a meaning of boredom or lack of interest.
- **Closed palm:** It can mean that the person is evaluating what is said or done.

Head high and chin forward

You have heard the phrase "go with your head up" on many occasions. When a person realizes this gesture, it is read in non-verbal communication as a sign that shows aggressiveness and power.

Touching your ear

On many occasions, this gesture means the desire to block or not listen to the words being heard. But if the context is a discussion between two people, it may mean that the person understands that you are hiding something.

Touching the ear means the desire to block out what is being heard.

Scratching the neck

When a person performs this movement while talking to you, they are unsure what they are saying.

Closed jaw + tense neck + frown

It is a set of gestures that happen when there is a position with which you are dissatisfied.

Nod your head

It is a spreading gesture, which in most cases has a positive meaning since it communicates interest and agreement. When the gesture is made numerous times and at high speed, it means that you no longer want to listen.

Body language Meaning of the gestures of the arms and hands in verbal language, arms can be very valuable in the non-verbal language since they are great allies when communicating something. Sometimes, they harm when communicating if we do not manage their movements, and they distract the public or give different signals to the message.

Shrug your shoulders

It is a universal movement within the non-verbal language, and it means not knowing what is happening. Generally, this shoulder movement is accompanied by open palms, a slight hunch of the back, and a raised eyebrow.

Crossed arms

It is a well-known preventive body language stance that signifies rejection or misunderstanding. But you have to be concerned with this movement because it can mean that the person is cold, so you must take the circumstances into account.

171

The movement of the hands is a great ally to communicate the message.

Arms crossed with thumbs up.

It has a similar purpose to crossing the arms, but the thumbs up denote that they want to convey pride.

Hands behind your back

It is a site that demonstrates determination and shows that the person speaking is not afraid. Besides, this posture can help you gain confidence in times of insecurity.

Aim with one finger and closed hand

It is an aggressive gesture that is transmitted to other people who hear negative feelings. For the person who completes it, it has a purpose of winning over the rest.

Open palms

Performing this move-in non-verbal communication signifies honesty and reliability. Generally, it is carried out as a sign that nothing is hidden from the people who carry it out, so it provides credibility in the communication.

Speaking showing the palms of the hands gives greater credibility.

Interlock the fingers of the hands

Generally, this position of the hands is negative and conveys an anxious or repressed attitude.

Join fingertips

Although it seems marvelous, it has the opposite meaning to weaving your fingers. In non-verbal language, this hands' position means confidence and security but can sometimes be confused with arrogance.

Non-verbal language Means the gestures of the legs and feet in non-verbal language. It may be the least visible body, but it can tell a lot about the person speaking. In conversations or conversations in which you have to speak, you must control what your legs and feet' movement says to make the viewers feel contradictory to your message.

Trembling legs

When a person has trembling legs, it can mean that they are in anxiety, irritation, or both.

Forward foot

Generally, when you put your foot ahead, you do so in the direction you want to go. This can take various readings, depending on where your foot is pointing.

Exit

If your foot is pointed towards the exit door, that means you want to leave and finish as soon as possible to leave. The same thing happens if you speak to have their feet facing the exit; they want to leave.

Person: If your foot is pointing towards a person, that means that you find them interesting and are paying full attention to them.

Sitting with one leg elevated and supported on the other.

It is the most common non-verbal language presence of men. It shows a competitive attitude or in preparation for an argument.

If you seem to dance with your feet while talking, you are doing something wrong.

Crossed legs

It is a defensive and closed attitude. When a person chooses this posture with arms and legs crossed in a social context, they are not immersed in the conversation. In a marketing context, it means that the person is closed mentally, emotionally, and actually.

Crossed ankles

This sign is still within protective body language, just like when we cross our legs. This gesture is made to maintain control.

Body language Meaning of postures in non-verbal language

Postures in non-verbal language are very powerful, both personally and professionally, when doing a job interview.

It is a circumstance that gives a lot of care to what you want to communicate and, in many cases, conditions the type of gestures that are used in non-verbal communication.

Hiding behind someone or something

When a person is speaking, either standing or sitting and puts an objective between himself and the person or persons he is speaking, he seeks to defend himself. This shows that you are not sure what you are saying and are afraid to say it if it fails.

Expansive stance

When we converse, our feet are separated (at the height of the shoulders), and the arms are slightly open showing the palms. In this way, there is a posture of honesty and of not hiding anything with which you gain trust among the public.

Imitate language

When you're speaking to someone you like, the positions and movements are related. This way, you can determine if the talks or meetings are going as intended.

If the person you are talking to follows your movements and postures, the conversation goes very well.

Jug pose

It is a posture that affords greater presence and power. It happens when your feet are at shoulder height and your hands are on your hips. In this position, the chest's position also intervenes; the more outside it is, the more aggressive it will communicate.

Stick out breast

This posture occurs when the person feels they have power and control. This is very important as it means that the person has achieved some accomplishment of which they are proud. In postures to increase superiority, it can also communicate aggressiveness,

Change your body language to improve your communication skills.

Body language speaks for us; that is why it is one of the others' most important aspects. At work, mastering body language is also essential to communicate properly and demonstrate your ability.

Interpretations of body language can be misleading. As Ginny Soskey tells us on HubSpot Blogs, "If you want others to understand what you want to say without confusion, you must ensure that your facial expression, your posture, and other non-verbal signals are in tune with your message."

A person is capable of generating 250,000 different facial expressions and more than 1,000 different body postures. 82% of messages enter us through the eyes, compared to 11% that we perceive through the ear. It took us only 7 seconds to pass judgment on someone just after seeing them. Incredible true?

This is why there are such numerous body language features that influence our work's success or failure, and of course, in our daily negotiations. In addition to the five tips on body language that we gave you to improve your negotiations, take note of these recommendations to improve your communication skills and develop your leadership skills:

175

Have a positive attitude and maintain eye contact with the person you are addressing; nods from time to time and smiles. Stand up and take up space; This posture shows security and confidence and is the way to establish power if you act from a leadership position. Coordinate your body language with your verbal message; avoid contradictions. Keep a correct physical distance with the person or group with whom you speak. Not too close to be aggressive, not too far to suggest contempt or indifference.

Let others talk, don't interrupt, and pay attention. Avoid distracting gestures (for example, looking at your nails or clothes). If you are forced to disagree, use your body language to support your position. Make proper physical contact without being threatening. Do not turn your back on others. Adopt a kind posture that inspires confidence and sincerity. Do not be afraid to gesticulate while you speak; it has been proven that following a piece of information with gestures serves to understand the information better because the words become visible to our understanding.

Mastering body language is part of the difficulty of developing communication skills, which are increasingly sought after in the business world, even above employees' technical knowledge. That is why it is important to work on our soft skills with Merchants and Triskelion programs for our individual and professional growth.

Body Language As A Weapon Of Seduction

The body allows you to seduce without a word. If you are one of those who, when you speak, the bread rises, it is better that you use body language to flirt.

All human beings can flirt using body language. There are several infallible techniques to achieve the purpose successfully. Men and women use different gestures to take their flirt to the garden, but how should we use non-verbal language as a Seduction weapon?

They: a movie hunk

Before starting to forge the strategy, the man must put himself in the woman's shoes and know what is expected in that meeting: discard the idea of talking, thinking, or looking at other women. She and nothing but her is the target.

She stares into hers as if there is no tomorrow: knowing how to look is almost as important as knowing how to speak. Through the look, a person will give more or less confidence to repeat a second date. When someone looks at you, it is because they are interested in you, in your conversation, and your experiences. Don't get lost!

Take charge of the date: women like to control the situation but at the same time feel controlled. Taking the reins means keeping the thread of the conversation, bringing up topics, choosing the menu, and of course, paying the bill. Be careful going from controlling the situation to trying to control the girl!

Hands-on the table:

You don't have to be too smart; some girls like a touch, but others don't even like the sound of the wind on the first date. Use your hands to emphasize conversations, touch your chin or just have it because of your flirt. A large, well-groomed hand says a lot about the type of man in front of it.

Don't be rude:

Girls who like bad men are an old-fashioned myth. Now what is carried are the men who put themselves in women's shoes, listening and sharing. Attentive! Do not fall into being too cakey because you will bore the girl, and she will run away. He wants to take her to bed, not be her best friend.

The half-smile is better than the laugh: if the situation turns out to be funny, it is always a point in your favor. The best option to be funny without being rude is not to go overboard with the laugh or the easy

177

(or macho) joke. On the one hand, you will be fatal, and on the other, you can be offended. A half-smile is always much sexier and more manly.

A picture is worth a thousand terms: it's true. Men who take care of themselves are increasingly liked, those who know how to choose their clothes well, and those who, despite their three-day beard, are perfectly shaved. Take care of your image. They are the alphabet letters of your body language.

A Goddess Of Eroticism

If women are looking for a sensitive and manly, and protective man, they want a tigress in bed and an elegant and discreet woman on the street. The gestures that will take a man to the garden are:

Make him feel like he's in control - Guys love to think they're in control. Take a few seconds before making a decision and let him expose it; on the topic of conversation, the first course, or where you will have a drink. In the end, even if you choose, he will grow up showing more open and true. It will allow you to get to know the person in front of you better. Tangled with hair: there is no better weapon of Seduction than a woman's hair. He was gently stroking it or curling between your fingers. They will love this sexy yet demure way of flirting.

Pamper yourself a lot: caressing your body is a sign that you love skin-to-skin rubbing. His sexual character reaches the subconscious that will burn with passion for being the one who can touch you. Basic instinct: even though doctors and mothers always tell us not to cross our legs because of varicose veins ... Do a cross-over from time to time to the more 'Basic Instinct' type! Imagination is much more erotic than indiscretion.

Seductive lips: bite your lips, but watch the way you do it. You can look like a wolf if the bite is sharp or too aggressive ... they will run away.

The Unconscious Signals That Show That You Attract Her

His eyes, body movements, and the way he smiles at you are symbols that he likes you. Mindful of body language

"Oh, God, don't make me misunderstood," sang the Animals in "Don't Let Me Be Misunderstood," a phrase that millions of women and men from all over the world could utter during their nights out in search of the company of another sex or a mere time of fun when despite putting all the effort possible, communication between both sexes regarding flirting is so complicated that it leads to violent situations ("I thought you liked it"), if not directly humiliating for the one who has dared to step forward. So, we need to be armed with a little pocket guide to decipher our potential partners' intentions and avoid those traumatic episodes that we have all experienced. Is such a thing possible? The truth is that women are much more difficult to decipher than men: as Peter Hutchinson points out in an article distributed in The Telegraph, his coach Jo Hemmings had reminded him that the signs that men emit to show their interest in the other sex there are barely ten, while in the women's repertoire there are about 50 different ones, much more subtle and, therefore, less obvious to the naked eye. Leaning forward is a posture that indicates that we are interested in the other person. But this does not determine that it is completely impossible to anticipate the other person's intentions. Proxemics, which the anthropologist Edward T. Hall used to talk about the distances that separate people in different social situations, can help us understand it. Also, kinesics (the meaning of body movements) or the analysis of body language, since books such as The Body Language of Flirting, Dating and Romance (Gestech Publications) by Raymond C. McGraime, Secrets of Sexual Body Language (Amorata Press) by

179

Martin Lloyd-Elliott or Body Language Secrets: A Guide During Courtship & Dating (Steel Balls) by R. Don Steele. From all this bibliography, we discover a series of signs that we must pay attention to if we want to know that woman's intentions that interests us.

–If she preps in front of you. Pushing the hair out of the face, licking the lips to hydrate them, or putting on Vaseline or lipstick are attitudes at first unconscious that suggest that the woman is interested in the other person, so she is quick to make sure that her look is flawless. Does your suitor not mind that you see her disheveled, dressed in any way, and without makeup? Bad news.

- **Suppose she leans your body towards you.** When we sit at the table in a restaurant or next to a bar counter, leaning towards the other person indicates that we are receptive to what they have to offer us. If, on the contrary, we lean back (let alone cover our faces or place our arms in front of us), we will be adopting a reserved and distant attitude.

- **Suppose her feet point to you.** We tend to adopt postures in which our feet are directed towards that area of the room to which we want to go. This means that pointing your feet at another person means that you are curious about them, but if your potential partner has turned their feet to the door of the bar, it is because they want to shoot out as soon as possible. Dolls are one of the most sensitive parts of the female body.

- **If you move your lips,** one of the unconscious signs of courtship for women is moving their lips or drawing your attention to them through a long series of actions, ranging from simple "sniffing" to continue drinking from a glass, going through chewing of slow way.

- **Suppose you roll up your arms.** Jo Hemmings points out that the wrists are one of the most sensitive parts of a woman's body and that rolling up the sleeves indicates that a particularly intimate part of her is being exposed (although it may not seem like it). The nudity of the forearms may be only the first step on the path to total nudity.

180

- **If your pupils are dilated,** when a person feels sympathy or interest in something or someone, their pupils automatically begin to dilate. So, in addition to making ever-helpful eye contact to build rapport, the eye test can help us find out whether or not a woman is interested in us. –If your breasts show you. Let's explain this, as we don't want it to lead to confusion. As with dolls, the breasts are among the most sensitive parts of the female body and, specifically, one of the most suitable for protection. This means that, while crossing the arms in front of them is a symptom of the need for protection, presenting a body posture in which the chest stands out to the eye shows us the way forward.

- **If she raises her eyebrows**, it is a gesture that indicates that we have our eyes open to what we have in front of us and that we are curious and predisposed. Of course, there is one exception: raising the eyebrows occurs in response to an indecent proposal. In that case, it does not mean interest. It means that you must go back where you came from.

- **When you do not look away in short distances,** one of the questions makes every man lose sleep: When to launch into kissing a woman while minimizing the risk that she will withdraw her face when doing so? Some experts point out that it is relatively permissible to launch if two factors are met. The first, that the distance between the two faces is close; that is, you have exceeded the limits of what is socially acceptable with a friend or partner. Second, that the gaze between the two of you is maintained for a more or less prolonged period without either looking away; see if he makes strategic moves to get to your side.

- **If she imitates you,** we end up adopting the same gestures as those we consider interesting, influential, or seductive. If we see ourselves reflected in the woman we are interested in, we are surely on the right track. It can also happen when, for example, we grasp the fork or the glass at the same time. Be careful, though: it may be that you are simply hesitating.

- **If she touches you in a non-sexual way**, it is understood because then why would we need this advice? Proxemics points out that we tend to be closer to those people with whom we feel comfortable - so see if in a bar they make strategic movements to be next to you - and we want to establish a relationship, at the same time that we avoid gestures such as cross our arms (if this happens, you have no chance).

- **When you win in comparison,** perhaps all the above points do not speak for themselves, as it may be that a woman is outgoing enough to do all of the previously listed with any man who crosses your path. To see how he behaves with others and think about how he behaves with you. Maybe it's just like that; maybe you've succeeded.

Non-verbal Signs That Scream "I'm Not Dominant. "And How To Avoid It!

What do you think makes a guy more attractive to girls? It is the impression that you are a dominant man, in a good way. And no, you don't have to snort, scratch, and slap women like a caveman to demonstrate dominance ... nor should you! You transport your dominant male state by simply acting in the way that dominant males do, consciously controlling the non-verbal signals they send out, thus creating an impression on the female that you are Alpha. This technique is called the association principle. Within a woman's mind, you associate yourself with desirable masculine traits while casting off the undesirable "good guy" traits.

This is how magicians act. On stage, the magician carefully controls the impression he makes on the audience. By diverting the audience's attention to things they associate with magic — like his wand — he prevents the audience from noticing the things that would make him appear non-magical: the fact that he is using his hand to do the trick! Similarly, you can use the direction of the impression to control what the woman thinks of you. And here's some really good news for you:

by adopting the proper mindset discussed in this guide, you will eventually grow up to be a full alpha male. And you can start walking in that direction today by choosing the behavior of an alpha male.

So what is domination? It is the social control that comes from being successful. As you go through self-improvement, you will internalize the concepts in this book and become an alpha male in the future. Right now, learn to act like an alpha male, giving the impression of dominance using your voice, your eyes, your demeanor, and your posture.

Your gaze is the first non-verbal signal that tells people that you are an alpha male. A dominant man is not afraid to stare at people. By looking away, you communicate submission. When you look down, you communicate shyness, shame, and a sense of low status. When you're speaking, there is no boundary to how much eye contact you can perform. Studies have revealed that the more eye contact the speaker makes, the more dominant the person is perceived.

However, when you are the one listening, the opposite happens: the less you look at the other person speaking, the more dominant you become. (It has been wondered why adults say to children, "Look at me when I'm talking to you?" It is a way of reinforcing the adult's dominance over the child.)

Of course, you do not want to be above the woman and think that you look at her from below. If you are perceived as too dominant, then start to suffer from her dislike. So give your eyes a break from time to time.

Another indicator of dominance is your voice. Assertive people control the dialogue. They also speak in a sarcastic voice and are not afraid to interrupt another person. Researches have shown that using a soft, quiet voice gives the impression that you are not asscrtive. When you converse, try to let your words run and not be afraid to say what's on your mind. People who hesitate and get stuck are perceived as less powerful than those who don't.

183

Look at their mannerisms and behaviors. Try to avoid the following non-verbal indicators of beta status:

1) Use "ah" and "um," partial sentences and incomplete words. Studies have shown that people consider those who speak well to be lacking confidence and not very bright. It is a sign of nervousness. The reason we say "um" is because we are afraid of being interrupted by another person. Instead, don't be scared to pause for effect. Hesitating before important points will make you appear more competent, and people will remember what you say.

2) talking too fast. This gives the impression that you are feeling anxious and have low self-confidence. A normal and comfortable conversation is in a moderate range of 125 to 150 words per minute. Slow down!

3) Speaking in a monotonous voice, also known as stuttering. People with a narrow range of tone are seen as shy, uninteresting, and lacking in confidence. So vary its hue, and it will be perceived as an alpha.

4) Pausing too long before answering a question. This indicates that you are overthinking his answer, which makes him seem indecisive. It will also appear that you are trying too hard to win the other person's approval.

5) Closed postures. An alpha spreads his arms and legs out and is open. When standing, you can reinforce your body language by hooking your thumbs into your back pockets.

6) Keep your hands in front of you. This is a defensive gesture. Instead, be open and vulnerable. (You are vulnerable because you are not afraid.) Let your arms relax and remain open. No one's going to hit him, so why does he need to crash?

7) Play with your fingers or hands. When you are at the table in front of someone, there is a natural inclination to play with the sugar packets or wrappers with your fingers. Do not do it. And don't hit the table with your fingers - women hate that.

8) Touching her face while speaking. This indicates that you are overthinking, indecisive, or shy. To confer confidence, hold your hands together in a needle shape in front of your chest or face. (Many teachers do this when they are lecturing.) Another pose that will help you when you need a great display of confidence is to hold their hands on their hips. Police officers do this when they need to establish authority over criminal suspects.

9) Bend or cross your arms in front of you. On unique occasions, it is reasonable to fold your arms into an alpha shape (see Brad Pitt in Fight Club for a simple example of this), but as a general rule, avoid it.

10) Stiff or stooped posture. An alpha male has a relaxed position, whether he is standing or sitting. Let go and relax.

11) downward gaze. Alpha men hold their heads high. It is a show of enthusiasm, energy. Looking at the ground conveys the "loser" message. Lift your chin. Expose your neck — don't worry, no one is going to strangle you! Look at the person you are talking to; remember what I said about using your gaze.

12) Nervous facial gestures. Such as licking, he was pursuing or biting lips, sharply pinching your nose. An alpha keeps a relaxed face and mouth because he is not afraid of anything or anyone.

13) smile excessively. Primate studies have shown that beta males will smile more to signify their innocence to stronger males. Beta humans smile to show they are not a threat. The Alpha, however, only smiles when there is something to smile about. And yes — he can be a threat.

14) Walk briskly as part of your normal walk. Instead, walk a little more gradually than normal, almost like you're bragging. You are Alpha — no one is chasing you, and you are not rushing to please

185

anyone. If you're not in a rush to get somewhere, walk around as if you're relaxed and confident. Think: "I am the man. I can make any woman happy".

15) Walk only with your legs. Don't be afraid to push your torso and arms. Try this: walk as you've just had incredible success and feel on top of the world. Watch what you do with your body. You may be moving your arms along with your shoulders and having a slight jump in your stride. Now, do it all the time.

16) Slack posture. You don't have to put up with standing uncomfortably straight, but you do have to push your shoulders back. Watch Brad Pitt in any of his movies for examples of how to keep your back straight comfortably.

17) blink a lot. Instead, blink slowly. Don't close your eyes awkwardly. Just allow your kids to relax. Let them drop a bit. Don't make insect eyes.

18) Alternate your eyes from side to side when speaking. That is very beta. When you are in a conversation and are speaking, stare into the other person's face. Nonverbally, this communicates that you are saying something important and worth listening to.

19) Maintaining too much eye contact when the other person speaks. Ignore the advice books that tell you to maintain continuous eye contact. The non-stop eye contact makes him seem needy, socially retarded, and frankly like a weirdo. Instead, allow your eyes to stray and then stare into her eyes. Look through it rather than at it. From extensive testing, I have found that staring at a woman about two-thirds of the time is optimal. By the way, just keep your gaze when she's saying something genuinely interesting to you. On the other hand, focus on another part such as your breasts, hair, things that happen around you, etc.

20) Uncomfortable eyes. The bottom line is that your eyes should be happy, relaxed, assertive, and sexual.

21) Look down or to the side before answering a question from a woman. If you need to look away before answering to think about the answer, look up and to the side. Studies have shown that this shows more confidence.

22) fear touching a woman. Be safe and confident when touching a woman - any nervousness can be fatal to your relationships with her. Be Alpha and physically move it when you need it. Hold her hand to guide her, etc. Be gentle — if you use too much pressure, it reveals your insecurity. (Since you're Alpha, she's sure to follow, there's so no need to be anything other than playful and cuddly.) It's natural to touch other people, like when you're emphasizing a point. So let the love flow!

23) Quickly turn your head when someone wants your attention. Instead, perform movements that you would do at home — slow and relaxed. You are not waiting for the call of others. You are the Alpha, don't forget.

24) Use long, twisted phrases. Alphas keep the conversation short and get to the point. If you tend to use long sentences, separate them.

Don't feel bad if you inevitably slip and use one of these non-verbal cues from time to time. Nobody is perfect, lest he is hard on himself, especially when talking to a woman. Let it go and keep the conversation going.

When you think too much about such things that while speaking, you start to doubt, and when that happens, you feel vulnerable and afraid and start to hesitate. Instead, work on remaining indifferent and sincere at all times.

It is enough to easily be informed of how you communicate nonverbally through everything you do. Being aware means that you will start to avoid negative communication much more from now on.

Practicing the Body Language of an Alpha Male

Look at a man with high status - Brad Pitt, George Clooney, or the President of the company where you work - and you will notice that they move differently than the rest of us. They give off vibes that they are phenomenal, and for that reason, women squirt for them.

You, too, can perform that aura that makes you beautiful to women.

Have you ever regarded the way your friends look when they feel like shit? They stare at the ground with their arms crossed, their shoulders slumped and emitting other non-alpha behaviors.

Now think about the successful bastards. They bring all the old ladies around them, and some go around with motherly body language.

Here are a few points for body language (which, by the way, if you think it's easy, you're correct ... you can make these changes as fast as tonight and have the horniest old ladies clamoring for your attention.)

1) relax. This is the most remarkable state of mind you should be in.

A) Do not feel worried.

Let your worries go as you cannot solve any problem by worrying. So don't suck, and stop thinking about what's wrong. Just live the crazy life.

Now, I know that it is easier said than done (I used an old phrase, but relevant in this case). You have spent your entire life now emphasizing the thoughts that make you feel most worried.

But what is that emotion that we call "worry?" When you think about it, it is simply the fear of what might happen in the future. You are essentially punishing yourself by feeling upset before bad things happen. So there is no logical sense to worry!!

So pollution is avoiding your worrying thoughts at all costs. Identify them for what they are - toxic to your emotional states - and let them go.

Simply NOT emphasizing negative results that make you feel upset will reduce your worries by 90%.

B) Breathe through your abdomen, preferably of your chest.

When you breathe, imagine that you are bringing air into your stomach. Feel your belly swell and deflate when you breathe.

C) Avoid non-verbal behaviors that are contrary to relaxation:

+ Elevate your shoulders.

+ Wrinkle your forehead

+ Nervously moving your hands or legs.

+ Tighten your facial muscles.

D) Relax your muscles and slow down all your movements.

Alpha males generally move slowly, as if in control of time. Beta males are nervous and make awkward movements. Imagine that you are standing and walking in a pool, where your movements are slow and fluid.

E) Relax your eyes and your eyelids.

Beta males keep their eyelids wide open because they are so nervous. His eyes flicker. Instead, let your eyelids rest. Look straight ahead. Only pay consideration to things if they interest you. While you are out and about, make the affirmation, "I am Sexual, I am Relaxed, I am in Control."

F) If someone requires your attention, move your head slowly.

189

A common trait among quite a few Beta males is, so eagerness to please that you see them turn their heads towards the other person strangely quickly when someone calls out to them.

2) Feel Masculine and Powerful.

Visualize that you are a masculine man. Do the things in your life that make you feel manly, like lifting weights and exercising with a punching bag. Watch your health.

3) Realize that you are a man of great value.

Focus on your classes and ignore your needs. To be completely confident, think things like, "I'm the mere dick, I'm a Chingón, everyone peels me."

Sound arrogant? See it as a therapy to overcome your lack of security. You will want to moderate yourself at some point once you have become successful and know that you are amazing (so that you don't act like an asshole), but until then, constantly think about your greatness.

Treat people as if they respect you even before you meet them. If you have to, visualize Elvis Presley: "Thank you, thank you very much ..."

4) Be comfortable in your skin.

An Alpha male is smiling with or without a particular female, as he regards women as the source of fun in his life - no more, no less. Take the attitude that, of course, women love you, but it's not a big deal either way.

5) Extend your body.

Take up your space with your arms, legs, and chest. Keep your neck aligned with your back so that your head is held high.

(Something that served me to get used to having my neck aligned was removing the pillow from my bed. After all, it is more challenging to have optimal posture when your neck is bent for 8 hours each night).

CHAPTER SIX

SEDUCTION

Generally, women don't make things easy for you. She is rarely going to give you an obvious sign of her interest to move forward, to kiss her, or even if she likes you or just sees you as a 'friendly' man with whom she would spend some time chatting.

Keeping her interest can be very difficult; if you see the chemistry evaporate, the longer the conversation lasts. Besides, since she's not giving you a signal, it seems impossible to start touching or isolating her or doing whatever it is that lets her know that you are attracted to her and that you want to kiss her.

Even when I was with a girl on a date, I could not enjoy it because I felt anxious before the kiss, and I always thought about how I would transition to my move. I will give you my "Chemistry Test," a simple play that you can use to test if there is chemistry between the two of you. (Simple as it is, I've found it to be incredibly successful.)

Right now, since you don't know how to bring the interaction to a sexual level, you lose the girls; And when you make a mistake with a woman, she will rarely give you a second chance. The 3-Step System to Slow Down Into Sex, which I will teach you, will fix your problem of not knowing when to play it (or if you should even).

As you flirt (don't chat, flirt; there is a big difference), she will be doing things that encourage you to jump for the close; And without you even noticing what it is doing, it will make things easier for you.

192

I decided to create this chapter because most of the questions a man can have are related to this idea of taking a 'normal' conversation and making it a flirty, sexual interaction.

Men always want to know:

- How to excite a woman from the beginning?
- How do you get him to see you as a possible sexual partner?
- How do you let her comprehend that you are interested in her sexually?
- Since she feels like she's attracted to you, what do you do?
- What to do if you have little experience or are even a virgin and he begins to ask you about your sexual life?

Serious Mistakes You Probably Make That Keep Her From Your bedroom.

There tend to be certain serious mistakes that are somewhat common, and I see that men constantly make with their women.

The first mistake is this idea of pretending you don't care. I think this stems from men heeding suggestions like "don't look too interested" or "you have to be arrogant."

Shy men often fall into this trap because they use "disinterest" as an excuse to dodge placing themselves in a situation where they have to be proactive. I know because before I was very shy and girls rarely had any idea that I liked them. For my ego, it was good because I was rarely rejected. However, it was lousy for my sex life because I hardly ever slept with someone.

But there is an even bigger mistake that men make. The mistake is that they believe that the more they talk to a woman, and the better she likes them, the easier it will be to start flirting and being sexual with her.

193

The truth is that it is the other way around. The more you talk to a woman or get to know her without becoming sexual; it will be more likely that nothing will NEVER happen to her. The correlation is the opposite: the better a woman likes you, the less likely she is to be sexually attracted to you.

The Main Reason Why Men End Up In The Friendzone

The main reason for this is that they don't want to spoil their trust with a woman. They sense that the woman likes them, and they are afraid that if they try to do something, she will think they are just another jerk trying to sleep with her. (Which you are) So it's much better, to be honest, from the start.

The reality is that a woman decides very quickly if you have the potential to be a lover, boyfriend, or friend, or if you are just another annoying man who does not want to talk to.

Most men introduce themselves as potential boyfriends and do things like:

1. You are setting too much effort into finding things you have in common.
2. Focus on showing her that you have a good job like traveling and other "boyfriend" traits.
3. Being on his side when he speaks ill of Don Juanes and acting as if he were the opposite of those "morons."
4. Respect her too much to make a move.
5. Listen to all your problems and try to solve them.

This is a huge mistake.

Why?

Because it does NOT create attraction with a woman, none of the things on that list create a single gram of sexual attraction. Even if you make her think, "you would make a great boyfriend," You keep losing because once she thinks THAT, she will start to show her "good girlfriend" qualities, which are just as boring and asexual as boyfriend qualities. Not only that, but you will build too much trust with her, and you will eliminate her urge to have sex. You presumably finish up in the friend zone.

So do we all agree that it is much better to be sexual upfront? Now that you know, when are you going to start doing it?

If you think it is not your personality, it is outside your comfort zone, and that it does not feel natural, do not worry. The 3-Step System I'm going to cover makes it very simple.

You Never Have A Second Chance To Create One First impression.

If this is strange or hard to believe, don't worry. It's not your fault. Movies, television, 90% of the books that talk about relationships, and most of your friends you unconsciously copy, are wrong.

If you're not careful, it's very easy to get this wrong. It is assumed that you nevermore get a second chance to create a first impression. This is true in the world of dating and relationships.

A few years ago, before I was good at it, I worked with a girl named Candice. She had the "girl next door" appeal. The typical girl that everyone likes. We clicked right away, and we had that all-important chemistry right from the start. The same sense of humor. It just all came together. When we were at work, we tried to pretend nothing was happening, but we would end up talking after a while. When we weren't talking, I caught her watching me, and I was sure she liked it.

This happened around Christmas time, and I knew there would be a work party for it; I decided to move on then. Since I thought she liked me, I took it for granted.

As expected, during the Christmas party we were together, talking. After the party, we all went out to a bar where Candice and I ended up together. I was saying to myself, "I'm going to make my play later when we're drunk, we're alone, and it's appropriate."

When the bar closed, I invited some to my apartment to continue the party. Candice and two friends of mine came over, and we were having a good time. Finally, when my two friends felt that they should leave me alone with Candice, they left. Now Candice and I are completely alone in my apartment. We are talking and laughing, remembering funny stories that happened throughout the night.

All the time, I was pondering about how I change the subject or get her to shut up so I can kiss her.' I was sitting on the couch, wanting to touch her and letting my hand caress hers, but I couldn't change the topic of conversation, so that instead of talking about our colleagues, we were talking about ourselves. Soon it was 2 am, then 3 am, and then 4 am. In the end, she said, "Well, I should be going."

The next time we were together, the same story was repeated: talking, laughing, a lot of confidence. However, each meeting ended up convincing me that I would do it next time. This continued for a few months until I couldn't take it anymore, and I texted her, "I think I like you."

The next day I got the speech "We better just be friends." The reason why I am telling you this story is that at that point in my life, I had already had a couple of girlfriends, and my flirting was good enough that people would assume I was good with girls, but I was keeping a secret. I COULD NOT CLOSE THE DEAL.

Some years later, after figuring all this out, some friends and I went on a ski trip, and there was Candice. Using my 3-Step System, which I'm going to show you, I was able to flirt with her, and we ended up being together all weekend. By then, it was too late for any of it to be born.

That experience made me see that that time, years ago, it was not she who put me in the friend zone. I put myself there because of the way

I acted. I want you to think about that girl you only ended up in the friend zone.

Was she the one who put you there? Or did you get there on your own because of how you acted? Don't beat yourself up; you didn't know it then.

What I'm going to teach you is going to prevent that from happening to you again.

Creating a Sex Character

I'm going to teach you how to make sure you are creating sexual tension from the beginning of a conversation. It is even more important to use that tension to make the transition that allows you to close the deal and bring it back to your room, so you don't make the same mistake.

It will also help you avoid those strange silences when you run out of conversation topics. This is because it will give you a roadmap to move forward and close the deal and get appointments. It will ensure that the girl arrives and that at the end of the date, you end up flirting with her and do not leave with a hug or a handshake.

You will notice that all these girls will change their opinion of you because of what I am going to teach you now. It is the concept of creating a Sexual Character. The initial thing to keep in mind is that women want sex; they just don't want the responsibility of making it happen.

So, women are looking for men who, according to them, can make things happen. I repeat: women look for men who, according to them, can make things happen.

That is why the same men have sex constantly. That's why this guy, who doesn't understand how he manages to have sex constantly, can do it; And he'll probably keep stealing the girls you love from you unless you realize this.

They have to believe that you can close the deal without causing things to get weird along the way. This means that you do it without giving her an ounce of responsibility. It means showing her that you are comfortable with sex and that you will not suddenly get weird.

Women sense this within minutes of talking to you.

So ask yourself: Am I that man?

Or are there settings I require to perform?

The great news is that these changes are not as difficult as you think.

Here is a tip you can use to show a woman that you are the guy who can make things happen.

The next moment you are presented to a girl, and you shake her hand, hold her hand a few seconds longer than usual. Let her be the first to retract her hand. With that, you subtly send a signal that you can make things happen. Try it today. Your first reaction will be discomfort, but trust me, you will be sending a very specific message to her.

Throughout the last seven years, my mission was to realize this. That incident with Candice brought me to a level of exhaustion where I couldn't take it anymore. I invested thousands of dollars dating almost every night with some of the best seducers in the world. I went to workshops and lessons, and I read thousands of books that had to do with the world of dating, sex, and psychology.

Then I put everything to the test with girls I met on the internet, through my social circle, in bars and clubs, and my favorite place, networking events. Through years of trial and error, sticking with what worked and taking away what didn't, I was able to condense it all into this simple 3-step System.

Getting To Sex In 3 Steps: The System

I know you want to get straight to the point. So let's talk about the System.

What I'm going to teach you will reveal:

- A simple trick to bring a normal conversation to a sexual plane naturally and discreetly.
- How to verbalize your wish without sounding weird, trying too hard, losing courage, or giving away your power. I'll even teach you one of my favorite "tricks" to accomplish all of this without you having to say a single word. He names it "The Playful Look."
- You will also learn specific techniques to bring out the wild side of a woman.

The reason why I put together a 3-step system is that if you don't have a map, it's very simple to get lost in the confusion of a conversation and, before you know it, get caught up in a boring, asexual conversation, talking about their jobs or politics. You have no idea how to get back on track.

I named this system "Slowing Into Sex" because I noticed different "speeds" at which you can be with a woman. It is very similar to having different speeds in a shift car. If you've ever driven a standard car, you know that you can't go from 1st gear to 4th gear without first going through 2nd and 3rd gear. Your car is going to turn off because you never had the necessary revolutions to maintain that change in speed.

The same thing happens when we are with a girl. Where most men get it wrong is that they spend all night on 1st (The world of the "good boy"), and when the night is about to end, he wants to skip at the highest speed, and they notice that at that moment it is impossible to make the change because it is trying to do too much, too late.

199

This System does create smooth transitions, so you don't ruin the progress you've already made.

This is the primary reason why men can't get out of "let's just be friends" with a girl. They are too kind to the girl for months, sometimes years, until they can no longer hold it and declare their feelings, hoping that she will feel the same. Just as I found out with Candice, it just doesn't work.

It all starts with:

Step 1: The C Rating Button

If you are losing girls, it is probably because they do not have a sexual connection with you. They do not feel sexual affinity when they are with you, and they are looking for a man who will let them express this side of her—someone to warm them up.

The Classification of C Button

Here you let her know that it's okay to let some of her wild sides come to the fore. Bringing out that 'wild side' is the first step in closing the deal and taking her to your room. You have to take the conversation to a Class C territory.

You must be having a conversation that a parent would not be comfortable with if their child were listening. Something exciting and real about Classification C: but most of us turn into your typical A-rated movie guy when we're around a girl. It's as if we're afraid to say something that has the slightest chance of offending her, or worse yet, revealing that we like sex.

So we talk about safe, neutral, A-rated topics. Have you seen a movie with that rating lately? They are boring and predictable; they are not sexual in the least. So the first mental adjustment you should make is to stop worrying about whether you will say something that offends a girl.

Here's a secret for you. Women LOVE locker room gossip.

When I was in school, my girlfriend at the time was in a sorority. I used to stay there to sleep and spend some time in that house where my girlfriend lived with eleven other girls. Since I was there so much, they lowered their guard, and it was as if they forgot that I was there. While I was there, you know what I heard? Gossip that is told in the locker room.

It was the same kind of conversation that I had with my friends where I lived. Gossip about who was having sex with whom, who they thought was good in bed, which was creepy and stalking. They also vented their frustration of which guys were too weak to be sexual.

So how do you take a conversation to that Classification C?

I have many techniques to do it, and each one is more comfortable with some and less comfortable with others. But this is something simple to get you started:

Make a Class C observation of something that is happening around you. For example, let's say you are in a bar and there is an older couple nearby, a man and a woman. You could answer something onward the lines of: "That couple gives you an air of being swingers. I picture them perfect at one of those fancy '70s parties where everyone put their keys in a bowl, and husbands and wives were exchanged depending on which key you pulled out. Do you notice it, or is it just me?

You see, what you just did is, jokingly, use a situation to introduce a sexual subject like the exchange of sexual partners in an innocent way.

You just came out of 1st and got 2nd.

What I like to do afterward is cast a hook to test the terrain and say something like: "Now that I think about it, you give off that swinger vibe too." I laugh and change the subject to see if she tries to bring up that same subject again. If she does, I can tease her a bit about it or talk about how the very innocent-looking ones end up being the horniest. I implicitly tell her that she has a "perverted" side.

If she doesn't take the bait, I wait a few minutes and then change gears using my techniques. All the girls I've dated, even the shy and innocent ones, love to talk about "locker room gossip" once they've gotten a little open.

Not only do they love to talk about it, but when you take the conversation to Class C, you immediately set yourself apart and differentiate yourself from the hundreds of guys who hang out on safe topics. It is refreshing for them to talk to you, and they will want to keep doing it. You show her that you are comfortable with sex, which helps her see you as a guy who makes things happen 'without getting weird or uncomfortable.

The most important thing is that you create an environment where seduction can occur, where she begins to think about sex, and you can manage to kiss her and take her home.

How else do you lead a conversation to Class C? Classification C has to do with the topic's content and how they flirt with them. It can be something as simple as changing your vocabulary and the words you use.

-She's not bad; she's naughty.

-You are not going to hit her; you're going to spank her.

-If she's bothering you, "don't make me pull the belt off."

-It is not a basement; it is a dungeon.

Even some words, or the way you describe things, can hit that C-Rating button. This is especially effective when you annoy her or make an observation about her.

-Her gaze is full of Lust.

-She looks excited.

The following words have a tone with sexual overtones:

-Tempting

-Thongs

-Dental flosses

-High heels

-Panties

-Fetish

-Vibrator (dildo is too much)

-Swingers

-Lubricant (or you can use the name of the best-known lubricant in your country)

-Wet

-Cougar

-Whips and handcuffs

-Naughty

-Snuggle

-Cybersex

These are all C classification words. These words with sexual overtones are what you will want to use at this point. You're not going to use any porn words. Those go later.

The funny thing is that since most of these words have double meanings, if she interprets them sexually, you can accuse her of having a dirty mind.

This is the kind of conversation you want in 1st gear. You're not going to stand there like you're 13 years old. You only establish the conversation rules and enter those topics, not to be surprised when you start climbing.

Since the conversation is in Class C, you must move on to the next step.

Step 2: Express Your Sexual Interest

A while ago, I told you the story of my colleague Candice, with whom even though we had amazing chemistry, I couldn't transition to kissing, and I ended up with her, "let's just be friends."

You see, on that first night, I missed a crucial step. I never expressed my sexual interest. I was just beginning to study all of this back then and was obsessed with not being the "nice guy" who buys her drinks, fills her with compliments, or is too nice.

As I saw girls' reactions like Candice change to being more positive, I began to think that the secret to attracting a woman was to appear as if I had no sexual interest in her.

However, I did notice a few things regarding how they acted with me.

1. Although they no longer saw me as a "good guy" who they could control and manipulate, they were still not sexually attracted to me.

2. Most women are NOT as confident as they first thought. Instead of persecuting me as the "great challenge" that I represented, they existed, and they went with another.
3. By hiding my sex drive, I was often seen as "asexual," or worse, closet gay.

That's what happened to Candice.

After the middle of the night, as we continued to laugh and joke, she probably suspected that he was not the kind of man who could make things happen. Yes, I was the funny guy she loved to hang out with and talked to, but she probably just assumed I wasn't such a sexual guy.

I grappled with this for a prolonged time. It seemed like no matter how hard I tried, and he couldn't find the balance between being the "good guy" and the "asexual guy."

One day I was with my friend Steve Weed, a naturally good guy with women. Until recently, I was astonished about how I could flirt when displaying "good boy" qualities, such as flattering a woman. Instead of criticizing his behavior, I decided to pay attention and find out why it worked.

It turned out that at one point, I saw Steve shamefully admit that the girl was 'turning on' him, and the next moment Steve was flirting with one of her friends and ignoring the other girl. He seemed to anchor her attention to Steve.

As I continued to analyze Steve, I noticed how he verbally expressed his intense desire for her, but at the same time, it gave the impression that if she left, his night would not be affected in the least; that he would probably be with another girl in a few minutes.

At some point, Steve started telling the girl what he would do to her later in the room.' A few seconds after he told her this, he turned around and asked me if I wanted to play pool. While we were playing pool, she was sitting in the corner, and she was watching him the whole time. As I put the puzzle together, I realized that it is NOT about hiding your sexual desire, pretending to be indifferent. It is about expressing your sexual desire but being indifferent about the result.

I mean that the girl Steve was flirting with at the bar knew she was sexually attracted to him, but she also got the impression that Steve was so used to picking up girls that he liked that if she disappeared, he would hardly realize she was gone. Before, I was so focused on showing disinterest that I completely failed to get her to care in the first place. There is no "chase" if the woman is not chasing you. You do not represent a "challenge" if she does not intend to have you.

What's more, your initial interest is what makes her take notice of you. However, it's how you RESPOND when she returns that interest that triggers the persecution or makes her think, "I guess I was wrong about him; he's in too much need of my approval."

"The Spontaneous Sexual Compliment"

I desire you to try this easy exercise the next time you go out: When you're talking to a girl, and you start to feel some flirtation or connection, make a strong statement of your desire for her. An easy way to do this is that when she says something funny, you can look at her and say, "Now I'm intrigued. You are incredibly sexy and nice. You don't see that very often. "

After telling her that, she returns to normal. Almost like you, she never said it. If her friends are around, start talking and flirting with them a bit. Don't ignore her completely, but do ignore her enough that she starts chasing you. You will see that, by making that statement, the natural tension between the two will rise a lot, and the tension amplifies the attraction.

This is why expressing your sexual interest is so crucial.

You let her know that you intend to make things happen and that you will not be satisfied with a handshake or a hug, much less are you looking for nothing more to be his friend. You warn her that you will do something to climb after a while so that she will not be surprised when you do. An added benefit is that when they start to notice that you are the type who makes things happen, they start to do things that will make your way easier. As if since the topic was raised, she doesn't have to act like Ms. Conservative afterward, and you won't have a problem kissing her or closing the deal.

It's important to make your sexual declaration after you've already had a bit of attraction. You have to make sure you do it before you get too confident with her, or you're going to get stuck in a conversation that won't allow that escalation.

If the first thing you tell her is that she has an impressive butt, you probably won't get very far because you haven't created attraction yet.

"The Playful Look"

If you have been talking to a woman for a while and you detect some attraction while speaking, you lean a bit, and while listening to her, you casually look at her butt. Do it in a bit of an exaggeration, letting her figure out what you are doing.

I call her "The Playful Look" because basically, you are letting her surprise you by seeing her butt, but at the same time, you will be listening carefully to her.

Women find this very naughty, and at the same time, the message is clear: I find you sexually attractive.

That is expressing your sexual intention.

A while ago, I ensured to give you a chemistry test to measure women's attraction towards you. Something very simple that I like to do while talking with the girl is to wait for her to say something I agree with and then say "play them." When our hand's touch, I let my hand stay there to see how it reacts. If there is chemistry, she will almost always leave her hand there for a second too.

If you retract your hand right away, it just means that you probably haven't created enough attraction. I want you to try it the next time you're talking to a girl. It is simple and discreet, and at the same time, it tells you a lot. For now, remember that if you want to take the conversation to a sexual level, to avoid the friend zone and be able to touch her, you have to express your sexual intention.

A few months after the incident with Candice, I was introduced to Valerie.

The date started innocently, meeting us over a drink, but in less than three hours, we were in the cellar of her house; she was naked, with her legs spread on her pool table, inviting me to join her.

How did it happen so fast?

That brings us to the next step.

Step 3: Intensify the Flirting

This is the core of the System. My experience with Valerie was not out of the ordinary. When you start using this, you will see that:

Seemingly innocent girls will start telling you what they like in bed, they will make sexual jokes, and they will ask you what you will be doing after a while. They are going to be more proactive in encouraging you to go for closure. You're not going to be left without knowing what she's thinking or if you should jump in. It's going to make it impossible not to close the deal and take her back to your room.

She's going to beg you for sex.

Let's go back to this "gearshift" idea. Earlier, we talked about how if you make the changes too fast, you will fail. If you've driven a manual car, you know there is an even more damaging problem, and that is staying at the same speed for too long.

Just as you can ruin a car's transmission if you always drive in first gear, if the pull revs get too high in one gear and you don't shift, you can scrub it up.

This is the reason why you noticed that a girl was very interested in you, and then that interest quickly dissipated. It may have been a girl you met at the bar, with whom you had great chemistry, but eventually, she forgot about you and went back to being with her friends. Or worse, maybe it was someone you dated, and you thought things were going well so that later she is no longer so available to go out with you and will eventually stop answering you.

You have to climb continuously and not reach a plane. It always reaches the next level.

How do you do this?

Sexual flirting

"Sexual Flirting"

that's the name of this new way of communicating with women.

The word "sexual" is of utmost importance because I've learned, over the years, that without adding a good dose of sexuality to your flirtation, you can fall into the trap of being the flirtatious type that women never take seriously. They will laugh, but they will think that you are still a safe and kind guy with whom they would never have sex. That is why there are very big differences in sexual flirting.

With this specific type of flirting, you will start to:

- Introduce sexual topics to the conversation
- Use stories to make an "innocent" transition to the topic of sex and start thinking about it.

209

- She uses certain games to make her open up and tell you her wishes and fantasies, making her feel comfortable feeling those emotions when she is with you.
- He was teasing her in a way that has sexual overtones. Even though she knows you are only teasing her, there is an element of danger and excitement in the conversation that begins to arouse her unconsciously.
- Be very aware of sexual tension, and manipulate and control it to quickly bring intimacy.

Even if your goal is not to have sex with her on the first night, this type of flirting ensures that you get to kiss her and position yourself in her mind as the type of man she is going to have sex with, not the type who she just wants to be friends.

Here are some examples of speed changes in conversation:

(The two have been flirting, and things that are said are taken lightly)

You: I can't believe you like Lady Gaga. It's so weird.

Her: Hush, you're probably a closet fan of Lady Gaga. I imagine you alone with your iPod listening to her music and singing. LOL

You: You better take care of yourself, or I'm going to spank you.

She: Oh, did I embarrass you? LOL

You: I'm going to grab you with pillows after a while, and I'm not going to be pious just because you're a girl.

She: I would beat you in a pillow fight.

You: I am the world champion of the pillow. I have to advise you that I am also known for my tickle attacks. If you get naughty, you will feel my fury.

Okay, did you notice how I made the switch to a more sexual frame? The conversation started with Lady Gaga and ended with us being in her bed fighting and tickling each other, being "naughty."

That would be a change from second to third.

Let me show you how I could make the change from third to fourth. Remember, you have to keep shifting because if the ride gets too high in gear, you're going to scrub.

Her: Don't even think about it; I hate being tickled.

You: (Pinky extended) I promise you, unless you're very naughty, I won't tickle you.

(As soon as she takes your little finger, tickle it.)

She: (smiling and laughing) How bad. Hate you.

You: You know that? I hadn't noticed that you have a very sexy smile.

Did you see how I changed gears again? It was a transition from joking about tickling to having some physical contact and first having her hand in yours to "promise" and then tickling her.

The most important thing is that at the end, you said,

"You have a very sexy smile."

What makes that last sentence so important is that it leaves no room for misinterpretation. Let her acknowledge that the two of you were flirting and that you find her sexually attractive.

You avoided "let's just be friends" objections that might come out later.

Here's a secret for you; women WANT to appear sexually attractive.

I've dated and had sex with multiple girls, and you know which compliment turned them on more than anything else? The one that

211

they would repeat to me, telling me how much they liked it and begged me to tell them again?

It has nothing to do with "You're beautiful" or "I love your eyes."

It was "Hell, you're so sexy ..."

A beautiful girl knows that she is beautiful, but she doesn't know if she is sexy.

When you manage to make her feel sexy, it brings out her wild side.

In the middle of work, a colleague of mine took my hand and tucked it under her panties so I could feel how wet she was. I hadn't even kissed her yet.

In the middle of the party, another girl followed me to the bathroom and let me shave her pubic hair because I told her that's how I like it.

After spending a day exchanging dirty emails, this girl showed up at my house wearing a trench coat and nothing else. She told me that she had to be quick because her boyfriend was waiting for her at home.

There is no limit to what they will do if you can bring out their wild side.

Do we agree that it is better to be sexual from the beginning? I hope you are saying yes because you are playing a dangerous game near the friend zone if not.

Can we agree that you should show your sexual interest in a girl?

I think you will agree that getting a quick kiss is crucial. On my first night with Candice, I didn't kiss her, and it took me almost four years to get that "just friends" vibe off and get her.

The first step in kissing her is to move the conversation to Class C. If you paid attention, you would find out how to use the right words, topics, and stories; it is easy to transition into a sexual conversation.

If you're not wearing this already, you're missing out on something big and probably losing girls' interest to guys who do.

You should also be convinced that you should constantly shift gears and use "sexual flirting" to maintain sexual tension. Like I said before, if you ever dated a girl and you thought everything was going well only for her to stop dating you, eventually, she wouldn't even answer you. It's because you didn't maintain the sexual tension.

The reality is that once you have a woman thinking about sex with you and imagining it, letting the tension remain is sure to pass.

Valerie spread her legs on the pool table, with her parents sleeping in the next room. From whom I learned this, my friend Jake has an iPhone full of pictures of naked girls. They are normal girls that he meets when he goes out or with whom he works, But he does such an excellent job of putting himself as the sex man that they send him these nude photos telling him they can't wait for them to see him. I was with him for so long that I could finally figure out what he does.

8 Point Seduction Guide

Look, if you have a woman attracted to you (which I assume you are), but you don't lead the interaction towards seduction, she is going to lose her interest in you ... quickly.

Once you have the attraction created, you have to take it to a seduction level.

I just gave you three steps to get to that "seduction level." Now let's talk about what exactly to do to close the deal.

Here's how you do it.

Slow her down to speed

Once you have that good vibe, you have to slow down. Speak slower, make your movements slower, breathe and slow down to joke speed.

213

Let the tension build

What you're doing is building some sexual tension. When a woman and a man are close, and there is silence, it creates some tension. Most always try to break that tension with a joke, flirtation, or more stories. You have to learn to enjoy that tension and use it to your advantage.

High Five sustained

I like to do this when a woman says something that I liked. I put my hand in a "high five" position. When she does, I kind of hold her hand a little bit and let our fingers stick together a bit. This will simplify sexual tension.

Create a physical connection

Now you have to create some kind of physical link. Again, the best way is to use your hands. Take her by the hand and take her somewhere.

Come closer

Let the sexual tension build by being closer to her. Whether you feel closer, stand closer, or lean in while they speak.

During all this, be neutral.

Stop joking, flirting, and be more uncertain. Look her in the eye. Exude your sexual power. Let her know that you are aware that you are the most dominant sexual creature.

Kiss her

Progress towards sex

NEVER decide for her.

NEVER assume that she doesn't want more privacy.

Always respect her if she says no, but try to make her say 'no.'

Look, the point is that you are responsible for creating that sexual desire in her. YES, it can be created.

Everything I just suggested triggers sexual attraction. This is why perhaps, at some point, you were sexually attracted to a girl that you did not really like, nor did you find physically attractive. It's because the two of them unknowingly transitioned into "seduction mode."

Remember, the attraction is not a choice. If you do what I suggested above (assuming you're doing a good job flirting), she won't be able to resist being attracted to you.

Going forward

As the months go by, you will discover that, after you have learned this, you will feel very relaxed talking to women, and any anxiety you felt when approaching a woman will disappear; Since that anxiety comes from the fear of not knowing what to do, or how not to get bored. That is not going to be a problem anymore, and then you will be chatting with more women, feeling in complete control. It will probably be you who turns down some girl. You will also notice that some women who ignored you or who disliked you are suddenly going to be available to you, sending messages on Facebook, or even sending me messages out of nowhere.

The best part about the short talk is that you can create a lot more attractive with a surprisingly small amount of time, effort, or energy.

It is the way the "Short Talk" is presented that makes all the difference. Say something one way, and you'll bore his brain. Say it differently, and she will imagine that you will be the father of her babies; She will imagine ripping your clothes off or giving you a handjob in a dirty frat house ...

This is the most important lesson you will learn about creating attraction in women:

The way you say it matters.

By stating something in a slightly different way, you can convey your value from a low level to a very HIGH level.

I mean that in the course of a conversation, certain information has to get back and forth between you and the girl you are talking to. This is just the natural flow of the conversation. Gurus try to make you understand that an entire conversation consists of these "hidden attraction" techniques but, the freezing and harsh reality is that most women will constantly steer the conversation into the short talk (because that's what they know) So. You can resist this and keep giving those clumsy evasive "Guess what I'm doing. Guess where I'm from ..." answers that are going to kill the attraction much faster than you think.

... even more unfavorable, you can do what I did with the "Gary Null" lady and grab a topic and blow it to death. You cling for life to that theme that you both have in common ... I call them conversational "lifeboats"... The irony is that ... They sink fast ...

... Or you can learn how to turn an entire conversation or short talk ... into something fun, playful, and sexy ...

There are tons of ways to turn short talk sexy, and I am personally fascinated by finding these techniques, methods, and opportunities.

Let me deal with you what I have discovered and some of my favorite ways to do this.

It has taken me many ages to find these techniques, identify them, test them, and produce systems so that I can train them for you quickly and easily. All I ask of you is that, please, respect the time and effort that I have invested ...

The Ultimate advice

This information is "Ninja Level" training. I am about to explain to you that it is so dangerous for a great and powerful reason: IT WORKS.

It works so well that you MUST be prepared for the response you are going to get. I say this because many of the men who have struggled to improve their conversations with girls are not used to receiving a positive reaction, and they look LOST when they suddenly get it.

Get ready when you change the way you broadcast to "Short Talk," your conversations will take on a whole new dimension.

It's very liberating, and when you finally realize that you can make a Short Talk Sexy, you will soon realize that you have the gift of talking to any woman at any time.

Even if you don't ever get the lady (any guru who tells you that their method is 100% successful is LYING to you), you will ALWAYS find that you can have a fun conversation with a woman.

Okay, let's go! A little earlier, I told the story of how a girl I had spent hours talking to got rid of me to give a handjob to another guy she met in a matter of minutes.

Answer this question, FAST: What was missing from my conversation?

Time is over. This is what my talk was missing:

Sexuality

The following question is: Why didn't I realize this?

I didn't recognize this because I had achieved massive COMFORT with the girl. We had connected so well on a topic of conversation that it flowed from our mouths.

217

And for me, this was AMAZING.

My three biggest fears about conversations with girls had always been:

1. Run out of topics to talk about

2. Awkward silences

3. Resort to "boring" Short Talk

The mere fact that I had avoided these three results led me to believe that I achieved some progress with this lady. But we all recognize how that story finished. Here's why

The # 1 error men make that limits a conversation from turning sexual

The number one mistake men make, preventing them from adding sexuality to their conversations, is:

Drumroll

Fear Of Breaking Comfort

And why are we afraid to break comfort? Because we confuse comfort with attraction. And they are NOT the same thing. We've all figured out that I screwed it up with the "Gary Null" girl in the previous story, but let's not talk more about what I did incorrectly. Let's debate about what I should have performed. Here's how to apply this knowledge to turn a sexual conversation right now.

The next time you are right in the middle of a conversation with a woman who appeals to you, stop for a moment and consider why you are talking to her.

And I don't want a crappy answer. I want the truth.

You're talking to her because YOU HOPE you can CONVINCE her into being attracted to you in a SEXUAL way.

And you can do it.

But to do this ... you have to ...

Burn Your Boat And Don't Turn Back ...

Leave no excuse to turn back ...

This indicates that you must pass the POINT OF NO RETURN if you intend to create sexual attraction in a woman.

You have to be prepared to lose it ...

I failed miserably with the girl from the previous story because I was unwilling to lose the comfort we had created ...

... but what I should have established was SEXUAL INTENTION ...

The first thing you have to do to create sexual intention is BREAK THE COMFORT when you feel like a woman is becoming too comfortable around you ...

Sexual tension comes from the will to be mixed with uncertainty, suspense, and even a little nervousness ...

If you're in the center of an hour-long conversation with a girl about healthy food (or the Yankees, traveling, or their jobs), there is no tension, uncertainty, and suspense ...

Yes, there is comfort and good value ...

But you have to BREAK that ...

So, for example, if a girl has gotten too comfortable with you and starts to get into a long lecture on how much she hates her job ...

Stop it and say:

"If we keep speaking about this, I'm going to charge you $ 200 an hour for therapy. Did you bring your credit card?"

219

In shorter than a minute ... you will have broken the comfort, you will have put some suspense to the conversation ... and you will have broken in half the thoughts that tell him "he is a good guy ..."

If you let the conversation get too comfortable ... Breaking the COMFORT will be much more difficult, and later in the evening, stealing a kiss will seem inappropriate.

Break the comfort ...

Adam Lyons once informed me of a story where he had a lady on his couch, and she wouldn't stop talking about an argument he had with one of his friends. He was sitting there guessing, "how the hell can I get her to shut up? enough to kiss her...?"

AND HIT HER HEAD.

I have done similar things if I have the feeling that a woman has become too comfortable, and I cannot change the subject to something more sexual.

I look at her and say: "Don't you ever shut up?"

She usually looks at me like I've gone crazy.

But the TENSION GOES UP TO THE CEILING. And the comfort will have been broken ..., and from there I will give her a small smile ... then I will push her lightly in a flirtatious way ... and say, "OH ... have I made you angry? ..."

And now we are FLIRTING.

How To Dodge This In The First Place

We have already established earlier in this chapter that your INTENTION creates a sexual attraction with her. So let her know your intention if you don't want a woman to feel too comfortable with you and see you as just a fun guy to talk to.

Don't give her that option …

LET HER KNOW YOUR INTENTION …

When I talked to the "Gary Null" girl, I never said anything to her that would imply that I saw her as more than just a girl with a common interest - in vegetarian and healthy food. So that was the "paper" she gave me ... the guy she talks to about healthy food …

I should have made a clear statement of intent from the beginning:

A standard of a statement of intent is: (if you show a smile) "You have a very sexy and naughty smile like you have bad intentions. Haha, I like ..."

OR ...

"That stuff you just did with your hair ... it's driving me crazy ... And I wasn't paying attention to any words you just said ..."

Leave no excuse to turn back …

Once you introduce a statement of intent in the conversation, you can go back to a SHORT TALK ... because now under the "table," there is an underlying TENSION that is being built …

I just distributed what the biggest mistake men make in their conversations with women is. Most men cling to comfort because they don't want and are afraid to break it, and they drive all sexual tension out of the conversation completely.

By breaking the Comfort relationship and using the "statement of intent," you are on track to get precisely what you require out of the conversation ...

Avoid the "comfort trap," and your chances of success will increase. Now, I'm going to teach you some of the TACTICS to do a Sexy Short Talk.

The most serious problem men face when it comes to making "short talks" with girls is that they continually run out of things to say or bring up "boring" topics, especially at the beginning of the conversation before both of them feel comfortable with each other.

But what if I showed you that you could take any "monotonous" topic and turn it into a fun and interesting flirtatious conversation ... and that you can have an endless supply of "conversation gear"... All of this if you take on the role of a character. ...?

Why does it work ...

When choosing a character, choose a role that allows you to create attraction.

Certain roles work much better than others. Here are some examples of functions that create attraction:

a) You are dominant; she is cute

b) A position that assumes authority. Your judge, coach, or consultant

c) The victim of his seduction

d) The cold type

e) The selfish, neurotic type

f) She is a girl who demands a lot of attention

g) You can imitate her

h) You are the Devil on his left shoulder

i) Overly cheesy. Artist of your seduction

j) You are the adult who supervises her

k) Is using you to have sex

Each of these mentioned roles works so well because they somehow position you in the girl's mind as the man who "knows."

And the mere fact that you have assumed the role shows that you control the conversation and make the decisions. In a moment, I'm going to reveal to you exactly how to use these papers to make something Sexy with a Short Talk ... but for now, I just require you to assume the purpose of the paper…

... the character writes himself ... once you learn the character then all the funny things will come by themselves ...

This function sets the "frame" for the entire conversation. Even though you will be moving in and out of this role throughout the conversation ... it will ALWAYS be there to use when you feel like the conversation needs a little updating…

What to do ...

There Are Three General Rules For Taking On A Role:

1. Take on the role from the beginning of the conversation

2. Own the role / be congruent

3. And know when to drop it

You want to exercise full control over the role you take on. From the beginning, you are more or less saying, "these are the rules for our conversation."This is very important, and you must establish the "role of your character" from the beginning. It will seem strange if you start practicing after 30 minutes of "normal" conversation. And then you must own the role and be congruent with it. This means you CAN'T back down if she gives you "shit tests." Don't wait for her to "support" the game you set; just jump right into it.

And finally, you need to know when to drop it. At some point, after the attraction has been created, there will come the point where the

223

paper must be used in MODERATION because if you never let go of the paper, she will never experience a deep sense of relationship WITH YOU.

How to take a position and use it immediately now in the real world

Okay.

Here's a character practice exercise:

Imagine a certain type of character you can work with .... Choose one of these three:

1. An overconfident Playboy

2. She is a girl who demands a lot of attention

3. You are the Devil on his left shoulder (the Devil who orders him to do bad things)

Once you have selected one of the above characters, get in touch with how he could respond, react, what kind of facial expressions he would make, what would his tone of voice be like?

Spend a few minutes getting into the mind of the character you have chosen. Become him as you develop this exercise.

Your reactions come off the character.

Now how would an individual character answer the following three things?

1. She accidentally touches your leg
2. She drops something
3. She invites you to order her a drink

Her: (Accidentally touching your leg) So what are you working on?

A lady who requires a lot of attention: Oh my god! How dare you touch my leg? I'm not the boy you think I am ... With me, you're not going to get what you want just by sweetening my ear ...

Her: (Casually touching your ass) So what do you work on?

You are the Devil on her left shoulder - (the Devil who orders her to do bad things): Just ... slowly ... put ... your hand back on his butt ... She won't notice ... do it ... meanwhile, bend over and show her something of your chest ...

More examples ...

Her: (drops her cell phone)

Overconfident Playboy: You're taking every opportunity to show me your belongings ... right sweetheart? I admit it ... I enjoy the effort you're settling into this whole seduction thing ... most girls don't try that hard ...

Her: (drops her cell phone)

A lady who requires a lot of attention: Oh, please ... DON'T THINK you're going to cheat on me ... you just want me to look at your ass ... I'm not that kind of man.

Her: (drops her cell phone)

You are the Devil on his left shoulder - (the Devil who orders him to do bad things): He's watching ... Just lean a bit more ... maybe pull your hair back a bit ... and then make a stupid statement about "how drunk you are ..."

Can you see how taking on the role of a character adds a more interesting touch to everything? ... And also allows you to introduce Sexy Themes

Do you see how easy it is to transform the atmosphere of a short talk completely?

225

And can you understand how EASY it is ALWAYS to KNOW WHAT TO SAY when you're performing a "role?" You just say what you believe your character would say

Just to illustrate the difference ... use one of the examples above (Her dropping her phone or touching your leg) and imagine how you would have acknowledged if it had been simply YOU (without assuming the role of any character) ...

You probably would have answered his stupid question, "what do you work on?" and carry on through a boring conversation.

But ... the "role" you were playing has allowed you to add a little spice and sex into the mix instantly...

So now you can still answer his question ... but you remained able to make the corresponding talk ... SEXY.

How to Make a Short Talk Sexy - Technique # 2:

Turn conversation into a "game" and allow mutual interaction to take on a life of its own. Have you ever had hours of fun just throwing a tennis ball against a wall and catching it when it came back to you?

Or, didn't you step on the cracks' when you were walking down a sidewalk?

Or, did you try to pass as many cars as you were driving on a highway?

Or, sit at your desk and rate "how sexy" the girls in your classroom were ... while your teacher gave a devious explanation?

If you've done any of these things ...

... You have found THE GAME to make something boring fun

We do it all the time ... because games are so much fun!

"Getting The Game"

Every cooperation you have with a gal has the potential for a game, and once you get that game, what used to be a boring, normal conversation becomes something you are a part of.

Whether as teammates or as competitors ...

You just have to find something that simplifies your interaction, that you can turn into a kind of contest and see who can beat the other.

Everyone likes to play games because the rules are simple and clear.

... And just like playing a "role,"... These games allow the occurrence of things to be much easier to say ... because the conversation comes from the game ...

Before we get into some examples of "games" you can play ... let's examine some of the reasons they are so effective at making sexy little talk ...

Why "Games" Work So Well ...

They create a sense of comfort between the two (for good)

They keep the conversation flowing smoothly ... creating the illusion of "chemistry."

They allow both of you to share information that you would not otherwise have.

They make it much easier to introduce the element of "sexuality" into the conversation.

They focus the conversation on feelings, emotions, and observations ... rather than facts. The truth is ... THE SHORT TALK MUST BE TAKEN ... there is some information that needs to be passed back and forth between you and a woman ...

227

... But just like sitting down to listen to a boring lecture, being stuck on the road, or taking a walk down the street ...

SHORT TALK can BECOME FUN by finding the game ...

What are games?

Any activity that can be used for fun ...

But to make this explanation much simpler, I will list some of the most popular games that the best Ligue Artists use regularly.

Each of these games is designed to provoke emotions in the woman you are talking to ... and create the feeling of comfort and ATTRACTION.

... Here are some of my favorites.

Just remember that just like when you use "paper," you MUST NOT explain the games. Just jump to them. Start with something fun and high-energy and slowly go deeper and more sincere.

Game of three questions

While talking to a girl, the game just starts ...

You: "Let's play a little game."

Her: "Okay, what kind of game?"

You: "It's very simple; we just take turns asking each other questions ... but there are rules."

Her: "Such as ...?"

You: "1) Each question must be acknowledged, 2) No question can be reproduced, and 3) you go first ..."

"So, I want to understand more about you ... What is ... your favorite ice cream? Mine is Ben and Jerry's Cookie ..."

Trade three questions back and forth. You ask, she answers. Then she asks questions, and you answer.

Start with very common or very funny things (for example, "what is your preferred ice cream?"), And be qualified to share your answer and get the game going.

The second question is a little deeper; you can talk about good childhood memories.

In the third question, go deeper; it can be about love, relationships, etc.

Since it is a game, she will be speechless when you ask her, "Where was the most unusual place you had sex?"

You just give her a smile that says, "Yeah, I just asked ..." Unless she's prudish, he's going to go the way you carved.

Can you see how simple it was to introduce sexuality into the conversation under the guise of a game?

Every time I use it, the girl asks something sexual in less than five questions.

Fascination Game / Like Game

This is another great way to share information fun and creates a playful back and forth between you ...

Fascinates me ...

I like it ...

Remember, start small. Don't go straight to the deep stuff. Make her speak first and go deep little by little.

E.g., "Do you know what I like about New York? Who has the best pizza in the world. What do you like about New York?"

Then once you've warmed up ... "I love girls who have an unusual side ..."

It's about the "VIBES" that comes and goes between you and the girl. Rather than relentlessly trying to create a deep sense of comfort ... just focus on the vibe that's going on between the two of you.

Interaction should be the center of attention .... NOT the TOPIC being discussed.

I repeat: Interaction should be the center of attention ... It is NOT the TOPIC being discussed.

This is where I had completely spoiled it in the previous story. I made "healthy food" and "Gary Null" the center of attention when attention must have been the playful interaction between the two.

Now I wonder - what if the interaction with the girl "Gary Null" had been as follows instead?

Me: I like peanut butter smoothies

Her: I like Graham Cracker Nutrition Bars

Me: (giving him those five) Me too ... I also like to travel to spontaneous places and strange dark places.

Her: Oh yeah ... Well, I like to watch people walking along the boardwalk and laugh at everyone who seems strange to me.

Me: Well, I like to have sex on the beach while "strangers" walk the boardwalk.

Her: I like sex after getting back from a really hard workout at the gym ...

See how planning a game allows you to elevate the discussion to a sexual level ... in a matter of minutes?

When you put something in the meaning of a "character" or "a game," the woman's statement goes downhill, and she finds herself playing along ... BECAUSE IT'S FUN.

Remember that a woman is looking for fun. And frankly, most men are bored and incapable of entertaining conversation (I know that because I was one of them), so when a woman meets a guy who can create laid-back fun ... she instantly will recognize "this guy is different "and will play your game.

Yes, she wants to play your game ...

She just has to be sure it's going to be something nice ...

Playing Roles

What is playing a role?

It is creating an imaginary setting and characters that the two of you can move out together. Let's say you're speaking to a girl, and you tell her you're going to Italy next week ... and she humorously says, "can I go ...?"

Instead of laughing at this ... you would say something like:

"Yes, I'm going to hide you in my suitcase ... When you get there, you have to be my paparazzi. I'm going to provide you a camera, and you just have to follow me around all the time, taking pictures of me ... and pointing at me like I'm someone famous. Then you can sell the images to a local tabloid, and we can use the money to take a yacht and play in Monaco. Of course, I'm going to end up losing you in a game of poker against some Iranian sheik ..."

You see how you just caught this absurd position and kept making it more absurd.

She was playful though, you probably got her to laugh ... and she predicted a future where the both of you were in Italy and Monaco.

231

It's very manageable.

Start a story about a daydream with you and her. Let me fill in some details and together create a fun game.

And for the love of God ... don't be afraid to introduce a little sexuality into the role play ... that's what it's all about ...

So... there you have it!

Some of my preferred ways to combine fun, playfulness, and sexuality to your short talks ... and MASSIVELY increase your appeal in the eyes of the woman you are interacting with. And what's great about all the techniques mentioned is that you don't need to change what you're talking about ... just how you present the information.

Now is the time for you to put these techniques into practice and get a little RESULTS. Take my word for it ...

Start Now!

Take action right now — don't wait. Do something with what you've learned right away, so you can start using it AUTOMATICALLY. Use these techniques every day, and soon you will realize that you will create the kind of vibe that women crave, and you can almost see that attraction shining in their eyes ...

How To Flatter A Woman Effectively

Suppose That a person admires him. Is this enough in itself for someone to like you? Probably not. If your value is too high than that of the others, they will get nervous around you, and you will perceive that both do not have good chemistry together because they do not feel very good around them when they are around you. This happens because they see you much better than they see themselves.

And this is a problem faced by many people who are perceived as "cool" or "cool." Although they look like very cool people, others feel stage fright around them.

As a consequence, many great people have trouble maintaining relationships (sex and friendships.) So your cool and cool must be balanced by allowing other people you interact with to feel good about themselves in your presence.

You are wondering, "How is this done?" You do this by freely handing out genuine compliments.

One method to do this is to make a flattering remark and then quickly ask a question below in a probing manner as if ensuring that said woman is qualified to be with you. Remember, you are a good match, so she will feel good when you impress him.

Examples-

You: "What? You have a good vibe! What do you do for fun?"

She: "Blah, blah."

You (thinking about it for a second): "That sounds like a lot of fun. I would love to hear more about that."

You: You look cool to me. What do you say you are studying? "

She: "Blah, blah."

You: "Interesting ... I have a friend who studied Bla Bla."

You see, when you say a genuine compliment, quickly follow up with a question. This also prevents the woman from denying compliance and puts her to the test.

She will be practically eating out of your hand and believing what you tell her as long as you make her feel qualified to be with you.

As an alpha male, you approve, and you don't need an approval return. So don't expect her to thank you for the compliment.

AlsoYes, women typically deny compliments or flattery while making them look less brilliant. And women may then think that you gave false praise, which is the last thing you want. So don't give him a chance to deny your praise.

I like to follow up on my compliments with a question because then that frames the interaction as that even though I found something I liked about it, my approval can still go away if I don't like your next answer. That makes me the highest value token, and it's her job to win my affections. She will be a little happier when she sees that you are interested in the answer.

Now here's something you need to know: you mustn't give false compliments because you would be trying too hard to get approved. Also, it's hard to give a fake compliment and make it sound sincere, and you don't want her to get suspicious. And this is what beats do, and alphas do not.

Another strategy I like, particularly with a new woman, is to change the subject or issue after paying the compliment quickly. "You strike me as a very interesting girl. You know what? Something happened to me on the way ..."

And this keeps me in control of the direction of the conversation and prevents her from having a chance to deny my compliment.

Another reason why I like to dish out compliments in my interactions with people that it keeps me externally focused. Because I am thinking about them, I do not care or burden myself to analyze my every move.

CHAPTER SEVEN

THE POWER OF EYE CONTACT

Eye contact is a very effective means of communication, relevant in practically all communicative contexts, except when this is not possible. It is important, for example, in job interviews, to socialize with strangers or when showing intense emotions of happiness, anger, or fear.

There are different types of eye contact, each having a different meaning. Through visual contact, emotions and thoughts can be exchanged, often supporting verbal language and fostering the connection between the sender and the receiver. In Psychology-Online, we explain the ins and outs of eye contact in psychology, the types, and the meaning of each one.

What Is Eye Contact?

Eyes are understood to be the situation in which two people's gazes are fixed on the other's eyes. This is a really powerful means of communication, being a clear case of non-verbal communication.

This eye contact allows us to interpret other people's emotions, as well as transmit our own.

For example, if we see someone with a flushed face and a frown, their gaze probably denotes large doses of anger or anger. In this way, a connection is established between their gaze and ours, and this anger

235

is much easier for us to interpret and even know the degree or intensity of it. Therefore, eye contact is considered as important as a source of emotional information.

The Importance Of Eye Contact

The fact that eye contact acquires such relevance at a communicative level is not mere chance since it allows many interactions between the receiver and the sender. It is very important when it comes to active listening or expressing emotions.

It is also necessary to talk about eye contact's relevance as almost a requirement for communication to begin. Normally, when we address or want to address someone, we unconsciously look them directly in the eye, thus capturing their attention and giving them the signal that we want to communicate something.

Eye contact is also relevant when establishing and respecting speaking turns. If another person speaking to us suddenly shuts up and looks at us, they are probably waiting for our intervention.

Besides, it is necessary to distinguish different types of eye contact, from the most intense and prolonged, the curious, or, on the contrary, the absence of eye contact or elusive glances. We will see all this in the next section.

Types Of Looks In Psychology

There are different ways of looking at others. Now we discuss some examples and their usual meaning. However, it should be added that the meaning of a look is sometimes difficult to catalog, as it depends on many personal and contextual factors and who interprets it.

The Types Of Gazes In Psychology And Their Meaning

Intense and prolonged eye contact denotes attention to what the interlocutor wants to convey or to his actions. A slight lift of the eyebrows usually accompanies it. However, if this look is too pushy or aggressive, it may be a challenging look.

Avoiding Gaze

What does it mean to avoid eye contact? If a person avoids looking another person in the eye, it is usually because they feel threatened, insecure, or embarrassed, for some reason. Looking away in psychology means insecurity or shame.

Eyes narrowed

If a person looks at us with narrowed eyes, it is usually because they are on the defensive or distrust us, or they expect an attack of some kind.

Blink excessively

This action is usually due to a high level of nerves, denoting restlessness, shame, or it may even be due to this person being attracted to the person they communicate with. If that's the case, the following information on how to calm your nerves before a first date may help.

Dilated pupils

Our students tend to dilate when something is interesting to us. We could even say fascinating; this usually occurs when there is a surprise or a genuine interest in the other person. Pupil dilation is a physiological reaction that occurs when a person sees something that attracts them. Another interesting physiological reaction is blushing. Find out in this article why we turn red when we are ashamed.

What We Say Through The Gaze, By Science.

It is said that the face is the mirror of the soul and, if there is any part that must carry that emotional charge, it is without a doubt the eyes. What does the look tell us?

It is said that the face is the mirror of the soul and, if there is any part that must carry that emotional load, it is without a doubt the eyes. More or less expressive, they usually give us away if we are tired or sad, happy or angry, in love and spiteful. The eyes have been the inspiration for songs and poems and have been characterized by the beauty they give to the face. We close them if we want to turn off the world, and we keep them open when we don't want anything to escape us. We put makeup on them, hide them behind sunglasses, and even change their color with contact lenses. But those are not its only functions.

The eyes are a crucial part of non-verbal language, and what we express with them is infinite. So says Ronald E. Riggio, the professor of leadership and psychological organization for well-known businessman Henry R. Kravis and a former professor at Claremont McKenna College. In an article published in Psychology Today, he claims to draw on the Research that science has carried out so far to extract some interesting data about the power of the gaze and what we transmit thanks to it. Its main conclusions are summarized in five points.

Contact Excites

EyeStaring into another person's eyes generates an arousal reaction, although its interpretation varies depending on the context. When a newcomer looks at us for a long time, we can see it as a threat and experience fear or anguish. This attitude is very common in animals, which feel threatened if a human stares them in the eye. However, it is also possible to become sexually aroused thanks to eye contact and interpret it as an invitation to have sex.

Eyes Reveal The Honesty Of A Smile

Psychologist Paul Ekman has distinguished between smiles representing genuine happiness and fake smiles used to fake happiness or cover any other emotion. The solution to distinguishing one from the other is to observe the gaze of the person in question. When the smile is honest, the eyes narrow, and the crow's feet are generated at the ends.

Pupil Dilation Is A Sign Of Interest

As Riggio explains, when something interests us, our pupils dilate. But, besides, that dilation makes us look sexier. The professor cites a study in which the pupils' size was artificially altered in a photo of the same woman. Both photos were compared, identical except for the dilation's size, and those that had a larger dilation were rated as more attractive than those shown with normal-size pupils.

The Reciprocal Gaze Is A Sign Of Love

Research studying topics related to love and attraction has concluded that looking closely at each other and observing each other is almost a guarantee that the people involved are in love.

Eye Contact Gives Rise To Deception

Normally, and as has been said, eye contact and looking at something is usually a sign of interest, love, affection, or derivatives. Thus, a liar does not usually look into the eyes, and that this is a fundamental characteristic of his non-verbal language. However, according to Riggio, Research has shown that people tend to lie and make more eye contact. They put more energy into trying to convince their interlocutor of something that is not true. On the other hand, the truth-teller does not need to prove anything and may be distracted if he is not looking at us.

Keys To Non-verbal Language: The Four Views That Work

We often hear about the significance of knowing the non-verbal language to identify what our interlocutors are telling us. This is what your eyes say.

We are what we communicate. They accompany us, follow us, and believe us because of what we say and how we move, gesture, look, and even how we smile. Your gestures give you away. The keys to being a good communicator (Espasa), Fran Carrillo raises some of the keys that we must know about non-verbal language to understand everything that our interlocutors suggest and know how to act to convey exactly what interests us. In the extract we collect, he talks about the messages we send and are sent to us through the eyes. It raises the existence of four types of looks, their meaning, and how to identify them.

What Your Looks Say

An intelligent development manager of a multinational company in the Insurance sector, he always lost business opportunities due to his inability to manage his look. However, with a friendly face when the moment of truth arrived, he would divert his pupils to the point that the interlocutor began to suspect if he was not giving her a hoot.

Their insecurity generates more insecurity. His eyes were dilated more than necessary when he became tense, and his eyebrows ceased to have a precise sense when they arched or wrinkled, highlighting the latent and patent lack of control of his face. Psychology tells us that the look is closely related to our state of mind. In our contact with the public, we participate in a challenge in which two gazes face each other, and ours almost always lives trapped by fear and the constant feeling of ridicule.

You can't help not looking because eye contact is the main element of connection with the listener. It is the most direct way to make you participate, to get involved in your intervention. Bad control of the gaze will cause us to express discomfort and discomfort to those who listen to us; a full mastery of it will turn us into stage winners of the moment. And it is that the eyes, as part of the facial language, express what the message is often silent.

We always say that we distrust someone who does not look at us when they are telling us something, whether it is important or not, who averts their gaze only once or twice, but always at the moment of telling us exactly what is so relevant that we want to hear, what they are for.

Has summoned us. You can't help not looking because eye contact is the main element of connection with the listener. That elusive gaze conveys insecurity. Like an edgy look, especially if we reinforce it with a frown, which induces us to focus our attention more on the paper, on the table, or on any secondary aspect of the room or object in the environment rather than initiating that contact visual with the audience - don't forget this - the true main actor of the intervention.

In the same way, we do not believe one hundred percent who stares at us, bringing his iris to the limit of tears, or who averts his eyes in a conversation more than once without explanation (exaggerated blinking falls into the category of courtship subtle, that moment of seduction between a man and a woman, two men or two women, which Flora Davis explains well in her masterpiece on non-verbal communication). I gave it the following analogy so that he would understand what I meant: when you communicate in public, and your gaze should function as the beacon for the ships that dock in port. If

241

you are writing a large audience, you should focus on a permanent lighting sweep.

You are looking from one side to the other, without concentrating on any one in particular, at a speed inherent to your message's rhythm. The slower you speak, the slower your gaze should be until you decide to project it onto someone in particular. If you do this, keep in mind that those present's attention will increase because they detected an evident decrease in your communication speed, and they will wonder why it is. That you fix your eyes on a specific person does not mean anything (regardless of whether you feel comfortable looking at them): actually, you do it because it makes it easier for you to specify your main message and, from that physical starting point, extend it to the rest of those present the contagion effect.

The Four Looks Of Power

Once sure that I had understood it, I entrusted her with a technique promoted by Rubén Turienzo, who will not mind if I borrow his original way of qualifying the three most frequent looks that intervene in a communication between two or more people. As a world benchmark for charisma and personal influence, he designed a powerful gaze control and management strategy to achieve the desired effect in an audience when communicating.

I got it to apply it in his internal presentations, meetings with VIP and strategic clients, and even open conferences before different audiences. To the three looks that Rubén proposed, I added a fourth. Now I entrust them to you, dear reader. With the following techniques, you will learn to look differently without losing an iota of your communicative power, although I warn that this type of strategies are especially applicable to contexts in which you must communicate before a not very large group of people - about fifteen or twenty-; in large audiences, of one hundred, two hundred or a thousand people, they have no reason to exist, and their effect is not as long-lasting.

The butter looks. We are defined like this because it mimics the movement we make when we spread slices of toast. We carry out the sweeping sequence that we do with our eyes when we do not want to focus on any specific focus from one side to the other. The goal is to involve the entire audience in our speech. When we apply this type of look, our words' speed must be moderate or even high, fluid, although without reaching extremes that impede their correct understanding and intelligibility. In the same way, our body expression must adjust to that rhythm, and we must gesticulate just enough so that word and gestural movement go hand in hand.

The cheese looks (melted). Name that refers to the analogy with that piece of pizza that remains stuck to its cardboard container by a glob of melted cheese that, no matter how much we stretch, does not break until we bring the pizza slice to such a height that it does not fit any choice but to shed its roots. When we communicate in public, we must apply this gaze at times of slowdown in our speech. From that comprehensive look with which everyone felt involved and that we drove comfortably at a controlled speed, we now move on to another that paces a less rapid pace of speech, in which we already increase the seconds we dedicate to each one, time slows down.

We remain for a few moments looking at each other's gaze. With this, we are warning our receptors that something important is coming because they observe how our body begins to emit more leisurely movements, less gesticulated, with almost perfect control. We flow from tranquility, and the pauses are more pronounced; it is the prelude to what will come next.

The caramel look. And what comes later is the look that serves to fix the messages - like that candy that you take out of your mouth to later retrieve it from the paper in which you left it and observe that it remains glued to it and that it is difficult for you to tear it from its base -, serves to focus attention and provoke memory. We have already swept the room with our butter gaze, we have focused the attention of those present with those melted cheese eyes, and now is the time to generate communicative tension.

We stop our speech, fix our posture and focus our gaze on a single person. Why does it attract our attention more than others? Because we like it? No, because that way, our message will come out better. When we feel it –the message– with our body and say it with our mouth, the second by itself is not enough. It would be best if you had facial and body engagement to validate what you say. You focus on someone, the alternating movement of light stops, and your words come out with the right speed towards all the interlocutors. You are saying to them, «Hey, this is important!, Remember it, you can forget the rest, but if this fragment you I have said it that way, and I have staged it for you in this detailed way because I consider it to be the fundamental part of my intervention, the one that you should not forget». It is a powerful look that generates power in those who know how to represent it well.

The bubblegum look. Finally, and in a later phase, we come to this fourth variant; The gum is chewed, stretched, and savored, but there comes a time when overexposure, the time to play with it, ends up tired your jaw (your gaze) and leaves your ability to persuade dull. You perceive that it is the moment to no longer focus the attention of those present on your non-verbal communication (eyes included) when you see that, progressively, their gaze begins to show fatigue: they deflect it, lower it or concentrate it on another object or another person in the room. At that moment, you have to conclude that message and, why not, your intervention.

Ways to use eye contact in a meeting to get what you want

Have you been in an interview where you felt like you lost the interviewer's attention? Good, attentive listening always goes hand-in-hand with good eye contact, it's a universal truth, and we usually find ourselves staring intensely at people saying important things.

Eye contact is not only a good indicator of a person's interest, but it also has the power to persuade. Think of an interview as an excuse to win over a new person. It is the same as when you meet a new friend or go to a networking event; the only thing different is the prior training that can be done.

To create a fabulous impression, the key is to become a personable person, aware of your surroundings, and you want to see yourself engaged without being obsessed. Eye contact is the best way to be personable and inspire confidence from the moment you walk into a room. Since 93 percent of first impressions have nothing to do with what is being said, body language is a critical component of the process...

These suggestions will assist you in making a positive impression on the next person you meet.

Make A Good Impression

Stable, smooth eye contact is best during business meetings. Keep your eye contact casual, something that is warm, connected, and engaged, but not fixed all the time. The moment you stare into someone's gaze, you make everything feel uncomfortable and unnatural.

For example, let's say you are having dinner with your friends and you are telling a story to four people, but your gaze is only focused on one. It is upsetting to others who are not getting the benefit of your gaze and can make them feel like they are not included in the situation.

A meeting does not question that if there is more than one person in the room, you will want to make eye contact with everyone casually, moving from one to the other, making sure everyone feels included, and making a lasting impression—Channel what you feel when you are talking to a person who seems interesting to you.

Establish Trust

The eyes are the window of the soul. So when you're meeting someone, use eye contact to appeal to their energy and enthusiasm. When you have that kind, open, willing, and friendly touch in your eyes, it's easy for people to trust you.

Confidence has a lot to do with your energy. When you meet a potential client, you have to establish who you are from the moment you enter the building, so it is important to greet the person who greets you at the reception in a friendly way and make eye contact with everyone. People want to hire employees they like and trust, so take a look at everyone in your path to establish the perfect energy to set you up for a great meeting.

Present

This has to be present and aware of what you are seeing, and you can demonstrate these skills in a meeting. Take a moment to scan the place and notice something interesting on the other person's desk (you can even mention it) and make sure you look it in the eye. This can help the person remember you better when the meeting is over.

When I was an actor and had just moved to Los Angeles, I walked into an agent's office for an interview and was blown away by the photographs on the walls. It turned out that he had taken those incredible images while on safari in Africa. Before I even sat down, we started chatting about his photos, and I genuinely complimented his work. The fact that I was interested in his part set a different (and positive) tone to the rest of our conversation.

Show Interest

When someone notices a twinkle in your eyes, they can realize that something interests you and create a connection that will continue to be on work-related and non-work-related topics.

Recently, a customer of mine in real estate acquisitions contacted an owner who he knew had been a senator. As they chatted, my client asked her genuine questions about the Vietnam War, and the former senator was immediately grateful for my client's interest in his personal life, which made them instantly connect, build rapport, and establish trust - all. With interest and eye contact. They found common ground that could be translated into business later.

Reduce Anxiety

Get used to looking up or to the side, but not down. The moment you look down, you show insecurity. When you look up, you are strengthening your energy, staying in line with optimism and curiosity, and keeping yourself open to receiving the other person's energy. In terms of eye contact, looking up developments and invites interaction, while looking down leads to fear.

Let's say that during an interview, you are asked a question that you cannot answer. Instead of looking down and cutting off your energy from the other person, look up to make it seem like you're thinking openly and confidently. Body language expert Anne Cuddy gave an excellent TED Talk about the power of your presence and how to boost the production of chemicals and endorphins in your body through your presence alone. Through muscle energy testing, we have found that eye contact is similar in energy production.

Body language and eye contact are often overlooked, but understanding the impact of each can help you master the art of persuasion.

247

Your eyes speak for you.

To a certain extent, we can check our faces, our gestures, and postures, but we cannot 'manipulate' the blink rate or pupil dilation as we wish. Our eyes' behavior concerning body language is the most unconscious of all; therefore, interpreting their movements will be reliable to establish real meanings based on the individual's non-verbal communication.

In general and in similar light conditions, Research has shown that the pupils dilate when faced with a stimulus that is attractive to us, that we like; The opposite occurs when something generates rejection, fear, or disgust, the pupil's contract. This resource has been widely used in product testing by large marketing and advertising companies.

Blocking eye contact, covering or closing our eyes, is one of the most obvious and common things we do when worried, frustrated, or struggling with something (emotionally speaking). When we feel shame or guilt, we stop seeing and believe that we can stop being seen by others; it is a way of disappearing and protecting ourselves.

According to expert Joe Navarro: "Research also shows that when we are nervous or in trouble, our blink rate increases, a phenomenon that is often seen with liars, but also frequently with people who are under great stress. I wouldn't call anyone a liar just because his blink rate is increasing, although while studying Richard Nixon, I noticed that when he was debating with the press, his blink rate ranged from roughly 12 per minute to 68 times per minute. During his deposition, Bill Clinton showed a high blink rate, sometimes over 92 per minute, but again these were people under a lot of stress. "

"When interpreting the behavior of the eyes, there are many misconceptions. Some mistakenly perceive little, or no eye contact as a classic sign of deception, especially during questioning, while the sincere person must "close their eyes." This is not supported by Research and is completely false. Alder Vrij and others have noticed that liars tend to have more eye contact because they know we are looking for deception signs. "

The Best Ways To Conquer Her With Just One Look

Learn to conquer it in 4.5 seconds; just one look is enough!

Eye contact is key when flirting is no mystery.

Although body language also sends messages, according to experts, eye contact is the most effective method to conquer. For something, they say that the eyes are windows to your heart and that your gaze is more communicative than you imagine.

80% of the information you receive enters through the eyes and is the most receptive sense. When someone is looking at you, you immediately notice, and your brain begins to take mental notes about that person depending on how they are looking at you.

For example, if your brain perceives that someone is looking at you simultaneously as many people, it stops recording information and discards it. On the other hand, if they are only looking at you, they will alert you, and you will feel the need to look at them again.

So eye contact is vital for communicating all kinds of emotions, particularly attraction signals, making it the most important resource when flirting. And there are five infallible techniques to achieve it (without looking crazy).

Maintain Eye Contact For 4.5 Seconds

When you look at someone, it takes your brain three seconds to scan their face, so doing it for a second and a half long is a way of letting them know that they held your attention longer than anyone else. But beware! Holding it for ten seconds will be sending one of two messages: you want to have sex, or you are about to fight over something.

249

After all, looks are one of the best foreplay to have good sex.

Sustained eye contact for a long time produces very strong emotional reactions. Besides, it activates the nervous system, raises the pulse, and stimulates blood circulation. So as subtle as it may sound, holding your gaze for a few seconds is a clear sign of flirting.

Look At It, Look Away, And Look At It Again!

When you are with other people, it can be more difficult to flirt.

The trick is to have eye contact with the person you are interested in, and while they are looking at you, look at the rest of the people, and then look at them again. This is the most effective way to let her know that he was the first person to attract you, and even if you have looked at the rest, he is still the one who interests you.

And if you are alone with her, you can also put it into practice!

Let her understand that you are interested in breaking eye contact by looking down and then looking up again.

On the other hand, if his gaze drifts to the side or up immediately after making eye contact and he does not look at you again, he is most likely not interested.

Follow this advice, and in 10-15 seconds, you will have your answer: either you have conquered it, or you should definitely take another look at the others - maybe there is someone else that you discarded very quickly.

The Triangle

According to various eye movement studies, when we make eye contact with other people, our gaze tends to rest on strategic points on their faces.

When looking at a stranger or in professional situations, we usually make a triangle from one eye to the other and end in the space between the nose and the mouth.

In friendlier situations, the triangle widens, and we look down at the mouth.

On the other hand, with people who seem attractive to us, we tend to lower our gaze much lower, including our chest (yes, you know why men cannot contain themselves, it's a natural reaction!).

And the more intense the flirting gets, the quicker, more passionate, and more constant eye contact becomes, followed by long periods spent at the mouth.

Blink

If the movies have taught us anything, blinking is a clear form of flirting, but it works! The truth is that when you're looking at someone you like, you tend to blink more than normal.

It's been proven that the brain associates blinking with attraction, so the more you blink, the clearer it is that they like you. And the greatest thing is that it is reciprocal; when you feel that someone blinks at you more attracted you will feel towards that person.

So use it to your advantage!

Increase the frequency with which you blink, and if he unconsciously likes you, he will synchronize with you, increasing the level of attraction between the two of you. Of course, now do not shy away if he blinks a little because it does not mean that he is disinterested.

When you are completely absorbed in a conversation, busy or very entertained, you blink less so you don't miss a second.

But what then?

Use common sense, analyze his body language and the situation, and it will be clear to you if he is flirting with you back or not.

Sting Her Eye

The classic, incomparable and infallible wink or eye sting.

Accompany her with a sexy smile; it is a very effective way of letting her know that you are connected with her. And if you want to be more daring, try it with both eyes at the same time.

Before you start juggling, what we mean is blink in practically slow motion.

But considering that blinking takes milliseconds in slow motion does not mean that you close your eyes (freak). Just consciously blink once a little more slowly.

Now, if you are ready to go out and conquer with your best weapon: your eyes.

Everything is valid in war and love, right?

The Secrets Of Eye Contact

Contact is very important when it comes to communication. Not only serve to modulate the conversation and convey feelings and ideas. Learning to crack their codes can give you a lot of information about others.

Eye communication is a powerful means of expression. Through looks, conscious and unconscious messages are sent that exert great influence in all kinds of encounters. They are part of that communication between the lines that mark so much mutual perception. The looks are a world to decipher that is worth taking into account.

Eye contact and its interpretation are strongly associated with the amygdala, a part of the brain related to emotions. Now, the fascinating thing about eye contact is that it is subtle and forceful language at the same time.

We are not aware of how we look, and sometimes we do not even reflect on the message we are communicating and what effects it has on interaction with others. This article's objective is precisely to elucidate some interesting points of the wonderful world of the gaze.

"Who does not assume a look will not assume a long explanation."

-Arabic proverb-

The Duration Of Eye Contact, A Fundamental Factor

The continuance of eye contact is one of the essential elements in communication through the gaze. For example, a person who avoids the gaze of another is quite emotionally upset. The complete absence of eye contact indicates a lack of control over what you are feeling. In others, it causes a feeling of discomfort and mistrust.

At the other extreme is the one who fixes the gaze and does not divert it. This type of eye contact speaks of a desire to control and perhaps dominate the other person. After a few minutes, this type of look can be truly intimidating. It suggests that there is a desire to instrumentalize the other.

Eye Reading

All eyes convey some excitement, even when they are not very powerful. In the latter, the aridity of the experience or the apathy experienced is reflected. However, it is not easy to observe at a glance. The other person may be upset. Now, when we do, we discover in her the traces of her emotional world.

253

Scholars of body language have managed to identify several of the encrypted codes in eye contact. Here are some of the most common interpretations:

If the blinking is excessive and noticeable, you probably feel insecure and nervous. People don't believe in leaders who blink too much.

They are looking to the left means to remember something and to the right to generate thoughts or ideas. If your gaze is constantly looking in that direction, that person may be lying. With left-handed people, this goes the other way around.

When someone looks into their eyes, they do not believe what the other person is saying.

If there is a concern in keeping good communication with the other, it is usual that the eyebrows are raised during the conversation.

Seduction And Instinct

Looks also perform an essential role during seduction. They are usually the inception of what later becomes a kind bond. Even if the contact is by phone, the people's eyes reflect a certain love interest. For example, it is usual that they shine more, that the pupil is more dilated, and reflect more sweetness.

According To Body Language Experts, Interest In Another Person Is Measured In Eye Contact.

If a person stares you in the eye, lowers their gaze, and then looks back at you, they are probably interested in you.

If the person looks at you, then breaks contact and looks to the side, they are not sure if they are brought to you or not.

If she makes eye contact but then looks up, she will most likely not feel any attraction to you. When you blink more than ten times a minute, you are interested in the person in front of you. Animals are also susceptible to the gaze of humans. If they are angry, they interpret the gaze as a posture of defiance. Looking away is one way to reduce the possibility of an attack.

In conclusion, looks are a world of infinite possibilities. A way of communicating that says a lot about ourselves and others. Therefore, it is worth getting into account when communicating with other people.

The Power Of The Gaze

They say that the gaze is a door to the soul. Through it, we can know many things about the person who is looking at us. There are all kinds of looks, and these also change depending on the moment and the emotional state of the person. It is not the same to look with anger as to look with desire, passion, or indifference...

Thus, the information that a glance can convey is enormous, especially if that look is sincere. This is so because the looks are usually very expressive, although it depends on their type. Eye contact is one of the weapons of seduction, which we use in many cases to transmit things to the other person and awaken something in them.

If we learn to use the gaze well and accompany it with other aspects or actions that we will see in this article, we will be able to seduce someone effectively, or if not, to awaken their interest in us. Flirting with your eyes but is not easy, and we must take into account several aspects.

First of all, clarify that this article in no way pretends to be a manual to flirt, far from it. We will talk about the power of the look when it comes to seducing and some aspects concerning it that you can enhance to have a more marked effect on the other person.

While we talk about seducing, we also refer to awakening the interest of another person beyond a sexual or love sense ... although it is true

255

that throughout the article, we will frequently refer to the action of flirting.

You were flirting with your eyes: how to do it effectively?

But, how to connect with the look? And above all, how to do it successfully? We are going to analyze some aspects that can help us to achieve this:

- Attitude

The first point that we must be clear about when connecting with the gaze is that the gaze that we project or direct to the other has to be accompanied by an attitude. This attitude must be consistent with what we are trying to convey with our eyes. Simply "looking" is not the same as looking with desire or passion, for example.

Thus, the attitude has a lot to do with the purpose of our gaze and with the emotion that we want to transmit and that we want to awaken in the other.

We must ask ourselves, what do we want to awaken in the other, exactly? Do we want to arouse interest? Desire? Curiosity? And based on this, "adjust" our gaze. For this, we can practice in the mirror.

- Time

On the other hand, the idea is that the look that we give to another person lasts only a few seconds (even thousandths of seconds). Very long glances are not effective because they can cause just the opposite effect, that the other person becomes overwhelmed or intimidated.

- Intensity

Another aspect to consider to link with the gaze is its intensity and how we modulate it. This characteristic is not easy to define since how do we measure the intensity of a gaze? This is, in a way, a matter of common sense.

We can look very intensely (fixedly, without blinking, with an accompanying facial expression) or, at the opposite extreme, look "without further ado" in passing and without being too entertained.

So the intensity of flirting with the gaze also has to do with the duration of the gaze and with the facial expression as a whole, among others. Ideally, then, it will turn out to find a middle point in this intensity; for this, we can practice in a mirror, for example.

- Body language

The look is one of the body language elements (within a non-verbal language), but more.

To link with the gaze effectively, we must also attend to other aspects of our body that accompany that gaze so that they are consistent with it (that is, the idea is that there is a certain harmony between our gaze and the rest of the body).

We must think that the look largely defines our facial expression and face since it is one of its key points. For this reason, we must look at:

- Smile

Do we want to accompany our gaze with a smile? If so, what type? A mischievous smile, perhaps? Everything is important when it comes to flirting!

- Posture

What body posture will accompany that look? Ideally, it should be a natural posture and never forced.

- Gestures

What gestures will accompany our smile? We must also keep this aspect in mind and modulate it to be consistent with our gaze and expression. Let us remember that if the different verbal language elements "agree," our message will reach more effectively and credibly.

- Hands

The position of the hands is also important, although not always excessively. It all depends on the context in which we are flirting with the other person. Thus, it is not the same to be standing as sitting, far as to close, in a cinema as in a museum, etc.

- Set your goal

But, as mentioned earlier, none of those is useful when flirting with your gaze if you don't previously set your "goal." This includes finding the time to look at that special someone, so you must get that crossing of eyes first of all.

How to interpret the reaction of the other?

Okay, okay ... we have put into practice our best look at that person who steals our sleep, but ... what happened then? What has she done? Different situations can occur. We show you some of them and how to interpret them.

- She keeps his gaze It.

Maybe that, while we are looking at her, the other person has also kept his gaze on ours. What can this mean? One possibility is that we have interested her, or at least, we have aroused some curiosity in her.

- Withdraws look

It can also occur just the opposite, and it looked to withdraw. If you do it right when eye contact occurs, this may be a sign of embarrassment or intimidation.

If you do it a little later, it may mean the same thing or simply that we have annoyed you or that you have no interest in us (although it is too early to judge). It will also depend on whether it was the first time we did it or not.

- Withdraw your gaze and fix it again

If the other person withdraws their gaze to fix it on us again, this may be an indicator of interest.

- Game of looks and smile

When it comes to flirting with the look, if the other person reacts "playing" with their eyes and accompanies everything with a smile, this seems to be a good indication that they like simply that he is interested in meeting you.

- Avoid your gaze and do not look again.

If the other person not only withdraws his gaze once we establish eye contact but also avoids your gaze and does not look at you again, this is a likely indication that he has no interest in you.

Logically, this and the previous tips should be analyzed in their global context and consider other aspects of the interaction, so they only offer guidance when interpreting the game of gazes and the other person's reaction.

How To Seduce Someone With Your Eyes

The eyes can be a powerful tool for seduction. There are various ways you can practice your eyes to show attraction and get someone interested in you. Make initial eye contact and make the most of your gaze.

- Take the initiative to make initial eye contact. This shows confidence, which many people find beautiful. People tend to be involved in those who are interested in them. Intrigue a person if you try to match their gaze from across the room. Try to make eye connections first, rather than waiting for her

259

to notice you. Look for signs that someone is interested in you. Use this as an opportunity to make initial eye contact. The cues can be subtle, like someone glancing at you. Women can sometimes run their fingers through their hair to convey attraction.

- Start with a few brief looks. Start things off with a few glances if you are a shy person. Looking at someone twice definitely conveys an interest. Try a few short glances at someone, look away, and then see them again. This can show a potential partner that you are attracted to and that you want their attention.
- Look at someone sideways. In addition to making direct eye contact, seeing someone out of the corner of your eye can be helpful. Only glance at someone for a few minutes if they haven't had a chance to strike up a conversation yet.

Spend about 5-10 minutes looking sideways at a person you find attractive. Be cool and make it obvious. See if that person also notices you.

It can help look at someone out of the corner of your eye while laughing at something a friend says. Laughter is contagious and can be attractive to the person you are trying to seduce.

CHAPTER EIGHT

INTIMATE RELATIONSHIPS: ATTRACTION, LOVE, AND CULTURE

Two phenomena associated with intimate relationships are personal attraction and love. The attraction is one of the reasons that can lead us to establish a loving relationship.

Some authors consider that affiliation is the basic phenomenon on which the processes of attraction and love rest. Affiliation is a basic human tendency that leads to seeking other people's company and whose primary function is to ensure the survival of both the individual and the species. In this sense, it is considered that one of the objectives of the affiliation is to enter into relationships, express love and sexuality.

Attraction

As defined by Baron and Byrne, interpersonal attraction can be understood as the judgment that one person makes of another along an attitudinal dimension whose extremes are positive evaluation (love) and negative evaluation (hate). In addition to this cognitive-evaluative dimension, this judgment is associated with behaviors (e.g., trying to do things with the person that attracts us), feelings (e.g., feeling sad when we cannot be with that person), and other cognitions (e.g., attributing to that person many positive characteristics).

261

Moya summarizes the main psychosocial explanations of the attraction that have had the most support in recent years:

The search for cognitive consistency. Theories, such as Festinger's cognitive dissonance, consider that people try to maintain coherence between our attitudes and between them and our behaviors. Therefore, according to this perspective, we will try to have the same ideas and hobbies as our partner, and in unstable situations, we could change our ideology or get divorced.

The consequences of association and reinforcement. The effects of the association on interpersonal attraction, following classical conditioning principles, consist of being attracted to those who appear associated with good experiences for us. We will dislike those associated with bad experiences. In this sense, the MUM effect consists of people resist transmitting bad news to others, even if we have nothing to do with them. When transmitting it, we will appear associated with the negative event before our eyes of the receiver. We will therefore be unattractive to them.

Exchange and interdependence. Authors such as Blau and Kelley and Thibaut consider that according to the theory of social exchange, a person will be attractive if we believe that the rewards derived from such a relationship are greater than the costs involved. The judgment of the person's attractiveness involved in a said relationship depends on the comparisons we make using two criteria: a) the comparison level based on past experiences. Any current situation will only be judged as beneficial depending on this comparison, which previous love relationships can form, and, b) the level of comparison with alternatives. A somewhat good relationship can be the best evaluated if it is the only alternative we have.

In addition to these psychosocial explanations, a series of factors play a fundamental role in the appearance and maintenance of the attraction that we come to feel towards certain people. Next, we will review the most relevant ones.

Proximity

Proximity doesn't just get people to know each other, and it often influences dating and marriages. Research by Festinger, Schachter, and Back showed that the three people with whom college students living in a dorm had the best relationships were the people who lived closest to each other. Likewise, authors such as Byrne and Buehler have verified that the relationships established by the students during the semester are a function of the distance between the seats, that is, that physical proximity influences the fact that the students get to know each other. . However, the correlations found between physical distance and attraction do not assure us that proximity causes relationships, it could be that people who share certain characteristics (e.g., religion, economic status, etc.) prefer to live close to each other.

There are several explanations about the influence of physical proximity when establishing relationships:

- The people who are closest physically are also, generally, the most accessible.

- With repeated exposure, feelings of anxiety about the unknown decrease, and that new person gradually becomes more familiar.
- Proximity can increase familiarity, and familiarity can, in turn, increase attraction. The effect of mere exposure consists of the fact that the repeated perception of an initially neutral or positive stimulus leads to a greater attraction towards the stimulus.
- Similarity can also increase this familiarity since people who share certain spaces tend to resemble each other in other aspects, such as ideology, aspirations, problems, etc.; we will tend to get together well because we are similar or because we have been doing alike as a consequence of being together.

263

- Finally, according to the theories of cognitive consistency, when we have to spend a lot of time with a person, and the relationship is unpleasant, we tend to restore balance, either by trying to get away from it or by discovering that that person was not as unpleasant as we assumed.
- Proximity positively influences attraction as long as the person is initially positive or neutral, not negative.

Negative And Positive Affect

Experiments consistently show that positive feelings lead to positive evaluations of others, likes, and dislikes, while negative feelings lead to negative evaluations, dislike, and antipathy. Affection can influence attraction in two ways:

- First, someone else can do something that makes you feel good or bad; people who make you feel good will tend to like you, and if they make you feel bad, they will be disliked.
- Second, suppose a person is present only when your positive and negative feelings are activated (for whatever reason) as a consequence. In that case, this person will also be nice or unpleasant to you. The general idea is based on classical conditioning. When an attitudinal object is associated with a stimulus that causes negative or positive feelings, the observer develops negative or positive attitudes towards the object. Numerous experimenters have shown that positive affect leads to liking others, while negative affect leads to dislike.

If positive reactions can be transferred from person to person, so can negative reactions. If negative emotions make other people unpleasant to us, and if affection is easily associated with anyone, then we transfer our negative feelings from one person to another if we see them together. Research on stigmata, negatively perceived characteristics (e.g., race, age, foreign accent, physical disability, etc.) indicates that this negative association occurs as easily as positive associations. Even if a stigma is overcome, the previous stigma's effect will not necessarily dissipate.

Personality Characteristics

Anderson found that the five most valued traits were being sincere, honest, understanding, loyal, and trustworthy. Likewise, in Moya's research, the best-evaluated personality characteristics were understanding, loyalty, ability to capture others' feelings, sincerity, and joy. Other studies have shown that the most valued traits in people are grouped into two sets: a) affection (e.g., affectionate, friendly, happy, and considerate), non-verbal cues (e.g., smiling, looking attentively, expressing emotions), and dispositions attitudinal (e.g., showing a liking for people); and, b) competence, which includes social skills and intelligence (e.g., having an interesting conversation, etc.).

Another series of attributes related to the power, prestige, or social position of the person we interact with is of considerable importance to qualify as attractive, especially for males. In fact, in press advertisements, women offer physical attractiveness and seek financial security, while men offer financial positions and request certain physical characteristics.

Likeness

The results of psychosocial research show that, in general, as the similarity between people increases, so does attraction. The two dimensions of similarity that have been studied the most by social psychologists are attitudinal and personality similarity.

Attitude similarity refers to how two individuals share the same attitudes on several issues. Byrne indicates that the greater the similarity, the greater the attraction. This result has been found in people of all ages, in very different groups, and different countries.

265

The study by Smeaton, Byrne, and Murnen confirmed the proportion hypothesis that predicted that attraction differed according to the proportion of similar attitudes shared. Despite these results, several investigations indicated a slightly greater effect of different attitudes than similar ones, in part because most people assume that a stranger, especially an attractive one, harbors attitudes similar to those of the same.

This assumption of general agreement with one's opinions is called the false consensus effect, and a consequence is that agreement is expected while disagreement is surprising. Suppose on some special issues, and individuals believe that they have a minority opinion and that most people disagree. In that case, the disagreement will be expected and will have less effect than an unexpected disagreement.

In the case of personality similarity, the research results are less consistent. Moya argues that the lack of relationship between personality similarity and attraction can be explained because personality characteristics are not usually publicly exhibited. Other times, the personality trait's very nature attracts both alike and those who are different. In general, it has been shown that similarity produces greater attraction than difference, at least in the case of the following characteristics: sexual orientation (that is, if the person is male, female, or androgynous), depression, type A behavior, seeking sensation and cognitive style.

The following explanations show how similarity can influence attraction, both positively and negatively:

- Similar attitudes activate positive affect, while different attitudes activate negative affect, and affect leads to attraction.
- According to cognitive consistency and equilibrium theory theories, people naturally organize their likes and dislikes in a balanced way. In this way, balanced relationships occur when someone is similar, and we like them.
- The similarity is reinforcing. The most valuable proof that others approve of our ideas, customs, and tastes is the fact that

they have them precisely. This formulation suggests that we are interested in other people's opinions not because we seek precision but solely because we want to verify what we already believe. However, when people resemble each other because they possess some negative characteristic, then it is possible that the similarity, instead of leading to attraction, leads to rejection. Sometimes the difference can be more reinforcing than the similarity since it allows us to learn new and valuable things. Also, feeling unique and special is highly valued

- The choice of people similar to us in certain dimensions (e.g., educational level, social class, or physical attractiveness) can result from comparing and evaluating the various alternatives we have and their costs and benefits. This is because, generally, the most valued people are the hardest to get. According to expectation-value theories, in real life, we will feel attracted to the most valued people within the field of those who can reciprocate us. In this sense, the pairing hypothesis refers to the fact that married couples and couples in love tend to become partners based on their similar physical attractiveness.

Finally, when questioned directly, university students do not consider social, ideological, and religious similarity as a relevant attribute in a partner's choice. Two explanations would account for this result: a) people are not aware of the importance of situational determinants of behavior; and b) this attribute may be important at the beginning of the relationship, but not for the choice of an intimate partner. However, it is relevant to note that according to French data, for people of high socioeconomic level, the meeting spaces for couples would be closed or reserved places. People of the low socioeconomic level would be public, open places all the world. This suggests that, even though certain similarities are not relevant when choosing a partner, it is more likely that couples have certain similarities (social, ideological, religious) to the extent that the meeting spaces for couples differ according to economic stratum.

Reciprocity

Once two individuals discover enough similarities to move toward friendship, an additional step is imperative. One of the factors influencing the development of effective relationships is the existence or not of reciprocity in the relationship, that is, that we too are attracted to these people. Almost everyone is happy to receive such positive feedback, and it is quite unpleasant to be evaluated negatively. An exception is that individuals with negative self-concepts sometimes respond well to accurate negative evaluations, possibly because these evaluations are consistent with their self-schema.

Although mutual liking is often expressed in words, the first signs of attraction can be non-verbal indicators. Gold, Ryckman, and Mosley found that when a woman responded positively to a man by looking at him, talking to him, and moving closer, he tended to be attracted to her, even when he knew that her attitudes were different.

Someone who has a bad image of us is not rewarding. According to cognitive consistency theories, someone likes me, and that someone I like is an unstable situation. Aronson and Coe found that when two people shared the dislike of a third, the attraction between them was greater than when they did not share that feeling.

Physical Attractiveness

As Hatfield and Sprecher indicate, given the same characteristics, a person with a pleasant physical appearance is more attractive than another with less physical attractiveness. Physical attractiveness is especially decisive in the first encounters or when the contact is superficial. According to the process of cognitive ignorance, the person that we initially decide has no interest, is not paid attention to, and is forgotten. Research has shown that men often ignore unattractive women.

In various studies, both men and women and people of different races have agreed that an attractive female face is one with both a childlike appearance (large, wide-set eyes, a small nose, a broad smile, and a small chin) and mature features (prominent cheekbones, cheeks narrow, high eyebrows and large pupils). Height has been valued positively in men's physical attractiveness but negatively in women. Another physical characteristic that seems to influence physical attractiveness is body build, the waist-hip ratio in women's cases. Alicke found that attractiveness decreased markedly when a very attractive face was matched with an unattractive body. Also, overweight people are generally perceived as less attractive.

The following explanations show why a pleasant physique is attractive to us :

- According to the implicit theories of personality, there are numerous beliefs about what people's characteristics are associated with each other in our society. In this sense, the halo effect considers that whoever has a good quality will also have other good qualities. Some research has shown that people tend to believe that attractive men and women are more stable, interesting, sociable, independent, dominant, exciting, sexy, balanced, socially skilled, and more successful than those who are not attractive. However, physical attractiveness can be associated with negative characteristics. For example, very attractive women may be judged as more materialistic and vain than less attractive. They may be considered more guilty than the latter when they are tried for a crime involving deception.
- Attractive people also attract us because our public image is favored when associating with a person of these characteristics. Thus, various studies have confirmed that

when a man appears accompanied by a very attractive woman, he improves the impression he makes.

- Attractive people can behave in a way that increases their evaluation and makes them more attractive. Reis showed that attractive men had more relationships with women and developed a greater social competence in this field than less attractive men. However, the most attractive women did not establish more interactions with men, were less assertive and more fearful in their relationships with men than the less attractive women.
- According to the affect-centered model, good-looking individuals activate positive effects, and affect, as already mentioned, is an important determinant of attraction.

People are not correct in estimating how others judge their attractiveness. Men (but not women) overestimate their good looks. Because many biases favor attractiveness, it is not surprising that many people care about their appearance. This preoccupation with one's attractiveness and fear of negative judgments by others is known as appearance anxiety.

Judgments about whether a person is attractive are not solely a matter of the person's physical details in question. Situational factors influencing the observer are also important. Kenrick found that if a person had previously seen several highly attractive individuals, the person in question is rated as less attractive.

Behavioral indicators also affect perceptions. People react more positively to someone with a youthful gait than someone with an elderly-like gait, regardless of gender or age. Furthermore, adults who seem very young are also judged as weak, naive, and incompetent, but loving and honest. Those who appear to be very mature are perceived as more dominant and attractive but less affectionate and friendly.

Attraction And Culture

Attractiveness, perception, and social behavior, contrary to beliefs that beauty depends on who is looking and that there are radically different patterns of beauty, fifteen studies have confirmed that people of different nations and ethnic groups agree when they indicate which types of individuals are physically attractive and which are not. For example, people of different cultures (13 countries and four ethnic groups) judged a female face as more attractive if it showed the following characteristics: large eyes with dilated pupils, small nose, high cheekbones, narrow face with thin cheeks, wide smile, lips thick or full and small chin. However, other results show cultural variability: blacks in the United States evaluate heavier women as more attractive than whites in the United States. This suggests that although there is agreement on the body structure and attractive facial features, there are ethnic variations in the parameters of body weight and size that define an attractive person.

Studies allow us to conclude that people perceive and evaluate attractive people more favorably; It is the effect called 'what is beautiful is good.' The review by Langlois confirmed that more attractive children were evaluated as more friendly, more competent, with a better fit and affective balance, and with greater interpersonal competence than less attractive children. The same was true of attractive adults: they were judged as more competent at work, more pleasant, and better fit or mental health.

Consistently, attractive children and adults were also treated more positively. There were fewer negative interactions with the more attractive children, more positive interactions, and more care. While attractive adults received more attention, were given more rewards, more positive interactions were established with them, fewer negative interactions, and more help and cooperation.

It has also been confirmed that attractive people act more positively (e.g., they are more popular, slightly more intelligent, have more

271

adapted social skills and behaviors, have better physical health) and possess more positive characteristics (e.g., higher self-esteem, better mental health, more extraversion).

Finally, attractive people self-perceive or judge themselves slightly better than less attractive people (they perceive themselves as more competent and better mental health).

Socio-cultural And Attractive Factors

The previous results confirm the socio-cultural explanation about attractiveness:

- Cultural norms and values determine the behavior and judgments of the judges and 'evaluated' through their learning;
- Expectations and stereotypes are learned ('there is no lame or one-eyed person good') and are confirmed through behaviors and self-fulfilling prophecy (e.g., when faced with someone unattractive, I treat him worse, to which he responds more negatively).

Although the tendency to perceive that "what is beautiful is good" is common in all the cultures studied, what differs are inferred positive traits. For example, in Korea, an attractive person is inferred that he cares more about others and is more integrated, consistent with that culture's collectivist values. In the United States, it is inferred that greater attractiveness, greater assertiveness, dominance, and strength are consistent with the dominant individualistic and competitive cultural values in those societies. Another study with

Asians (Taiwanese Chinese) confirmed that attractive people were evaluated positively on both socially desirable and undesirable traits. Still, there was no relationship between attractiveness and judgment on non-normative traits (of medium desirability). That is, physical attractiveness is associated with traits that are normative in a given culture.

272

Now, three facts question the socio-cultural explanation about 'what is beautiful is good':

- The relationship between a person's attractiveness and the judgments and behaviors attributed to him is not greater in adults than in children. However, according to socio-cultural arguments, people learn beauty patterns and their correlations as they socialize in a given culture, so adults should show this effect more intensity.
- Likewise, the relationship between attractiveness and the judgments and behaviors attributed to a person is similar for men and women. This fact questions the socio-cultural idea that this effect is based on different gender roles that emphasize more female physical beauty than male.
- Finally, the self-perceptions of attractive people are only slightly more positive. This fact questions the socio-cultural perspective that indicates that perceptions and interactions are internalized in the self-concept.

Appeal and Evolutionary Explanations

The high cross-cultural agreement in judgments about attractive features (infantile face, amphora body for women, regular face, and muscular triangular body for men) is consistent with an evolutionary explanation.

However, a series of facts also question the evolutionary hypotheses:

- Given that attractive traits similarly influence men and women when it comes to inferring judgments and behaviors about people, the evolutionary hypothesis that states that when choosing a partner, attractiveness is more important for men is questioned. since it indicates the greater reproductive capacity of women while resources are for women since it indicates the ability of men to ensure the survival of their descendants.

273

- Given that the relationship between the person's attractiveness and the judgment and behavior attributed to him is similar for children and adults, the evolutionary hypothesis affirms that attractiveness must be important because it is related to reproduction. Say, with adulthood.

The results are congruent with the evolutionary hypothesis that attractiveness is a general indicator of good health - the so-called good gene theory. The fact that it associates the attractiveness of a person with their better evaluation and quality of interaction in childhood is also consistent with the evolutionary theory of parental investment, which suggests that parents invest more in children with greater survivability and reproduction - healthier because they are more beautiful, regardless of whether they are boys or girls.

Love

Love is such a complex phenomenon that it has given rise to many broad and vague definitions applied to other intense emotional events such as bereavement or rape. Besides, love is a dynamic process that is constantly changing during the relationship, so its definition will vary depending on its state. The data provided by various investigations carried out from different disciplines clearly show that there is a progressive decrease in initial passion and that this, together with the gradual growth of commitment, gives rise to a cycle with an initial phase of passionate love strongly associated with sexual desire followed. of a phase of partner love that lasts for about two years in most cases.

Types Of Love

One of the basic types is sexual or passionate love that would be characterized by:

1. Strong uncontrollable feelings of attraction towards the desired person and anxiety and discomfort in his absence.
2. Strong physiological activation and sexual desire.
3. Obsessive thoughts or rumination about the loved object;
4. A certain pattern of behaviors, such as expressing affection for the desired person, supporting them physically and emotionally, and unconditional acceptance.

On the other hand, non-passionate romantic love would be composed of:

- Thoughts of need, of "caring for" and of trust in the partner;
- Feeling of well-being, difficulty concentrating and 'floating in the clouds' and, to a lesser extent, intense physical reactions; and,
- Behaviors of intimacy, support, and tolerance of the other.

Of all the love typologies, it will be Lee the first to try to validate his proposal empirically. Lee distinguished three basic love styles: Eros, Ludus, and Storge. The combination, in different degrees, of these primary styles, would give us three other secondary styles independent of the first: Mania, Pragma, and Agape:

- Eros or passionate love is characterized by an irresistible passion, intense feelings, strong physical attraction, and sexual activity. Lover Eros values love highly but are not obsessed with it or pressure his partner to intensity, but rather allows things to develop mutually. The characteristic of this type is self-confidence and high self-esteem.
- Ludus or playful love, with little emotional involvement and no future expectations. This loving style does not have a preferred physical style but rather likes all kinds of partners. Even though many people see this love as morally negative, Ludus does not try to hurt other people. He usually makes the rules of the game very clear before starting the relationship.
- Storge, or friendly love, is characterized by a long-lasting commitment that develops slowly and prudently and is based

on intimacy, friendship and affection. The similarity in terms of values and attitudes is much more important to Storge than physical appearance or sexual satisfaction. The orientation of this love is more to seek a long-term commitment than a short-term passion.

- Mania is obsessive love, with a strong dependence on the partner, intense jealousy, possessiveness, mistrust, and ambivalence. This lover tries to force the couple into commitment without waiting for it to evolve naturally.
- Pragma refers to pragmatic love, love based on the rational search for the ideal partner. The pragmatic lover considers age, education, social status, religion, or the ability to be a good father or mother. Unlike Storage, in which love can grow without being particularly concerned about the partner's future projections or the partner's family background, the pragmatic lover is likely to establish conditions before developing a relationship.
- Agape or altruistic love, of absolute renunciation and selfless surrender. It is a rather romantic love in which sexuality and sensuality are not relevant.

The Hendrick and Hendrick scale of attitudes towards love is the one that evaluates this typology from an individual approach to love relationships. With this scale, Hendrick and Hendrick classified the romantic stories described by university students in these six different styles: eros or love at first sight (34%), Storage (66%), Ludus (2%), mania (2 %), pragma (17%) and agape (2%). More than three-quarters of the stories described corresponded to partner love, followed by a third of them framed in passionate love.

From the point of view of gender differences, Hendrick and Hendrick found that men, compared with women, attach more importance to passionate love (eros) and playful or entertaining (Ludus). Women, compared with men, are more inclined towards friendly love (Storge), logical (pragma), and possessive (mania). These results have been described from the perspective of the functions that these forms of love have had for each sex in the species' evolution.

Functions Of Love And Evolution

The evolutionary conception provides us with arguments about the biological functionality of loving behavior for the individual as a member of a species.

This approach sees love as a natural part of the human condition and, perhaps, natural to other species. Love is biologically relevant if it helps promote species' survival, a central theme of evolution theory. Five million years ago, the survival of species depended on reproductive success. Sexual desire and commitment, respectively related to previous aspects of reproductive success, were reinforced in higher primates whose biochemistry led them to seek and obtain pleasure not only from sexual activity but also from female-male bonding and parent-descendants. Ancestors who acted this way were more likely to pass on their genes than those who were not motivated to sexual activity and establish stable emotional bonds. As a result of this evolutionary process, humans are genetically pre-programmed to have sexual activity (sexual desire or sexual love in terms of Oatley and Johnson Laird, 1995), to fall in love (stable emotional relationships with a partner), and to care for descendants (parental love). The evolutionary perspective admits that current environmental factors influence.

Social and non-genetic aspects of the body determine sexual activity. The historical influence or the ten thousand years of civilization established as in which we currently live has acted only during 5% of the species' existence or over 400 of the 100,000 generations of humanity.

This socio-biological theory allows us to explain the sex differences in sexual behavior and love based on two central processes that have to do with differential parental investment and sexual selection:

277

- The sexual selection consists of two different processes: a) Intra-sexual selection refers to the pressure that members of one sex exert on the other through competition. In a species in which males compete for females through their hunting ability and strength, the strongest and best hunting individuals are more likely to dominate the competition and survive; and, b) Epigamic selection is the other part of sexual selection. If one sex selects its other-sex partners based on certain attributes such as physical strength and aggressiveness, these attributes must be more characteristic of one sex than the other.
- Parental investment is defined as the expenditure of time, energy, and risk of the parent in the offspring that increases the probabilities of survival of the latter (and therefore reproductive success) at the cost of the father's ability to invest in another offspring. While the typical parental investment may have been highly variable throughout our evolutionary history, the minimum possible parental investment of females, due to nine months of gestation and subsequent months of lactation, has been much greater than that of males in our species. A woman can have a maximum of 25 children, and the average number of children in simple hunter-gatherer societies is five. Ancestral males might have benefited reproductively from copulating with any fertile female if the risk was low. Therefore, it is fair to hypothesize that natural selection favored males who had low thresholds for sexual arousal and reactive to new sexually attractive females. On the other hand, our female ancestors had little to gain reproductively and much to lose if they copulated randomly with new males. Selection is unlikely to have favored females who were sexually attracted to a wide variety of males or solely because of their presence .

According to the socio-biological theory predictions, in the case of the human species, since women must be fertile, they will be better sexual objects when they have a youthful and maternal appearance.

278

For example, the narrower the waist is relative to the hips, the more men will prefer them and value them as more attractive, healthy, and reproductively valuable. It can also be assumed that women would be more selective in selecting their mates since they have a higher parental investment in their offspring than men and can father a few boys in a limited period. Therefore, women go looking for men who stick with resources to protect them and their children. In particular, when choosing potential sexual partners, they will pay more attention to the attributes of status, dominance, and aggressiveness. They will select those with a greater ability to obtain resources.

Predictions from socio-biological theory regarding gender differences in behaviors are common with role theories that emphasize that women are assigned and socialized in passive, lower status, and communal roles while men do so. They are inactive roles, of higher status, and agentic; therefore, women should be less approving of casual relationships, and they should have fewer different partners. Sociobiologists argue that, although men may be somewhat more permissive than women in extramarital affairs, men especially disapprove of women having such relationships since they must guarantee paternity with the utmost certainty.

From this perspective, it is predicted that men will value playful love more, consistent with their lower parental investment and their positive orientation towards casual sex and obtaining the maximum number of possible partners. Women, given the greater parental investment and the effort necessary to raise a few descendants, will tend to value more pragmatic and friendly love, as well as the criteria of social power and status to choose their partner. Therefore, men's playful love and the pragmatic love of women would favor the species' reproduction.

According to these predictions, cross-cultural research has consistently confirmed socio-biological hypotheses that women prefer older sexual partners and evaluate them based on their resources. Men prefer younger and physically attractive partners. In this sense, the cross-cultural research of Buss confirmed in 37 different countries that women tend to evaluate their male partners based on their economic capacity, ambition, and perseverance, while the attributes positively evaluated by men to choose a female partner are health, beauty, and youth. They will choose those who have the greatest signs of reproductive capacity. Likewise, in the meta-analysis by Oliver and Hyde, men presented more permissive attitudes towards sexual relations, earlier initiation of coital sexual relations, a higher frequency of intercourse, and a greater number of sexual partners than women. This greater male centrality in sexuality is supported by anthropological research. Of the 849 societies examined in Murdock's Ethnographic Atlas, 708 are polygamic (one husband for several wives), and only 4 are polyandrous (a woman can have two or more husbands). In addition to the four polyandrous, they are all polygamic, the reverse being not true.

According to the socio-biological augmentation, the differences between genders will be reinforced, especially in cultures that impose fewer social constraints. These allow exploring the entire behavioral repertoire and allow innate differences to manifest more strongly.

The universal character of love and cultural influence from a cultural perspective, some authors have postulated the transcultural existence of romantic or passionate love. Thus, Jankowiak and Fischer, in a review of 186 cultures, have found that 88.5% of them have indicators of passionate love. In particular social constructionists and relativists like Averill, other authors postulate that passionate love is a phenomenon constructed by social discourse at a given historical and cultural moment. Thus, Hendrick and Hendrick, among others, argue that it is exclusive to Western culture and emerged around the 12th century. However, some authors such as Berscheid emphasize that there are descriptions of desire and passionate love in much earlier documents such as the Bible, Hindu, and classical Chinese texts.

More and more psychologists, anthropologists, and other scholars believe that love is a universal phenomenon. However, its concrete meaning can vary markedly from one culture to another at different times. Before the modern age, it was not a prerequisite for marriage, so in many societies, it was arranged by parents or relatives, perhaps hoping that love would arise in the couple in the future. Still, there were no great expectations of romantic love. Studies conducted in Western cultures have found that the relationship between marriage and love has changed over the past thirty years. A generation ago, especially women wanted to marry even in the absence of romantic love. Still, since then, men and women have agreed on the idea of romantic love as the basis of marriage. It seems that in the twentieth century, in Western societies, romantic love has become the fundamental reason for maintaining long-term marital relationships.

The belief that one should marry only for love becomes an ideology when a society widely shares it. Since people today share this belief, it is difficult to understand how marriages in previous centuries could have been happy. Perhaps the people of other times shared another ideology. Perhaps there was often early anticipation of sharing life with a partner, sexual fulfillment or coming to love the partner more deeply over the years. However, some of these anticipations sound a lot like today's anticipations except for 'falling in love.' It is possible that the bond between love and marriage has not changed that much; what may have changed is the ideology of love from 'marriages must be arranged to 'marriages must be based on love.' To some extent, this depends on how love is defined.

Socio-Structural Factors And Intimate Relationships

Some authors have insisted on social structure factors in the sphere of beliefs and loving behaviors.

Guttentag and Secord stated that the demographic ratio between men and women is an important variable to explain the dominant type of love. When there are more numerous men than women in the population, the few women are valued. An idealized vision of women, of the family, and a non-passionate romantic vision of love prevails.

281

In this context, a more partner style of love would probably dominate. When there is an excess of women, the family and marriage will be devalued. Extra and pre-marital sex, singleness, and separations would be frequent, committed love would not be dominant, and a playful and erotic love style would predominate. These authors reviewed demographic data from different countries and historical periods, such as ancient Greece, medieval Europe, and the United States, that confirmed these hypotheses during different centuries.

On the other hand, Eagly and Wood argued that sex differences in the criteria for choosing an intimate partner should be smoothed out in societies characterized by greater gender equality, since men's preferences for younger women, capable of being good attractive housewives, as well as the importance given by women to men's social resources reflect the differences in status and roles between men and women. Reanalyzing the partner selection criteria, it was confirmed that, the greater equality between the genders, evaluated by a UN indicator on the degree of labor and institutional insertion of women, as well as salary parity with men, there were fewer differences between the sexes in the importance that was assigned to financial resources and being a good householder as criteria for choosing a partner.

From this socio-structural perspective, the differences in beliefs about the love between nations and between genders depend on social resources, demographics, and distribution of power and status among gender roles. Socio Economic development will directly reinforce the importance of passionate love, love as a criterion and prerequisite for choosing an intimate partner and marrying. It allows the person to value subjective rather than practical aspects. Social and economic development, which is associated with a lower difference in status and power concerning gender roles, will cause more similarities in men's and women's responses about love. Levine concluded that economic development would reinforce individualism, the relative equality of opportunities between men and women (higher education, greater female labor participation, and legal equality), would increase the importance of subjective feelings and personal decisions in the formation of couples, which would be associated with an increase in divorces and a decrease in birth rates (greater control by the woman of contraception and greater planning of the offspring, not experienced as an obligation). Therefore, the differential distribution of resources and roles would explain the differences between men and women and between nations.

Cultural Factors And Intimate Relationships

Other studies have shown the influence of cultural values on beliefs about love. Dion and Dion suggest that different cultural orientations strongly influence how people conceptualize love and intimacy. The more individualistic cultures, in which intimate relationships are established face to face and more or less symmetrically, value the passionate romantic component of love more. In contrast, in collectivist societies, intimate relationships are organized through the extended family's intervention, and the pragmatic and friendly aspects of love are valued more. Thus, romantic love is a more important basis for marriage in individualism than in collectivist cultures. In the former, two people's love and individual decisions seem natural to form a stable couple. In the latter, in general, the formation of the couple is a decision of the elderly. It is based on arrangements that respond to the families' wishes, and it is a duty for the individuals. Most of humanity lives in collectivist cultures, and in general, the family has a great influence on marriages. Most of the brides are adolescents; in two-thirds of the societies, a dowry is paid for them, and the marriage is conceived as a socioeconomic contract between the families. In 1980, in China, only a third of marriages were free from family influence. In 1989, in Korea, 40% of marriages were arranged, as 72% of Turkish women interviewed in the '70s. Parental arranged marriage was very common among Indian and Pakistani immigrants.

From this socio-cultural and normative perspective, more than the differences in resources and roles.

They would explain the differences between genders and between nations. Even controlling the level of economic development, cultures whose values emphasize autonomy and individual decisions and value internal attributes and feelings (individualistic) will reinforce the importance of passionate love, love as a criterion and prerequisite for a partner's choice. And marriage. Collectivist cultures, which are characterized by greater differences in status and emphasize family decisions and normative duties, will give less importance to love as a criterion and prerequisite for forming a stable couple and will value more the practical and friendly aspects of the relationship. Love. It can also be assumed that normative cultures, which emphasize the need to obey rules, will reject more playful and pragmatic love and emphasize criteria such as innocence and social status. These cultures that do not tolerate uncertainty and emotions should also emphasize the style of love mania - strong emotional and possessive activation. Hierarchical cultures, which emphasize the legitimacy of status asymmetries and obedience (from children to fathers and from wives to husbands, among others), and masculine, competitive cultures that emphasize gender differences, will also reinforce differences in response between men and women, in particular by reinforcing people's support for traditional gender criteria (e.g., women will value social status more and men will value chastity and feminine characteristics such as being a good housewife). Let us remember that according to a socio-cultural argument, the cultures that impose more constraints will reduce gender differences in normative responses (e.g., there will be fewer differences between men and women in the valuation of pragmatic love if it is normative in collectivist cultures).

In summary, the phenomenon of love presents an inter and intra-individual variability and a cultural and historical one.

Types Of Love And Socio-cultural Factors

A study on the importance of people from 15 countries and regions of the world to the different styles of the love of Hendrick and Hendrick has confirmed the influence that economic, social, and cultural factors exert in the valuation of these types of love.

Considering that the more under the score, the better the type of love, and that scores above three indicate disapproval. Using the national averages, it is confirmed that the erotic style is the most valued, followed by the storge mania style. Ludus and pragma are the least valued styles.

Besides, cultures that emphasize the friendly and partner style (Storge) also value practicalities (pragma) and place less importance on possession, jealousy, and strong emotional arousal (mania). In this sense, cultures that emphasize passionate love also value manic loveless.

Erotic love is more valued in female cultures, in uncompetitive societies, which value the quality of life and in countries with high social development and in cultures with low avoidance of uncertainty that are characterized for being less normative and anxious.

The storge and pragma love styles, which do not have such passionate overtones, are more valued in collectivist cultures where intimate relationships are based more on family obligations and duties and cultures with low avoidance of love. Uncertainty, intolerant, intolerant societies, which are less emotional and value gradual and calm love. Countries with less socioeconomic development and greater hierarchical distance give more importance to love's social and practical aspects. Therefore, these results corroborate what has been found in previous studies, that is, the higher prevalence of the pragmatic and partner love style (Storge) among African and African countries. Collectivist eastern and less developed nations.

In individualistic cultures that value the individual more and with high avoidance of uncertainty that is more normative and emotional, the manic style related to possession and high affective activation occurs more intensely.

Finally, the playful love style is more valued in collectivist cultures, with low socioeconomic development and low uncertainty avoidance. For example, in these cultures, in African countries, both due to the absence of resourceful male partners and a certain greater tolerance and acceptance of casual sex, extramarital sexuality is more frequent.

Types Of Love And Gender Differences

Concerning gender differences, the results show that women, compared with men, agree significantly more with pragmatic love and storge love. At the same time, they value Ludus love and agape love more negatively. It is in feminine (vs. masculine) cultures where there are more differences between women and men in the valuation they make of the playful love style. Therefore, men value playful love more, and in particular, it is men from feminine cultures who value play love more than women.

It has also been found that collectivist countries and less social development show a greater difference between women and men in their storage love valuation. Although women show more agreement with the style of friendly love in all cultures than men, this type of love was more emphasized by women from collectivist and less developed societies, probably to compensate for the lower resources and autonomy.

The results also indicate that men and women in individualistic countries show a greater difference in their pragma style valuation. Women show more agreement with the practical aspect of love than men in individualistic cultures, although, in collectivist countries, both men and women value it more importantly. Likewise, the differences between men and women in their valuation of the pragma style were greater in masculine than in feminine cultures. Therefore, pragmatic love was emphasized more by women than by men in individualistic and competitive cultures, probably as a way of adapting to their environment.

Love and physical attractiveness are more valued as criteria for choosing a partner in individualistic cultures, emphasizing personal feelings and decisions when establishing intimate relationships and in cultures characterized by establishing more egalitarian or less social relationships, hierarchical and greater social development. On the contrary, the valuation of innocence, social status, and good health is more important in societies with fewer resources, less social development, and strongly hierarchical. The higher valuation of the more material and realistic aspects of love seems consistent with the socio-cultural context since the components of survival and social adaptation of intimate relationships are more relevant in these contexts.

50% of people from collectivist cultures say that they would be willing to marry a person, even if they were not in love. Studies have confirmed that the majority of people (66%) refuse to marry someone who has all the requirements without being in love with him/her, and only a minority (13%) accept it (see table 3). But, especially, the individuals from individualistic and masculine countries state that they are less in agreement with marrying a person who has all the qualities but with whom they are not in love. Besides, the countries with greater social development and less hierarchy give more importance to love as a prerequisite for establishing intimate and couple relationships. Therefore, these results confirm the studies that indicate that love tended to be more important in westernized, more developed, and individualistic countries, such as the USA, followed by Brazil, England, and Australia, and less important in less developed nations. More hierarchical and collectivist from the East like India, Pakistan, Thailand, and the Philippines. The two least collectivist and economically most developed countries of the Asian countries, Japan and Hong Kong, attached greater importance to love.

287

These studies suggest that basic needs' satisfaction allows developing more self-fulfillment and self-expression, such as romantic love. Individualism and egalitarian cultural relationships increase the importance of internal attributes and personal decisions regarding and marriage.

The Truth About Women's Love and Sex ... It May Surprise You

"Women are too complicated."

"Women have many needs."

"I don't understand women."

You hear this all the time. And honestly, it makes sense. Other men say that because it is easier to raise your hands and simply relate to women as black boxes that cannot be understood than to try and wrap their minds around women who can understand. Here's what you require to learn about women, and the good news is: they are creatures at first and, on a biological level, very sexual. In fact, they presumably appreciate sex yet more than we do. Have you noticed how women moan during sex a lot more than men?

What All Women Fear To Live

(and the trick to alleviate this anxiety and get them to do anything you ask)

Regrettably, society states women to believe, in the relevant portion of their minds, (not the emotional portion), that it is "wrong" to enjoy sex.

Because women manage to be social creatures (more so than men, for reasons of evolutionary science), labels like "slut" or "prostitute" have a strong negative effect on them.

Neither of these fines applies to men who have a lot of sex. Thus, the supreme tragedy of the misogynistic system put in place by religion and society to repress women's sexuality is that men have more of a challenge in getting sex than they would if they went back to pre-civilization ages when ladies were wild and uninhibited.

Your job as a guy in contemporary society is to go around the woman's social conditioning and bring out the natural woman within her.

Sounds difficult? Believe me, it is not! In a way, women are like padlocks. They seem impossible if you are using the wrong keys, but once you find the correct key, they open easily. And yes, you can do this. I'm going to show you how.

To bring out the natural woman that lies deep within each woman, you must always keep in mind that, on a subliminal level, ladies love sex, and they want it as much (and perhaps more) as we want it.

And as if the social conditioning that women are subjected to isn't bad enough, a more powerful force lies within them: their biology. A perfectly natural consequence of sex is children, and every gal knows it. And she knows that if she goes pregnant when she's not supposed to get pregnant, people will talk. This is the supreme tragedy of women; Despite loving sex, they cannot be free with their sexuality without being labeled a slut.

So while you — as a sexual man — direct your encounters with women toward sex, you need to keep her from feeling like a slut.

(By the way, it's to your own preference to be discreet with women. The last point in life is to be like the approval-seeking beta males who brag to their mates about the women they've brought to bed. You don't need the approval of your peers, so skip the locker room talk! Real men don't need to do that.)

Have you talked to guys who say to you, "We men will never understand gentlewomen?" Well, ladies really aren't as strange or
289

hard to follow as those guys think. Nor are they different from us, as some of us might think.

Since we know that women want sex, it is okay for you to write down having sex on your agenda when you interact with them. In fact, it really is a great idea.

What you should bypass doing at all costs, however, is verbalizing their intentions. You DO NOT want to say something about sex, or his attempt to have it, to the woman.

Whenever you share your sexual purposes to a woman by saying something about him, you engage the logical portion of her mind, causing her social conditioning to skyrocket. "Oh-oh," she thinks. "This guy is vulgar, gross, and it gives me the creeps. And I couldn't end up being a slut here. "

So avoid being explicit about sex, and hold back the back of your mind how much women adore sex, and work on extending sexuality without saying anything at all about it. Use the language of your body, not your mouth.

What Women Like

Don't listen to what women say when they talk about the type of men they like; instead, look at their demeanor and look at the kinds of men they really throw themselves at.

If a woman were honest, she would say that the type of man she likes is "a sexual man who will create an opportunity for sex and will persist despite my barriers." However, she doesn't dare say this because she is terrified that someone will call her a "slut."

Women like relationships, but they don't need a man for that. After all, women have very intimate relationships with their female friends. I can't repeat it enough- Women want a man who gives them great sex. And here is another biological tidbit: women normally take on the passive role in sex. This means that you, the man, need to take responsibility for the sex by pushing the encounter firmly into readiness.

Don't make her take over. I mean, think about it: she lives in fear of being labeled a slut, and are you waiting for her to start sex? It's no wonder so many guys have trouble getting to bed. It's too much to wait for something like that - the woman just isn't going to act on that plane. To take her to bed, you will have to create a situation where the woman feels as if she could have sex with you without consequences for her.

For example, last month, I hooked up with a woman at "happy hour." We talked for a couple of hours, the topics I will reveal later to be a great conversationalist with women.

We get along really well, and then (two hours into our conversation!) She tells me that she had a boyfriend.

At this point, there were several ways he could have reacted. Most types would:

      a. Upset and leave her, feeling bitter about how the woman had led to this.
      b. Trying to talk and convince the girl to ditch that other guy.

Most guys would either have chosen a) or b). Trust me, I did that too. Instead, I've learned that the best thing to do is what I call "Option C": react nonchalantly, maintain my alpha male composure, and show that what she said didn't get me out of control.

"Good," I later said cheerfully. "He will keep you busy when you are away from me."

She laughed that it was a breakthrough between us that night. I don't normally go for girls with boyfriends, but she had been flirting with some guy in a bar for two hours; how good could that relationship be?

291

(And by the way, if a woman comes up to you and is in a relationship, mark my words ... if she doesn't have sex with you, then she'll find some other guy to flirt with her and satisfy her carnal desires. Her current boyfriend won't, or she wouldn't be flirting with other guys.)

As the night progressed, the perfect excuse was given to go to my house. She was a huge fan of the British Royal Family, and I told her about my collection of magazines from the time I spent my summer in England. "Come see them," I told her.

Once in my apartment, of course, it was simply a matter of me to maintain control of the interaction and allow her to slowly warm up sexually.

Around 2 AM, she decided to leave, not wanting to spend the night. All she had ever wanted from me was sex, no strings attached. (She knew that no one would ever know what we did that night.) In other words: sex without consequences. That is what women ask for. You've probably heard of women on vacation looking for adventure outside of town. Have you ever questioned why they do that? It is because there is no responsibility for them; they are not going to be called sluts. Sex happens spontaneously because the conditions are right. A woman thousands of miles away from home can satisfy her carnal desires, and no one in her city will ever know.

Do Not Talk Explicitly About What You Are Going To Do

There is a certain mating ritual that humans do. This is like a dance that goes on for several hours. The mating ritual must follow the appropriate steps for sex to take place. We men have an unfortunate tendency to always want to clarify the environment and find out from the woman what is happening directly, where everything is located between them, and how she feels about having sex. This is a huge mistake.

Never verbalize anything about wherever you are in the mating ceremony with a woman. Do not explicitly tell him what your intentions are. That is a logical thing that men do. Logical things kill sensations, and passions are crucial for a woman to be sexually receptive to you. Don't talk about your intentions about having sex; you should make it appear that the two of you had spontaneous sex. It will keep the emotional part of her activated while the logical portion of her mind remains deactivated. And that's good — it's the logical part of your mind that says, "No!"

If you come for her as a true gentleman who she really hooked up with, then she will rationalize in her mind that even though she doesn't normally have sex on a first date, you were an exception.

Just remember: a good time for a woman is good sex with a man ... and she wants you to take over.

The Number One Mistake Men Make In Dating, And How To Avoid It

At the ripe age of 23, a colleague of mine got his first girlfriend. Even though he was just a law scholar, while he barely was with her, he spent more than $ 3,000 on the girl in just the short time of a month, investing inexpensive wines, restaurants, and other unnecessary gifts.

Although he slept with her several times in that short period, she left him for another guy. My friend was distraught for months afterward, not to mention that he had to get a part-time job to refill his bank account.

I've been there, and I've done that. I spent time on dinners, movies… I even bought a $ 500 ring, saved in high school for support. I often bought the girl a $ 30 bouquet of flowers on our first date.

All that money spent, and not much received in return. All I had wanted to get out of the deal was sleep with her. It seemed like a very simple bargain ... the girl would get the gifts I bought her, and in return, all she would need to do was spread her legs.

Sound familiar? Get frustrated when you can't get to bed after spending so much money?

Well, here's the thing: You are operating on a false assumption. The money spent does not necessarily equal the opening of the legs. The problem with wasting cash on a woman who hasn't earned it is what it communicates. And what it says to her, loud and clear, is her value is higher than hers, so you need to obtain her approval by buying it.

It's like saying, "Okay, I know my worth is less than yours; how about I attach a dozen roses, an upscale dinner, and some very nice diamond earrings?" Do you get the point? However, the reality is that if you know that her value is high, you don't need to buy her favor.

I know that saying "don't buy anything for girls" goes against what we men logically think, and indeed it goes against what all of us have not been taught. After all, we have been led to believe that if there is something of importance that we want, we want to be willing to do whatever it takes to buy it, correct?

Well, in the state of inanimate things that don't think for themselves, that's true. But in the case of women, it is not. Consider the common super-hot woman. Most men see her as highly valuable, and thus they lower themselves before her and worship the ground on which she walks.

She walks into a place, and her money is not good. But what kind of guy does a woman like that throw herself for? Usually, one with high social status sees no need to buy you things to win your concerns. Oh certainly, he does it later, after he has her, so she has nice stuff to show off… but not while he's taking her.

The bottom line means that there are three definite rules of spending money on women (screw them up, and you'll not only go home broke but with blue balls as well). Always ask yourself before paying the following questions:

1) What is my value and hers? If you make a personal effort to pay, you communicate to her that you think she has a higher value than yours.

2) Has she earned what I am going to give her? As an alpha male, you reward good performance. So make positive the woman has done something to win your approval! (I squandered a $ 100 meal recently on a lady I'm dating. I did it because she has provided me the greatest fellatio (oral sex) in the world. Make no mistake about: the only time you should get a woman out on an expensive date is when she has done something significant to earn it, like pleasing you sexually.)

3) Am I funding for this in an Alpha way? Make sure you don't frame it like you're shopping for a woman in your bed because that's Beta, and it shows need.

I want you to start preparing a mental representation of yourself as a man of great importance. Now, as a gentleman of high value, you need to play the mind game that yes, you are interested in the woman, but your interest is conditioned on her good behavior.

By the way, never say things to a woman like this: "I'm buying this for you as a prize." Just reward healthy behavior and bypass encouraging bad behavior, and you will find that things will work out for you.

When buying things for a woman, never overdo this. State something like, "I'll pay for the coffee. It is not a big thing." what that tells her is that you're more interested in the social interaction the two of you are having and that you're not thinking about the drink you bought her.

This also means that there is nothing in mind. By saying, "it's not a big deal," you make her understand that you are not pressuring her for what you have done for her.

"Buying me things because he wants something later" is behavior that many women consider manipulative, and as a result, the man was denied sex. And to be honest enough, many men fall into that trap by spending a lot of money buying women nice things. Don't be that kind of man.

Unfortunately, the average woman has dated so many men who have bought her things to try to get into her pants. When you start buying her something nice, it triggers an automatic negative reaction within her. "Hey, he's trying to buy sex," she thinks, and when she rejects him. The normal woman is not a prostitute and does not want to be treated like one.

Okay, but then what to do when the bill comes? Well, first, you shouldn't take a woman out on a fancy date until after the two of you have sex. So take her to an expensive restaurant as a reward for her good behavior. Your first date should be something cheap and informal, like coffee. So when the check comes in, it's really no big deal.

A fundamental precept of thumb is to ask yourself if you would pay if you invited a casual friend instead of that girl who sits across from you. If the answer is yes, then by all means, go ahead. And don't feel like you just got accepted because I pay the coffee bill. You don't want to miss an opportunity because you were too cheap to buy a $ 3 cappuccino.

The main stuff you need to know is to understand why you are doing the things you do. Never buy things or do favors for a woman because she thinks you need to win her approval. Instead, take the Alpha male stance: anything you do for her is conditional on her earning it.

The Secret Of Knowing How To Listen

Here's a dirty little secret: almost everyone is a bit shy and introverted to some extent. People talk to you because they think you are a high-value person (as a woman will think if she is attracted to you and talks to you), they will feel good if they think they have gained attention from her.

To instill in others the feeling that they have earned their attention, seek the deeper meaning of what that person is saying to you. Once you have deduced this, locate what they really communicate to you.

Let's say someone says to you, "What percentage of our genes do you think we share with chimpanzees?"

What is the deepest meaning? On the surface, they are testing their knowledge. But the real meaning here is that they are trying to show off their knowledge and amaze you with an interesting tidbit.

Assume you are a person who likes to read and be informed. You remember seeing something in National Geographic about how humans and chimpanzees have approximately 98.5% of the same genes. Should you answer, "98.5%?"

No. Alpha males don't play other people's games.

A much better answer would be, "I don't know; we can't be quite similar. Will it be 50%? "The person will then feel like they have gained their attention when you tell them how interesting it is that it is 98.5%. (If you feel like you need to demonstrate your intelligence, you seek approval from other people, and that is a sign of low status.)

Suppose someone tells you that they just went to the beach in Panama City. They tell you this because they are excited about the trip they recently took, and they want you to share in that excitement. So the most dangerous thing you could do is say, "Man, that's nothing. You should see the beaches and waves in Hawaii !! "This statement shows that you are indifferent to the other person and makes them feel like they are not special.

Instead, have them tell you about the things they enjoyed on the beach in Panama City. Say, "How cute! I've always wanted to go there. What was the best part of the trip? "

And although alpha males interrupt when they need to, don't try to interrupt people when talking about something interesting to you. And don't worry too much if people interrupt you. People tend to interrupt because they are very involved in the conversation, exactly what you want.

When speaking, focus on them instead of yourself. Observe the reasons that people say and then validate those reasons. This leads to strengthening your state of internal joy and makes you more attractive and pleasant in others' eyes.

Genuinely think about what a woman tells you and show interest. Every woman is a new exploration, and you have a lot to discover from her. So take your time in your conversations and be a good listener.

The Magic Word That Reinforces A Woman's Good Behavior

Observe successful people, and you will find that they are more generous than the average person when it comes to saying, "Thank you." When someone does you a favor, they do it because they have a good image of you. By expressing their appreciation for you, you maintain their optimistic projection of you.

Don't say things like "You shouldn't have bothered," as that indicates that you didn't deserve what they did for or for you. If a person gives him things, it is because he sees you as worthy of the best. If you kill their attitude towards you, it leads to being unworthy.

Yes, whenever a woman compliments you or does something nice for you, never belittle or ignore it. Instead, thank her with the mindset that you have that well-deserved good treatment.

298

¡Remember — reward the woman's good behavior!

By the way, whenever a woman compliments you, see it as if she's really saying, "I like you. And I want you to keep bringing all of this to sex."

Tell her "Thank you" and almost hypnotically guide her to her bedroom!

Non-Verbal Signs That Say, "I'm Adorable"

I have already listed the non-verbal signals that lead to dominance. Many of those cues, like staring while talking, and showing dominance, make you more adorable. However, sometimes dominance signals (like leaning back) can make you more distant.

So as appropriate, you need to balance his dominance with his Adorableness. (Too much dominance doesn't make you desirable.) Be aware of the following silent techniques that will magnetically attract a girl to you:

1) Lean forward when you sit in front of someone who is saying something to you. This communicates interest in what they are telling you. However, it is crucial to make sure the woman is very interested in you before doing this, as leaning back is a non-verbal way of playing "playing tough." Once she's interested in you, lean forward to give the impression that conversation is easy with you.

2) Directly orient your body and face towards her. Note that you must have established dominance before doing this, as you lose some of it by being more direct with your body language.

3) Smile, but not too much.

4) Maintain a relaxed and open posture.

5) View your group similarly, but only slightly more striking than the others. If you meet the dress expectations of the people you interact with, they will quite like you.

6) Wear casual and brightly colored clothing. (However, such clothing also diminishes the perception of his dominance.)

7) Maintain mutual eye contact — encourage yourself to look her straight in the eye, and she will like this, and she will like you. Don't do it more than 70% of the time, however, as previously stated.

8) Make sure your voice is pleasant, expressive, relaxed and that you appear lively and interested in what is being discussed.

9) Avoid unpleasant facial expressions and the absence of gestures, showing indifference, closed body language and appearing in an uncomfortable posture.

Again, be sure to strike a balance between dominance and attractiveness. If you never smile, the woman will not like you. But if she smiles excessively, it makes her seem like she has a low status — that she tries too hard to please.

Like a relaxed posture, some things go a long way with simultaneous dominance and attractiveness, so you need to stay relaxed at all times.

Evoke Mercy

Many guys make the mistake of trying to make a woman feel sorry for them. They will obsessively call out to you, saying things like, "… I'm so lonely, and I really want/need to see you tonight."

On a psychological level, much of this points to the mother-child relationship. As children, we could often get what we wanted by evoking our moms' maternal nurturing instinct.

Don't do this with the women you date. Whenever you evoke pity in a person, that person will despise you. They will frame you as a loser in their minds, and then they will treat you accordingly. Have you met those unsuccessful salespeople who evoke your pity? ("Please buy this car so I can eat this month!")

Psychologically, people can't help but make fun of those pathetic people. Successful salespeople are those who safely make customers (and not salespeople) feel like they are making a profit by buying their cars and not just feel sorry for someone.

CHAPTER NINE

HABITS & SELF-DISCIPLINE OF A REAL ALPHA MAN

Why Should You Become A Better Male?

Making a specific effort to improve can have lasting benefits regardless of the result. See my example: Sometimes, I am even more introverted than I would like to be; even in general, I have greater social skills than I used to have. I am not 100% of what I wanted to be, but I am infinitely better than I was. So remember this: even if you make big strides, after all, you still fall short, but you will still be a better and happier man than if you had never tried anything at all.

Look Better Than You Ever

The physique is important, but not as much as you think. And not how you think. Women don't rely on how you look to judge men the way we men judge how pretty our girlfriends are. Look at it this way: imagine you are on vacation and meet a chubby girl at a tropical bar who is just as hot as you. You don't have prospects for the night, so what would you rather have, have sex with this fat girl that no one will find out about, or masturbating alone in your room?

Most guys would choose the above. Assuming it's not unpleasant - just a little overweight.

Women act the same way. As long as they reach a particular standard — that is, you are not morbidly obese or deformed in some way — you will not be eliminated due to their ugly packaging. Appearance makes up perhaps 20% of your level of attractiveness. (level of confidence, how comfortable you are with yourself, how high your status is in society, and how you make women feel in your presence are the other factors.) If Johnny Deep — a guy who is a 10 in appearance (according to my girlfriend) —were currently a depressed "rag" who is gangly all the time and trembles at the thought of talking to the girls he just met, he would have nothing. Of success.

So, balancing it all out, looking good will certainly add a lot to your appeal. And in this chapter, you will discover the secrets to change your appearance, which will immediately double or triple the looks towards you.

Shoes

women notice them much more than men. Many guys only have a few pairs of shoes in their closets. Have you seen how many pairs the average woman has? Girls, pay attention to what you wear. So make sure your shoes are pretty and stylish and even a bit bolder than the plain shoes the average guy would wear.

When in a shoe store, definitely ask women about shoes before you buy them! You don't want to make a costly mistake. Just say, "I need a quick female opinion. What shoes do you like, this pair or this one? "I recommend picking the two pairs that you like the best and asking for their opinion then.

Don't worry if the woman doesn't like any, and she will probably find other shoes in the store and let you know which ones she prefers. (In the meantime, you will have an opportunity to start a conversation with a girl, you naughty dog!)

At a minimum, you will need four pairs of shoes:

1) casual chestnut.
2) casual black.
3) elegant/formal chestnut.
4) elegant/formal black.

For formal shoes, I get the type of shoes that need to be polished. You will pay a lot for such shoes like that (my elegant black shoes cost $ 150), but they last for years so that they will be worth the expense. When they're polished up well, I get a lot of compliments. (I've noticed that women like polished shoes.)

Hair

If you're like most men, your hair doesn't look very good right now. Maybe you've had the same hairstyle for years or are trying to do the same thing with their hair that their friends do with theirs, even though their hair is different. It is time for a change. Check out what Hollywood actors and rock stars are up to now, find a hairstyle you like, and style yours later. Experiment. As I write this guide, the "sex hairstyle" (messy hair that makes him look like you've just been in bed with a woman) hits hard. Consider going to an expensive stylist and giving him carte blanche to style your head shape well.

If you want to look sexy (and you're not homophobic), I highly recommend going to a gay hairdresser, as these guys have an almost uncanny sense of what looks good for women. And honestly, if your hairline has gotten to the point where it's too noticeable, then shave your head. A significant percentage of women consider a shaved head attractive because baldness exudes masculinity and vigor. If you are an older man, having your head shaved will make you look a few years younger. Combing your hair is fooling no one, and few women find horseshoe-shaped hair sexually attractive.

The Skin

One of the simplest (and free) things you can do to improve sex appeal with women is to get a tan. You don't want to go overboard with this as there is a risk of skin cancer, but sunlight is also necessary to get the proper vitamin D dose, which helps your body produce testosterone. (Also, a lack of sunlight has been associated with a depressed mood.) If anything, though, get a good tan, and women will think you are sexy. You can kill two birds with one stone by exercising outside.

The Shave

Beards or mustaches are generally out of style these days unless you find a certain look that goes with their features or if you have any deficiencies that you need to hide. For example, a goatee or beard can work wonders to disguise a weak chin or acne-scarred cheeks. Consider shaving your testicles and the pubic hair that grows around the base of your penis. If you do, your penis will appear cleaner and more attractive to women. They will give you blowjobs more often. Just as we prefer women to shave their vulvas (since all that hair gets in the way), women also prefer you to shave. And as a bonus, your penis will appear to be longer without all that hair around it. Don't get picky. Shaving your scrotum is much easier than you think. Try it with shaving cream and a razor. Shaved hair will come out smoothly. Shaving your armpits can reduce the number of bacteria that grow under your arms, reducing body odors.

Also, make sure you do not have hair from your nose or hair sticking out of your ear. Many women lose any stimulus when encountering this. You can find an electric nasal hair clipper at your local grocery store for less than $ 20.

Many men shave their breasts these days, as more women seem to prefer shaved breasts to hairy breasts. However, that is an individual option. If you don't mind this, I suggest you try to see the reactions you get when you shave your chest and wear a shirt that exposes it. If you are tempted to shave your arms or legs, fight the urge and don't. The bottom line is that the vast majority of men who do this are a) professional bodybuilders or b) gay.

Stretch

For casual occasions, wear shirts that fit well, not shirts that appear too baggy. This can be harsh, as most clothes that you like will not fit. Just hope that about 10% of the clothes you try on in a store will be favorable to you. I can't stress enough the importance of not wearing baggy clothes and tents in vogue in ghetto high schools or among youngsters. Such clothes will not hide your tummy.

The best way to hide that rim is to wear shirts that draw attention to the chest, such as shirts with a horizontal stripe at the nipples. If you are fat, it goes without saying that you should also go to the gym (weight lifting and cardiovascular work) and eat correctly to lose weight. This also helps you with your testosterone levels. Carrying excess body fat (about 20% or more of your ideal body weight) can cause your body to have elevated estrogen levels. (Have you noticed that really fat guys sometimes have "woman's boobs"? Now you know why.)

Wear clothing that makes you appear as close to the ideal body as possible for a tall man with broad shoulders that descends to a narrow, slim waist. This is the look that women find attractive! Avoid clothing that makes you look different from this ideal body type. For example, fat guys should avoid shirts with horizontal stripes around the waist. If you are tall and slim, try a long-sleeved unbuttoned jacket or shirt over a tight T-shirt. The horizontal stripes are good; vertical stripes are bad. Common types should avoid horizontal stripes, however, as they make them look too wide. Instead, they should think about tight clothing options: tight shirts and pants.

Stay away from something too common like skinny stripes or the ubiquitous polo shirts frat boys wear. No, girls won't think you're original by flipping the necklace since too many guys do that.

Company or sports logos on your shirts? That makes him look like he's trying hard to fit in with the group. That's fine if you want to be a funky guy rather than a loser, but it's more attractive to girls if you stand out from the pack of guys who roam around like signs. By dressing casually, you want to give the impression that you just dressed after having good sex with a woman. So don't wrap your shirt completely unless you're wearing a suit. And leave the top two buttons unbuttoned.

Avoid weird designs or whatever makes you look like you're trying too hard to look cool. Consider wearing a suit and tie sometimes, especially when you're in situations where other guys dress like lotus, like in college. Have you ever noticed how women go out of their way just to flatter dudes in suits and ties? Suit and tie are important executive clothing. And they communicate status and ambition, and there is no counterpart for wearing them. Of course, you have to make sure you are an alpha inside, or you will be taken by a nerd trying to make a good impression.

When wearing a suit, wear a cotton shirt (plain, no stripes or anything), cufflinks, a dark jacket and pants, and a black leather strap, shoes well polished. Wear a nice silk tie, which can even have a bold design. Notice the type of compliments you get from people. Nothing expresses authority better than a dark suit. Vintage clothing is in, as long as it is not too flashy. Jeans are also good. Try to get a pair of expensive jeans. Go for a slim size because you want to make your legs look slim.

Combining

I'm continually in awe of how many guys I see make obvious mistakes like wearing brown belts with black shoes, so please pay attention to how the colors of their outfits go together.

You need to match all your clothes. You can do this two ways:

1) Through similar colors.

2) Through significantly contrasting colors.

Colors tend to affect people's spirits and energy levels, so think about what you want to provoke when you dress up and then combine the parts of your outfit accordingly.

There are two main sections — hot and cold. Warm colors include yellow, orange, and red. Cool colors include purple, blue, and green. If you want to wear similar colors, wear different shades of one color, such as light jeans and a darker blue shirt. You can also try colors that are closely close — red and purple. For example, both colors are close to each other on the color wheel. Also, dress in opposite ends of the color wheel — dark blue pants with a light brown shirt. Neutral colors — black and white — go with almost everything. Also, consider using colors primarily white or black — like beige, white tinged with brown or gray, a combination of black and white. But not beige with gray.

The color of your accessories (belt, watch, etc.) should match your shoes as much as possible. Pants should never contrast too much with your shoes, although your shirt can. Another rule for clothing that should be obvious, but often is not, is that clothing should be clean. Girls more easily detect stains and unwashed clothes.

How do you know if your clothes need to be washed?

1)On shirts and pants, look for stains. If you see stains, wash them by rinsing the stain under a tap and rubbing it off with the stain remover. Then put the garment in the washing machine.

2) Socks and clothes should only be worn once before being washed.

3) Jeans need to be washed when they stretch, even if they are not stained.

4)Nothing should smell. If it smells, put it in the laundry basket.

Ironing is not as necessary as it used to be, except in extreme cases. However, some things should always be ironed, like Oxford shirts (the long-sleeved cotton shirts you wear a suit with). When dressing in a suit, make sure your shirt is slightly starchy, or else you won't look good. You don't have to do the ironing ... just take your things to dry cleaning and let them do it.

Another thing that women appreciate is attractive underwear, as they wear flashy panties. So get something with something written on the garment or a drawing.

One night, with my current girlfriend, she was fascinated by my SpongeBob shorts. Short, dark-colored garments are also an excellent option.

Accessories

Most guys don't pick their accessories well, so this is a good area for distinguishing yourself from the rest. The main thing is that these are subtle but intriguing. Avoid overdoing it or trying too hard. Find interesting things that fit your personality. A $ 30 watch with a wide leather strap displaying a unique design will send you more compliments from women than a multi-thousand silver watch as the former displays much more originality.

A pretty $ 15 faux silver ring with an eye-catching pattern will turn the heads of women 100 times more than a $ 500 college class ring. There is wide latitude for accessories, as long as they make you stand out from the other types. Try to avoid things that tons of other guys already have, like white snail necklaces and bracelet tattoos. Be unique.

Your Style

There are two types of subjects — those who have sex and those who do not.

To have sex, figure out which demographic of people you belong to (e.g., high school guys, corporate executives, ghetto boys, college kids), observe the alpha males' dress in that group, and dress similarly. In particular, just try to be a little "cooler" than everyone else when it comes to shoes, accessories like your belt and watches, and the way your clothes fit. (Make sure you resemble the ideal of the male body described above.)

Don't look much "cooler" than everyone else, or you might seem out of place and weird, or even gay. Just be a little bit better dressed than the best-dressed guy around. Take a look around, and it will be obvious how you should dress and what you should avoid. For example, T-shirts with sports logos, beer bottles, or phrases that you wouldn't say in a decent company are not attractive to women and are typically only worn by guys who will be out of luck that night.

Watch the latest blockbuster movies with popular actors for fashion advice. (The movie "The Big Scam 2" has some good examples of it currently being hit.) Also, check out TV and magazine ads targeting 18- to 35-year-old demographics. I'm not talking about ads for clothing per se (as these tend to go for very expensive clothes), but ads for things like cell phones and airlines. The models in these advertisements generally dress subtly well so that they attract a larger audience.

When you're shopping for clothes, listen to the opinions of the women in the store.

Simultaneously, create your unique style and avoid styles that are too ordinary and too flat. I like to shop around and dress in brighter, tighter 80's clothes. This is because it fits my personality. So go for something unique and trendy that is appropriate for you, but don't get too complicated by how it looks either. Because while looking for good bits of help, it's not your looks that drive you to bed; it's your alpha male behaviors and thought patterns.

Women are not just after a handsome man. They also ask for a man with high social status and excitement, passion, and romance. They want a man who will give them a good time and make them feel good. Along with style issues, it is also important to develop a strong male body. That means going to a gym and having a good diet.

Going to a gym will not only make you look healthier, but it will also make you feel more energetic and attractive to women because you will have much more confidence. The most important thing about how you look is that it should be consistent and congruent with who you are. Your clothes create perceptions of you in women. So if you can't support such created perceptions, they will lose interest.

If her clothing expresses "excitement" in the way Lamborghini styling does, then women will be disappointed if the engine inside is anything conventional like that of an SUV.

Your Body

Women could guess my age before I started practicing six years ago. Sometimes they thought I was older! So about six months after I started working out at the gym, the women I knew were shocked at my age — they thought I was younger.

A few months ago, a very pretty 26-year-old woman who took me into her home swore she couldn't be over 28. (I'm 39 years old.) She genuinely didn't believe me when I told her how old I was. He used to be fat and lazy; I am now lean and muscular. On a scale of 1 to 10, my appearance would round up a 4. Whenever I put my picture on sites like hotornot.com, I generally rated around 4 to 5. Today I am rated 8 to 8.5, and for the compliments that I get from women, I would say my rating on hot or not is pretty accurate.

You can't do anything about their genetic heritage (yet). However, your fitness level is totally within your control, and it's a significant part of what makes you look good to a woman. This is good news, don't you think? Being in shape will make you look good in many ways. Your stomach will flatten out, and you will notice more defined abs. With muscles growing throughout your body, your facial muscles will also grow, making your skin firmer and less wrinkled.

A Basic Guide To Work The Body

The training I'm going to give you focuses on heavy compound exercises that work many muscles simultaneously and include isolation exercises that work many muscles that compound exercises miss. Compound exercises will be the core of your training. Away from those many guys in the gym — the ones who only work before spring break and aren't serious about it — who mostly do push-ups and bench presses ignoring their legs and back.

This leads to poor posture, and no matter how big your upper body is, skinny chicken legs don't look good. Women look at and admire men's legs. Compound exercises dump tons of testosterone into your body. Besides building muscle, having elevated natural testosterone levels are associated with dominance and power traits — two sexual traits deeply attracted to women. Do this in a typical week:

Monday-

• Three sets of squats. Do 20 reps, 15 reps, and then 12 reps.

(Your leg and abdominal muscles are primarily made up of slow-stretch muscle fibers that respond better to higher reps than your upper torso and back.)

• Three sets of stiff leg raises. Do 20 reps, 15 reps, and 12 reps.

• Two sets of twins raise. Do 20 reps, 15 reps, and 12 reps.

• Two sets of arm push-ups. Do 12 reps and ten reps.

(For each exercise, use a weight such that the last 3 to 5 reps are extremely difficult)

Tuesday-

• Rest or cardiovascular work.

Wednesday-

• Two sets of forwarding bent dips. Do 12 reps and ten reps.

• Two series of the press with weight to the slope. Do 12 reps and ten reps.

• Two sets of lateral raises. Do 12 reps and ten reps.

• Two sets of overhead dumbbell presses. Do 12 reps and ten reps.

• Two sets of squats with weight. Do 20 reps and 15 reps.

Thursday-

• Rest or cardiovascular work.

Friday-

• Three series of deadlifts. Do 12 reps, ten reps, and eight reps.

• Two sets of weighted chin suspension. Do 12 reps and ten reps.

• Two sets of push-ups with weights. Do 12 reps and ten reps.

• Two sets of stringing weights. Do 12 reps and ten reps.

• Two series of bends and side raises. Do 12 reps and ten reps.

Do a warm-up or before entering the main sets, using roughly 50% and 75% of your working weights. For example, if you squat 200 pounds during your main sets, you would warm up by doing eight reps of 100 pounds, then four reps of 150 pounds. You should feel the warm-up to enter your work sets. If not, then you should do 2-3 more reps with a weight closer to work. In the example, you would do three reps with 175 pounds. It is important that you feel that your strength is failing in the series. When I tell you to do sets of 20, 15, and 12, I mean do the maximum weight to support that particular number of reps.

Limit your workouts to 50 minutes. Studies have shown that after that, your muscles start to break down too quickly.

Give yourself two to three minutes between sets to recover, but remember that you want to complete all of your exercises within the 50-minute limit. Immediately after your workout, eat a mixture of protein and carbohydrates. This stops the formation of lactic acid generated by lifting weights and shifts your body towards building muscle mass.

The training I have outlined is geared towards muscle growth. If you want to emphasize strength, do half the reps. On Tuesday, Thursday, and Saturday, you should do cardiovascular work if you need to lose body fat. I recommend doing high-intensity interval training. High-intensity interval training (HIIT) is short but intense, and studies have shown it to be more effective than moderate-intensity training. Moderate training consists of activities like jogging for half an hour, etc.

HIIT lasts for 10 minutes, but it has you alternate between sprinting for one minute and jogging slowly for another minute, alternating back and forth until the 10 minutes are up. Although HIIT is much shorter than moderate-intensity cardio, you are going to feel it. Finally, watch your diet. A popular saying among serious bodybuilders says, "Muscle is built in the kitchen, not the gym." To build muscle, your body needs about one gram of protein per pound of weight each day. Well, the sources are meat, chicken, nuts, tuna, and whey protein powder.

Eat smaller portions frequently rather than three large meals a day. This ensures that your body has enough protein for protein synthesis within your muscles. Eat clean, healthy calories. Avoid fats. (Look for "partially hydrogenated" oils and labels with reducing ingredients.) Avoid junk food like soda, fried foods, and white loaves of bread. Carbides are not bad by themselves; what you need is the right, complex carbohydrates, like those found in oatmeal, whole wheat bread, fresh legumes, and fruit. Avoid starches. Finally, be sure to drink plenty of fluids, as your muscles are mostly water.

What It Means To Look Good

Since roughly 20% to 30% of your attractiveness to women depends on your appearance, the more handsome you are, you'll find that every aspect of your interactions with women will get a boost. Dressing well, exercising hard, and eating with proper nutrition will help the older guys (30 and over). Men get the highest alpha status naturally with age, so if you have a flat stomach as well, this will pay off tremendously.

You will look more trustworthy, but when you dress well and have a good body, you will have more self-esteem and feel higher confidence. Whenever you need an ego boost, look in the mirror. This will help you in many small, self-built ways and significantly increase the joy of life. So hit the gym, eat right, and wear nice clothes.

Important Techniques To Control Your Mindset And Build Your Ideal Personality

I have been revealing many valuable secrets to you, but now it is time for you to take control of yourself. You, and not others, are in charge.

This means that you need to develop an internal nest of control in your life.

Most people have an external site, implying that they see forces external to them in charge of their lives. They believe that success is beyond their control. In a way, this is convenient as they have someone or something else to blame when things don't work out.

For these people, it doesn't matter how hard they try; life is a game of chance and luck. If the people around them are in a bad mood, then they are in a bad mood. People with an external site have trouble with motivation. Usually, they don't want to put in the effort to be successful unless they have already been successful. They also tend to take risks in life. When they make mistakes, they assign the responsibility to others instead of learning from what they did.

As we go through life, we assign explanations for everything. It is deeply embedded within our psyches. Psychologists have a term for this phenomenon: Attribution Theory. Studies have shown that successful people tend to have an inner place. This is because a person with an inner site believes that they make their luck in life. They believe that the harder they try, the more successful they will be. Whatever they want to achieve is totally within the realm of possibility. Having an inner place of command means being confident and self-motivated. It means being optimistic because you know that your destiny is in your hands.

Your Powers Affect Your Conduct.

This is the biggest reason why people who attribute things internally are more successful. Self-made millionaires tend to be people who trusted themselves and did their part to improve the situation. If you think you are attracted to women, you will find yourself displaying attractive behaviors naturally. Let's say you chat with a woman at a laundromat. You feel completely outgoing and have a great conversation with her.

After you both finish folding your clothes, you go out with her for something to eat. After a couple of hours of conversation, they head to a bar for a drink. Then they go to her house to finish everything in the bedroom. She found you attractive for many reasons, but most of all, it was his high confidence level.

So, where does your confidence come from? Does it come from having previously had sex with other women? In that case, that would be an external attribution. The problem with external attributions is that they make you vulnerable to a system of rewards and punishments. As long as you get their prize (i.e., sex with women), their confidence stays high, and you remain motivated to work out in the gym and wear good clothes.

If you have a string of failures with women, however, your confidence will plummet. So you leave the gym and wear whatever it is. So it's better to be safe because "that's the kind of guy I am" rather than whatever cause happens in the external world.

If you are confident because of your internal attributions, then you will stay that way no matter how many women don't have the good taste to choose it. (Did you notice how I didn't say, "It doesn't matter how many women reject you"? Think positively!)

By the way, there was a time when I was so terrified of talking to women that my vision would blur, my face would turn red, and I would stutter like an idiot. It was all caused by worrying about what those women thought.

The permanent solution to this is to stop thinking that women are important.

Yes, you read that right. Thinking that women are important only gets in the way when it comes to the love game. Instead, see them as a source of excitement, arousal, and sex ... no more, no less. Don't see every woman as a potential girlfriend because that causes you to act too hard to win her approval.

317

Simple Alpha Male Exercise-

If you find yourself with an external control site, you can help yourself get out and grow outside of it by creating a list of targets you criticize so that your life is not what it is. Go ahead and make your list right now.

Did you make your list? Very good. Some things you could have written down are:

1)Other people, like his parents, who did a bad job raising him or his boss who is keeping him right now. The people at your high school made fun of you and made you feel bad. These people taught him to be irrationally afraid of strangers, which is why today he is shy.

2)The circumstances. You were born into poverty, your uncle beat you up, you went to a bad public school, and you missed many educational opportunities that other people got.

3)Your genes / God. Your face is asymmetrical. You are short, etc.

I am not trying to simplify your problems at all. The key is that very often in life. We become immobilized due to circumstances that are beyond our control. Then we cannot effect a change.

We can't change how our parents raised us, so being so upset about it today is a waste of time. No matter how upset you get, you can't change what happened.

Looking at your blame list, can you see any real reason you must be so pessimistic that you do nothing to improve your life because of the people on the list?

Why do you give them that power?

Study after study has shown that firmly believing that we are in control of our situation will significantly impact our actions. The more we believe that we are not in control of our situations, the more likely we will give up.

As you move toward having an inner psychological site of control, you will become a more positive thinker. You have the power to take action to improve the things you are currently weak at. If you're ugly by example, then hit the gym, improve your diet, and work on your clothing and conditioning. You will also take responsibility for motivating yourself. You will find that as you are more determined to improve and persevere in pursuing the things you want (such as sex), you will increase your chances of getting them.

Your Thoughts

You are constantly thinking. Most of your feelings come from thoughts. The good news is that, as thinking beings, we can choose our thoughts and thus our feelings.

We can choose to think (and feel) positively or negatively. The bad news is that it is often easier to think negatively, so we have to be positive. For example, suppose you attend a quick dating event where each woman marks "No" in the box representing your name to indicate that they do not want to see you again.

A negative view of this would be to think that you are scum, so of course, women would not want to talk to you. And what about all the other guys who were way more flashy than you? Maybe it would have been a better night if you had stayed home and played Halo 2. A positive view would be to realize that, with each girl, you wrinkled your forehead and leaned too far toward her, indicating that you were nervous and trying too hard to get her approval. Fix those two major body language mistakes, and you'll convey a better impression of yourself next time.

What you think about often becomes a part of your life. If you worry, then you will find things to worry about. If you are optimistic, then you attract good people and things. So if you want to be a successful man, you need to have positive thoughts. Remembering the past creates many negative thoughts. You have certainly erred before; it happens to all of us. The key is to forget the past.

I want to make you recognize this: the past doesn't exist anymore, except in your mind. Bury your past mistakes and don't think about them after you've learned lessons from them. Try to eliminate negative thoughts. Identify the origins of negativity in your life and do not allow them to influence you. I find negativity in certain individuals, songs, and television shows like the news. (Don't feel like you have to be a news junkie. If the world is ending, someone will let you know!)

Develop Positive Thinking

Everything is in your mind. That, and your attitude. *"Why would a girl be attracted to me?"* you think. "I'm too short." You go to class and sit in your usual place. The girl sitting across from you notices you and then suddenly turns around and says, "Can you lend me a sheet?"

"Sure," you say, handing him the sheet. You don't say anything else to him for the rest of the class. That night, you remember that girl, dreaming about her while alone in bed, thinking you are a loser. What you didn't realize was that this girl was going the extra mile to talk to you. He didn't need a blade ... he could have asked another girl for it and not have to worry about the male-female play. But she used it as an excuse to talk to you because she was interested in you. She thinks she sent you an obvious signal. But you didn't realize.

For something to happen to you, you have to believe in it first. In our example, if you had believed that you are attractive, then you would be receptive to the girls that appear in your life. But if you don't think it's a possibility, then you are psychologically blocked, even when it's obvious, like the girl who asked you for the folio.

Good things happen to you. That way, you will take advantage of the opportunities. Identify negative thoughts when they arise and let them go. As you eliminate negative thoughts, let positive thoughts flow. Choose to be confident and happy on the inside, no matter what happens on the outside. Feel comfortable with yourself and realize that you will be happy no matter what happens. Your confidence comes from yourself, and you will improve every day because that is fundamentally who you are.

Here are a few ways to develop positive thinking:

1) Constantly imagine yourself as the person you want to be. Imagine how you would behave and what kind of happiness you would reap in your life if you were that ideal person. Visualize the amount of money you would earn, the house you would live in, and the physique you would have. Avoid negative influences in your life, such as friends who make pessimistic comments.

2) As you look back, think only about your successes. Realize that any failure you have is only temporary and more the result of bad luck than any inherent problems with you.

3) assume success(but don't link to it). See yourself as relaxed and count on that because you are the lover of every woman's dreams; of course, you will eventually have the success you want. Smile while having fun what makes you feel like a man who is attractive to women.

4) Start to identify the thoughts you have. Recognize that your judgments are under your control, so you can visualize everything you want. Because your reality is what you believe in, use your visualizations to encourage rather than discourage you. As Albert Einstein said, "your imagination is the preview of the attractions of life that are to come."

5) Make affirmations, which I will explain below.

321

Overcoming Your Insecurities

Have you ever said this to yourself?

"I hold a lot of blisters on my face."

"I am very fat."

"I'm very poor."

"I live with my parents."

"I do not have a car."

"I am very shy!!!"

I want you to think about any belief that makes you think you are not attractive to a woman. Because your reality is what you have created, you need to destroy the bad thoughts that make you unsafe and unattractive to women. I am not going to say that this is easy because it is not. I used to be extremely shy. Although my real problem was my fear of talking to people (especially girls), I used to say things like, "I appreciate privacy, and I want everyone to stay out of my business."

It wasn't until I lowered my ego, and became aware of my life, that I realized that shyness was my biggest problem. This required breaking down those thoughts. I realized that I was paying a lot of attention to what people thought of me. The thought of being rejected scared me. Once I identified the problem holding me back, I was able to drop my ego and confront those thoughts. For me, that was an incredible break because once I let my ego drop, I forever got over my shyness around women. This happened overnight.

From that point, whenever I talk to people, I work on focusing externally, for example, on what the conversation was about, and not on internal things like, "I want this person to like me." In the same way, you will have certain thoughts that make you feel good. Identify them too and reinforce them. I was genetically gifted when it came to muscles. So thinking of myself as a muscular man helped my confidence level.

Easy Alpha Male Exercises

1) Identify the beliefs that are good for you.

2) Reinforce them by amplifying what is good for you

3)Identify their bad beliefs. And eliminate them.

OK, this won't happen instantly unless you fully open your mind to this and make a full effort to do these three exercises. Even if you are skeptical, if you work slowly but surely, this will pass. Take baby steps to observe your behaviors and thoughts, and isolate those thought patterns that are good and those that you want to change.

And do yourself a favor and save all your tests for later, when you're home alone, not when you're with a woman. When with a woman, stay outwardly focused and only think about the conversation at hand. This will cause you to feel relaxed and, therefore, more attractive because you are projecting confidence, which increases your likelihood of sleeping with her.

Drowning Your Fears About Rejection

Picture this: you are about to try to talk to a beautiful/sexy girl. You see them standing there in the magazine section of the supermarket, entertaining themselves with Cosmopolitan magazine. Her blonde hair is silky and soft. His skin is clear and radiant. His waist is slim. And wow, look at the delicious shape of those tits! You feel the tension.

Excuses explode in your head: "I'm too tired;" I'm not well dressed; "I don't know what to say to him; "I don't carry condoms. "

323

That negative monologue you have in your head makes you decide not to approach. Now, your chances of having sex with her are zero. You get your groceries, you go home, and you sleep alone that night. You just shot yourself; the girl did nothing.

You didn't hesitate because you were very tired or badly dressed, or the words didn't come to you (and you can always buy condoms on the way to a sexual encounter).

Your real problem was fear. You didn't approach because you were afraid of rejection. "I wish I could hurry up and get over this anxiety of chatting with women ... I don't know," you say to yourself. "Once I get over it, then I will approach them eagerly / enthusiastically / smoothly."

The problem with this kind of thinking is that it sets you up for failure. The truth is that we always feel scared when we enter a new, unfamiliar situation. It is a psychological reality of human beings. The only way to free yourself from fear is to do what you need to do - for example, approach a woman - despite the fear. You have to make a great effort. If you've ever done it in sports, it just is. I was so afraid to communicate with girls that my vision blurred. I continued to make these excuses that I would only approach women when my fears are gone. I kept waiting and waiting.

My fears never went away. I was immobilized, unable to figure out why I was so scared of talking to women, and I spent many days and nights refusing to do so until I could feel good instead of scared. The truth is, virtually all men have anxiety about talking to women because, let's face it, rejection sucks. We all have an internal sense of ego (e.g., self-esteem), which we wish to maintain at a high level. Ideally, your self-worth will come from within yourself, and you won't have to depend on others to have it.

When this happens, it will become irrelevant what any woman thinks of you. If he likes you, great; if not, then what does it matter? You can't control what she thinks.

Don't let a woman's opinion matter too much to you. We all feel fear in an unfamiliar situation. It is normal and natural. Fear only goes away when the situation becomes familiar. If you don't make a great effort to overcome fear, you will be extremely vulnerable and paranoid. Surely, you can withdraw and stay away, and then you will never be rejected. But then you'll be lonely; you'll always be a sad loser who never slept with a girl. Here's the underlying reason: we all have an imaginary partner who will be with you your whole life. Its name is fear. If you allow this partner to control your life, he will put you in a straitjacket.

But fear can also be your faithful companion. When you jump on the exciting spinning slide of life, engaging in a myriad of challenging tasks/adventures, fear will be with you. He won't get in your way, but he will always be there as long as / as long as you're doing new things. When you feel scared, it is a sign that you are doing something new and exciting.

How to Eliminate Your Fears

To eliminate your fears about chatting with women, you need to do three things.

1. Don't have expectations / Don't expect anything. Be friendly for the sake of being social. Nothing more.

2. Talk to the women. Remember that the only way to overcome your fear is by doing what you are afraid of. The more you do it, the more easily you will get there because your attitude about any kind of negative experiences like rejection will turn to something like, "I've been there, I've done that, it's not a big deal."

3. Identify the thoughts that make you nervous. Then delete them.

Because fear is normal, most guys feel anxious when talking to girls, especially if they are not used to it. That is why it is not about not being afraid, but that you simply go straight to what you are going to. So what sets guys like you apart from the rest is the way they handle fear.

Most of the men are paralyzed by fear. And they were necessarily concerning girls, but also in other aspects such as their career. This is why many types do not achieve the success they want.

The reason most men never confront they fear that they fail to discover where they came from. The fear comes from within you. The problem is with you, not with the woman who rejects you. So the next time you talk to women, just treat them without any expectations. Don't set goals. As I mentioned previously, I used to be an introvert. To overcome my shame, I would force myself to converse with everyone, no matter who it was.

He spoke with pretty girls, with ugly girls, with fat girls, with older people, guys, children, families walking with their dogs. It didn't matter who they were. He talked to them about neutral issues, nothing to do with raising women. The result of all this was that I became an excellent conversationalist. I never felt fear again because I could continue doing what scared me until the time came that it no longer bothered me.

Then I made a mistake. I said to myself: "Now that I am a good conversationalist and have become an easygoing person, why do I have to waste time in conversations other than with beautiful girls." After all, as an alpha male, I thought, "He was a man of high value, and I would dedicate my time only to beautiful women.

So I limited the circle of people I would talk to. And my anxiety about speaking to casual women swept me away. It was as if I had never spoken to strangers in my life. At that moment, I realized that this was. I had a dependent attitude because I had thoughts about having sex with women before I opened my mouth and said "hello," which was devastating and frustrating for my purposes.

This is the point. Here's something I want you to try. No matter where you go, talk to two people (or groups of people) only for practice. Take it very seriously. Don't try to pick up girls through these conversations. Precisely because it is to practice, do not limit yourself to talking to the best women. You are looking for simple conversations. I have found that older people (men and women over 40) and fat people are easy to start conversations with. Perhaps because that demographic tends to be lonely.

If it helps, set a time limit for your interaction practices, such as talking to one person for 30 seconds and then end the conversation (you can say something like: "OK, I'll meet a friend. It was a pleasure chatting with you And then as if it didn't matter at all).

Once you have done your internship, you will feel comfortable, and it will be easier for you to converse with the good girls. Even when and even if you feel aroused, do not think or act in a way related to sex.

For example, if a girl walks in front of you, just say something spontaneous like, "Hey, I need a female opinion on something." Then ask a question that you want their opinion on. As you gain practice, you can apply another one of my tricks to say something funny before starting a conversation with a stranger. Tell yourself a joke and then laugh. That will put you in a good mood when you talk to someone else.

Ultimately, you will get to a position where you have spoken out and gotten so many negative responses from women that it won't affect you even one bit. You will have an attitude like, "Oh, how original. I've had hundreds of women give me the same cruel response."

In the movie "Fight Club" Tyler Durden presented the following phrase: "Let things go as they should go." Stop trying to control your attitude with girls. If you don't have an attitude in mind, it won't be relevant if the girl acts like, "Now I turn my head and I remember the

327

rejections I've received, and I laugh. I have spoken to so many women that rejections bore me, but they entertain me because of my sincerity.

To understand this more psychologically, we will say that "There is no such thing as a" State of nervousness "as something genetic. There is no such thing as "butterflies in the belly" of the "nervous virus" invading your body. All those nervous feelings come from within you. You have a series of mental processes flowing through you, and in the end, you are inclined to feel the emotion you decide.

Recently, I led a boy named James, who told me, "I would reject myself if I were a girl. So with thoughts like that, you don't have to be a witch to know why you don't succeed with women. He has a failure-oriented attitude.

We then work on the following:

1. James visualized a girl rejecting him.
2. James felt the tension in his body that was previously relaxed.
3. James evaluated every moment of the entire process, preventing him from having a fluid conversation.

Perhaps it seems very familiar to you to feel nervous about a woman who is close to you? Do not be sad. Thousands of guys - even those who consider themselves "Women Charmers" - have felt it at some point. You will be there just like them.

What to do to manage nervousness: Identify your negative thoughts and then change them. Instead of thinking, "There is my God, this girl will reject me because I will not be able to speak well ... Think: How wonderful it will be to talk with this girl I just saw in the store because, even if she rejects me, I always have the will and the conviction that every day I am one step closer to the woman of my dreams. When you are nervous, notice the parts of your body that become tense and relax your muscles in those places.

When I get nervous, I feel the tension in my face and my jaws. So I try to relax my facial muscles by mentally telling myself to relax instead of being nervous. In conclusion, there are many ways to reduce anxiety with a visualization exercise. Before you open your mouth and say something to a woman, visualize the situation as if it is happening, and then she rejects you.

Look at it this way. If you're not feeling relaxed and sexual, how do you expect the woman to cooperate? As an Alpha Male, you are obliged to lead, which means that you must feel relaxed and sexual for the girl to react favorably. That way, you'll be happy because. At least you went for it, like an alpha man who goes through life without apologizing for his wishes.

Each rejection means that you are one step closer to success. Each rejection makes your ability to converse that much better since you have completely desensitized yourself to the process. Focus on how you will feel later, and speak to the woman as if she has already rejected you (and you are happy about it) instead of making yourself nervous before you even open your mouth.

Making A New Way You Talk To Yourself Through Statements

I have been very successful in changing my attitudes, and much of it comes from saying Statements. Statements are statements that you repeat over and over again until you believe them. Throughout the day, you constantly say things to yourself.

They are often harmful statements, such as:

"I'm a loser."

"I'm not good at talking to just any woman."

"I'm depressed."

"I'm in a bad mood."

"I'm lazy."

"Life sucks."

"I am stuck in a job with no prospects, and there is nothing I can do about it."

Ouch! I can't write any more examples because it's conjuring up old painful memories of how I thought! But you get the idea, and perhaps if you take the time, you may come up with a long list of negative beliefs that you hold. The issue with bad thoughts is that they have a reinforcing effect. The more you think about them, the more you support them with feelings, the more they take hold of your mind.

The more you repeat a statement to yourself, along with visualizing and feeling it, the more you begin actually to believe it. Too much bad self-talk and your problems and insecurities grow. The good news, either way, is that you can start making positive affirmations. By repeating new affirmations over and over to yourself, you can program them into your mind.

Take the statement, "I'm more outgoing." At first, your mind may get confused and try to block it because it is such a radical new thought. After all, you have spent lots of time saying to yourself that you are antisocial. One day, after a few days of making your affirmations several times a day, you do something you would never have done a month ago - maybe you're waiting to pay at the grocery store and automatically decide to play a little prank with other people in line. You do this without even considering it because it is becoming part of your new personality. It is truly incredible to feel it when this happens.

Then recognize that affirmations work gradually. They are so slow that it is difficult to see that they are affecting. Just keep working, keep saying them, and before long passes, you're going to notice yourself behaving in new ways.

Affirmations can do three things:

- Change a statement about yourself, which fits according to your personality.

For example, if you affirm, "I am becoming a positive thinker," this will make you more optimistic. You will start to have thoughts like "that wasn't so bad" and "let's look" on the bright side.

- Reinforce a statement about yourself.

I was always happy with the way my hair looked. So if I say, "I have spectacular hair," it helps me become the type of person with inner confidence who always sees the glass as half full.

- Motivate yourself.

You can use the affirmation, "I talk to women that I find attractive." Then your mind will focus on the ways that you can chat with such women. You will have thoughts such as, "I need to go to the mall to see if I can find a woman" or "I wonder when the next dating event will be." At the supermarket, when you see a beautiful woman, you will think of any excuse to talk to her like, "Excuse me, do you know which watermelons are good?"

Statements work because you become what you think about. They force your mind into a certain way of thinking, and when you use affirmations long enough, those new thoughts become your new reality. Not only should you say the words of your affirmations to yourself, but you should feel what the words are saying and visualize the new reality. In that way, you experience your affirmations using your three major senses (sight, hearing, and feelings).

For example, one of my affirmations that I think to myself when I'm walking down the street is, "I enjoy having full alpha male confidence." When I say this, I feel myself relax my muscles and move more slowly, with my head held high. I visualize my ideal self, and I get happier.

331

When you are alone at home or in your car, say your affirmations out loud. You completely occupy your hearing when you say them out loud. Of course, you should occupy your eyes by vividly imagining them then, and your feelings, when you have a wave of emotions running through your body as you imagine your statements as true.

When you first begin to program yourself with a new characteristic, express the present progressive verb's statement. This is why I say that, instead of saying, "I feel happy with my life," it is better to say, "I am feeling happier with my life as time passes."

This overcomes many of the resistances that you can put up to your new affirmation. Even if you say, "I feel happy with my life," you think, "I am not a happy person." Using the present progressive, you overcome that. Once you feel much happier than you used to be, then you can switch to affirming that it is true: "I feel completely happy." As you keep saying your affirmations, your personality will always reflect this increasing until it has been virtually completely ingrained in the new you.

From period to period, you will need to review and repeat your old affirmations. This prevents you from slipping into your old mental models. Affirmations are like lifting weights with your mind. Just as you need to keep lifting iron to maintain your physique, you also need to maintain your new thoughts to maintain your ideal personality. When developing your affirmations, use the technique that you find that works best for you. Some people are auditory-oriented, so they benefit from recording their statements and then listening to them.

If you are on a Windows PC, the best way to do this is to create your audio files on your computer using a microphone and the sound recording program that comes pre-installed on most Windows systems.

Others are more visual people and will need to visualize their affirmations while saying them to themselves. I am kinesthetically oriented (motivated mostly by physical sensations), so people like me should try to feel their statements as if they were true.

Even if you have your main way of making affirmations, try to reach all of your senses. An additional method that helps everyone is to write the affirmations on paper.

When you make your first sentences, your mind will be full of doubts, but as you put them on paper, it is almost miraculous how much your mind will change to adopt the new belief that you are affirming.

An Easy Alpha Male Exercise

It's making your statements. As you make them, here are some rules that will help you:

1)Assert natural characteristics, beliefs, and accomplishments that you can motivate yourself to have. (If your State, "I have 10,000 girlfriends," then you program yourself for disappointment since it is physically difficult. Five or Ten is better.)

2)You have to make your statements very strong. "I am fully confident" is better than "I am confident."

3) Try to say each statement in no more than twelve repetitions.

4)The mind responds better if you say positive prayers. "I feel relaxed in social situations" is preferable to "I don't feel nervous in social situations."

5) When you want to STOP a feature, use the phrase "release the need," i.e., "I release the need to feel threatened by other guys."

Some of the affirmations that have worked well for me are:

I am laid back and confident. Remember, if you are not entirely comfortable and confident, the phrase is "I am becoming comfortable and confident."

333

I have phenomenally high self-esteem.

I am an alpha male.

I like having light talks with girls.

I am the best lover of every girl.

I think of good times.

I am sure of myself.

I free myself from the need to care what a woman thinks.

I pass through life with elegance, dignity, and style.

I am happy with myself.

I feel relaxed, calm, and in control.

I move my body slowly because I am alpha.

I relax and stretch out.

I feel highly sexual with women.

I love myself.

I'm good in bed.

I am an ultra-confident fascinating boy.

My life is fun.

I feel comfortable talking to other people.

I take my space wherever I am because I radiate confidence in myself.

I feel serene when I enter people's personal space.

I touch girls when I talk to them.

My facial muscles are relaxed.

I have rich standards, so I am a challenge for girls.

I'm interesting.

I am unpredictable.

I am equal to God.

I am handsome.

I am an attractive man.

I gain trust with everyone I talk to.

I am great and powerful, equal to a boxing champion.

I am so incredibly attractive and adept at the bed that women become wringing moisture around me!

With girls, I persist towards either get sex or rejection.

I enjoy rejection because that means I try to get it.

I am an adventurer.

I freed myself from someone else's need for approval.

I am a winner.

I am aggressive/aggressive.

When it comes down to sex, I'm a devilish bad boy.

I'm good at catching any woman.

I focus on positive emotions.

I am fun and interesting.

I am sexual.

I am completely satisfied and relaxed.

Simple Secret To Being Dominant

Domination is the number one trait that lures women. What I'm going to show to you in this chapter will be the secrets that will make women beg to have sex with you where "anything goes." It's about this: to be dominant, control the frame. It is as simple and straightforward as this.

It is important to understand the value of this concept of frames. As I said, there is no objective reality. All reality exists in people's minds. So, if a woman creates drama over something she thinks is a big deal, and if you go along with it, you've lowered your beta status by being sucked into her frame. If, on the other hand, you reframe the drama as something funny and silly and that it's not a big deal, then it is she who is drawn into its reality.

To give an example of my current relationship, my girlfriend wanted me to go to her parents' house with her to meet them. I preferred to go out with my friends that night, so I told him that those were my plans. She reacted badly and said, "John, it is very important that you come with me."

Most men are caught in the frame of having a long discussion or fighting over the issue. After all, you have extensive discussions regarding things that are important.

But if you pretend (frame) that her wanting you to meet her family isn't a big deal, you'll just react by saying, "Sure, let's do it someday," and then quickly changing the subject to something more interesting. That's what I did, and that brought her into my reality. Use this strategy in every situation. You, as a man, have the most powerful reality.

Because now she has a strong belief system, "I am a good match" and "I am the prize, not her," the woman will swallow this frame. One of the jobs I did for many years was part-time pizza delivery. (By the way, avoid pizza if you want to keep a slim waist!) This was before he learned and developed the proper mindset. And I always managed to get incredibly nervous whenever I knocked on a door, and a beautiful woman answered. This was because I viewed them as potentially great conquests for me (and not the other way around).

So when I tried to please them, I became a guy who tried too hard, damaging any attraction such women might have felt for me—but then adopting the attitude that I am a good match. Consequently, he was indifferent whenever he delivered an order to a beautiful woman. He would simply say, in a relaxed tone of voice and posture, "Hello. They are X $. for pizza." Sometimes women blatantly flirted with me as a result. (They had never flirted with me before.) I had sex with some of them, including one I dated for over a year — she was amazing in bed. She worked very hard to win my affections, as it was a tough challenge for her.

Women don't like to be put on a pedestal. Even though they sometimes claim that they like it. Men who are successful with women don't see them that way. They just act naturally. Women can be wonderful beings who want to have sex with you, but they put their pants on one leg at a time just like you do. After all, women are much more similar to men than most guys think.

The problem with getting girls on a pedestal is that I frame a situation of need or dependency. Think of people in your life who have been in need. They suffocate him every moment, trying to get his attention. They constantly demand your attention because they are unable to have a good time on their own. Psychologically, this makes you reject them rather than make you want to spend more time with them. So consider what a woman's perspective is like when you feel or show need.

How can you avoid such feelings? Hold on and stop every time you have a thought like these:

• "If I don't get this girl, I won't have sex for months."

337

- "I want this woman to like me. What should you do to achieve it?

- "Should I call her already?"

The irony about wanting people to like you is that trying too hard to achieve it has the opposite effect — it makes them turn away from you. So stop putting women on pedestals. A better and healthier way of looking at this is that you need to get on your pedestal. You are in the prize. Take these two examples of a man chatting with a woman. The first is a man who thinks that he needs to win a woman's affection; the second knows that he is the prize.

Beta (nervously): "May I have the honor of taking you to lunch? I invite you. Where would you like to go?"

Woman: "Thank you" (smiles) "I would like to have lunch at El Supero Carizzimo Ritzo. Go"

They go to lunch, the woman sees him as a good guy and a good friend, and he will never take her to bed because she just isn't attracted to him that way. Even though men complain about the money spent on women in exchange for their getting nothing, women don't see this as taking advantage of the guy. After all, if you're on a pedestal and someone is nervously asking you to do them favor with your presence for lunch, wouldn't you feel like you're giving them exactly what they want by indulging that favor? If a man has hidden intentions and the woman discovers it, that will make her not see him well.

Alfa (relaxed and comfortable in his skin): "I feel like having lunch at my favorite place, El Restaurant Barattero." (So, as a game, almost like an afterthought): "You are very nice, come with me."

Woman (giggling): "Bla Bla" (He doesn't care what the woman says because as long as she feels comfortable around the guy, she will go with him.)

Notice the framework this second example raises. Man is in his reality. He wants to have lunch, and he knows where he wants to do it. Because the girl has won his attention, she can accompany him. He's the prize, and not her — she's nice, so she's welcome. In the first example, the woman is the prize, when the man has a weak will (he does not have a place to eat), he knows that his value is less than hers (so he is nervous), and he has to bribe her into talking to him practically.

Also, notice how the phrase "come with me" is a command. You see, alpha is not afraid to risk his balls and say things like this to women or other people. Be sure, however, to soften the sentences by expressing yourself playfully. You don't want to come across as moody or bossy. Finally, notice how lunch is not framed as a date like it is in the first example. This prevents her from categorizing the man as serious relationship material who will have to wait months for sex.

Instead, if sex takes place, he will take an active role in creating the right conditions for this. The way the brain works is that when you believe something, your mind increasingly searches for more and more evidence for that belief to be true. That is the value of the previous exercise for the kickoff to believe that you are the dream lover that all women want. As you adopt the mindset of being a good match, realize that all women are naturally promiscuous when conditions are right (that is, a confident man leads them). You don't need validation or approval from the woman; instead, she does need you.

To sum it up, as an attractive man:

1) Make women enter your reality, and not the other way around.

2) Take the lead role, as women are normally passive when dating *and sex.*

3) Emotionally awaken women.

4) He is a man of high value, so it is up to women to win his affection.

339

5) He doesn't take women too seriously, nor does he take life too seriously.

6) Have your own beliefs, be assertive, and think to yourself.

7) you don't need the approval of others.

Most of the men I know who are good with women are aware of these things and set themselves high. Why? Because they (and you) know how to take women to the highest heights of pleasure!

Seven-Step System

I am analyzing by boiling them all down in the following Seven Step System of Seduction that leads you to say "hello" to a new woman to share orgasms in bed with the herb in just one afternoon.

1) You will walk up to a woman and have a quick, neutral conversation.

2) At the end of the conversation, you either get his phone number to set up an appointment, or you then terminate the interaction and get the rejection on your

3) When you meet her for your date, take the attitude that you are getting to know the woman before the two of you have sex. Talk about neutral topics and just vibe with her.

4) On the date, they will start to feel horny. As the two of you continue to vibrate towards you, she will gradually feel horny as well.

5) As she is gradually feeling horny, you should intensify your touch towards her, starting with her fingers, then going to her hand, to her wrist, to her forearm, to her upper back, to her upper arm.

6) When the moment feels right, suggest a neutral reason for the two of you to get alone together, like listening to a CD.

7) When you get the two of you alone, intensify the interaction toward sex.

None of these steps is very complicated, and all seven steps will be discussed in detail later.

Being Persistent

Through your interaction with a woman, you must take advantage. You must have a strong will and want to have sex. Lack of humor on your part can cause him to leave you if the interaction becomes difficult. (More so, it's important to be horny if you want her to feel the same way!)

Talk to a woman while you can. If you have to wait for something, wait to be openly rejected by her instead of saying goodbye. Countless times I have successfully ended up with the discomfort of a pause in conversation rather than walking away.

That also goes when you have a single woman with you in your house. You must persist with her token resistance, or else you will find yourself at best fond of her all night long (that is, she gets the emotional validation of getting your attention while you barely get a kiss.)

You have to perform your goal to get screwed or get their opinion, "no" with you. Don't run away. Running is what beta males do, so they don't have to get rejected.

Most men are scared to death talking to women they don't know, so talking to them anyway separates you from most of them. Other men You will get to be rejected quite a bit, but that's fine. The rejection of a woman is a victory. It means you had the guts to go for it.

Being an alpha, you have the will to do what you want with your life. Because you want to get screwed, you will persist with the women you want.

341

Understood?

Great! So remember - with the woman you want to have sex with, your goal is to persist until you get screwed or rejected.

The Boarding

Now I'm going to reveal one of my secrets to you. The woman of your dreams, never while you live, will knock on your door to enter you. That sounds obvious, but unfortunately, many individuals live like that is happening. They never go out and talk. Instead, they believe that if they work hard and make lots of money, they will one day attract the woman of their dreams into their lives.

Please do not be sad; I was describing myself. Rule number one is that men must make an effort to approach women. You should go out and take command and work on it. Women are not going to show it to you on your doorstep.

As they make up 50% of the human population, you can find and meet women everywhere. The rules are different for each place, so you need to adjust accordingly.

CHAPTER TEN

HOW TO SUCCESSFULLY SEDUCE A WOMAN FROM ZERO

At the very smallest, you should be able to have a basic conversation with a woman. Therefore, you should make it a rule of thumb; you will have at least one long and meaningful conversation a day with a woman. It could be your sister, a platonic friend, a co-worker, or anyone. The main objective is to get used to talking to women and do it easily and naturally. By the way, when you talk to them, don't try hard to make them feel good about you. Just have a normal conversation where you can be yourself.

To get used to talking to new women, do the same; from now on, you will enter a conversation with at least four attractive women a week for a few weeks. This can be easier than it sounds if you make sure you have something to talk about beyond "Hi, where are you from?"

I said to a woman, "Hi, I need a quick feminine opinion. I'm buying my sister (mother, whoever) a perfume. What do you prefer, Fragrance X or Fragrance Y? "Unconvincing, I know, but at least this will get you in conversation with a woman you don't know. Practice your openers tackling for success; now I'm going to focus as I explain how to talk to women.

The Approach And How To Do It

To do the boarding, you need to be in the right emotional state. You need to feel a strong sex drive and relaxed confidence. If you are

343

nervous and fearful and thinking hard about things to say, the woman will not find you attractive and even a little creepy. I know, in an ideal world, women should be flattered that guys have a hard time talking to them about what to say to them. Perhaps, as a man who wants to sleep with her, we must adjust to reality. You must be confident, warm, and relaxed - not panic and asexual.

Remember, all girls want sex. Some have psychological blocks like frigidity, but most will have sex with you if you are an alpha man, create the right conditions for sex to occur, and lead the interaction towards having sex. Where a lot of men screw it up with women is by using an approach phrase. The problem with opening openers is that they reveal to the woman immediately before you've even had a chance to speak that you are attracted to her.

And unless you have something that makes you look handsome, you don't want her to decide whether or not she's attracted to you instantly. Instead, it is better to come under their radar. Show your alpha man personality, and then you can assume there is attraction. (I talk more about what it means to assume attraction below) Not only do you want to be under their radar, but you also want to grab their attention at the same time. Get her interested by talking to you.

Lastly, you want to have a neutral conversation with her at first. You know how defensive you get whenever you're out there walking, and some homeless man comes up to you asking, "Hi, how are you?" You get defensive when this happens because you know the bum wants your money. He is seeking trust with you too soon... since he doesn't know you, he has no reason to want to connect with you.

Well, it's the same kind of reaction with women. When you approach a girl trying to seek confidence immediately, her defensive shield blocks you. On the contrary, when you have a normal, neutral conversation with the girl, she doesn't have those initial shields. And once you have that initial shield with a woman, as long as you have a normal conversation and take on the report (more on this later too), then you will find yourself having breakfast in your underwear with her the next morning, as long as you are persistent and sexual.

For that reason, there is what I like to call "Nine Hypnotic Words." These cover all of the bases I've listed before (putting yourself under a girl's radar, getting her attention, getting her interest in the initial conversation, and being completely neutral). The number one thing you have to say to a girl you randomly meet is, "Hi, I need a swift female viewpoint on something."

If you get their opinion on this, you can be extremely flexible, but make sure this topic is interesting for women examples:

- Did you read something in the last issue of the Cosmopolitan
- What do you think of this shirt?
- I am thinking of buying this painting. What do you think of it?
- When a woman asks me if her clothes make her look fat, what should I say?
- Tell him about a date situation that a friend (man) of yours had in front of a girl.
- My friend only studied with this girl all day.
- She tore a sheet out of her book and threw him like a paper airplane. She laughed, and he smiled. Then he wanted to do the same, but she suddenly got serious and said, 'No' don't do this; he told me he looked like an idiot. And he wondered, what should he have done?
- Ask. "If your lover plays video games all day. How would you feel about this? Then go inside the story about how your friend's girlfriend left him because he played every day.
- Start a discussion about what is going on back then. For example, if you are going to a dog rescue event, talk about the animals up! Adoption
- Nice weather today (especially if it isn't). You have to try this kind of peppermint (Say this at the grocery store). What do you think?

- You can converse with a girl about virtually anything, as long as you are neutral.

But be sure that it is a topic that interests you as well. That way, you seem genuine and not like you are trying to win her over. Also, never recite the memorized material! I only use the above list as topics of conversation, not as scripts. Trust me, and this took me a while to learn; if you look like a stage agent reciting lines, you will crash and burn.

Another key point (which took me a long time to finally figure out) When you start the conversation, make sure you don't seem too polished or like it's too easy to talk to her. If not, she will say something like, "Are you a seller of something?" or "I had to meet him sooner" Instead of just being normal (laid back and carefree)!

Your main thing to talk about can be as simple as your immediate environment. If you are in a movie theater, ask her if she has ever seen a particular movie and what she thinks of it. Tell you a story about something interesting that happened to you before the movie. One of my stories from the movies I told a girl I conquered in a movie theater and eventual romance:

I took one of my previous girlfriends to see a movie, and it was just the two of us and these eight teenagers. They were all loud and annoying, but before the movie started. My girlfriend got upset and said, "You can shut up. I want to see the movie, thank you!" They all gave me a bad look because, as men, you cannot fight with women, but you can fight with other men.

After a while, I went to the bathroom, and there they were all. I felt like they were all about to hit me. But then they told me, "Sorry, we didn't want to upset your girlfriend, we don't mean to hit you, you have enough with that girlfriend!" It turned out that they wanted to apologize for the way they behaved. I know the story doesn't seem logical, but that doesn't matter to a woman. You have to be sure it was real when you tell your stories and convey your emotions. (In the example above, it has more of an impact to use a complaining voice when imitating teenage boys, for example.)

Don't use my stories, use yours!

If you are in the waiting room of a dental clinic (as it was a few months ago), ask her if she has seen that particular dentist before and what is her opinion of him (as I did with this girl, I got her number and we were ... for ... the next day, have a great time, first to have a coffee - then to go shopping - then to a bar.

Then-my-house-followed-sex-and after-several hours on my couch watching movies of romance). Tell yourself that you should be cautious these days about dentists because of this, a dentist named Dr. Finger who had the fattest toes you have ever seen in your life. (At this point, she should laugh.)

You can talk about how you think it is interesting that people make their occupations adjustable with their last names. Dr. Finger was a dentist. You also knew a girl named Amy Salmon who went into fish conservation. At this point, if the girl is worth talking about, she will share strange, similar coincidences or talk about something else to keep the conversation going. This is a way to gauge their availability to you if the conversation becomes two-way.

(The woman who does not make the conversation with you is not interested in you, she will not even give a choice, or she is just nervous. If it is the last one, please just take the girl's phone number and see another opportunity. It is difficult to have sex on the same day with a nervous chick.) Once you've made your opening comment and she answers, let the conversation flow. Change the subject. Talk about anything else that is on your mind, such as something that interests you; just read today's psychology. The key is to talk about more than one topic.

Why do you want to do this? Because you want her (and you) to have the feeling that the two of you can talk about anything. You have always been in a conversation like the one that seems to last for hours because you and the other person keep thinking about the new links about the conversation. That is the kind of rapport you want to create.

You can perpetually go backward to the previous conversational links, open them again, and talk about them further. This is to give you a perfect opportunity to avoid awkward pauses. No matter how alpha male you decide to talk about yourself, your attitude will be the most important thing. If you feel fear, she will detect that and will be rejected by you.

Approach, with the full wisdom that women love sex, and thus there is a good chance that a woman will appreciate you when you talk to her. Even if she doesn't, it is her responsibility to let you know, not your attempts to read her mind. If you have a normal conversation, be relaxed and let it flow.

The dirty little secret about your interactions with women is that it doesn't matter what you say. You want to vibrate with her and get the report. Go for the good report.

When it comes time for her to ask your name, say your name with pride and give her a chance to say hers. If you feel like her, shake your hand at this point. This presents the dynamic that it is comfortable to touch. Ask questions; do stories, and just vibrate for a few minutes. You will know that she is interested in the conversation as soon as she begins to do stories on herself answering your previous questions (in other words, as I say, the conversation will become two-way.)

At this point, you have a kind of normal conversation that you would have with friends you have known for a long time. (Although you have not known this woman for more than several minutes, you want her to feel comfortable as if she knew about you.) When you've known someone for a long time, don't bombard them with questions. Instead, you make stories (talk) about what's going on around you, just like you can't believe how much junk food people buy at the store in the afternoon.

Lean back and vibrate with her. I find that I am more prosperous when I am with lower energy than high energy. The reasons are:

- She won't feel as if she has to match your emotional state if you come in very energetic.
- Women are more sexual when they are relaxed.

Making The Appointment

When the conversation flows from both parties, and you feel a good vibe, it is time to seal the deal. You can go right then or get a phone number and have your date later.

Base the decision on whether the two of you have time for this point (the date). As a common rule of thumb, it's best to avoid going on a date unless you have enough time. So if she has an appointment in mind, get her phone number and set a date later.

Setting the date (the good one) makes it informal and makes it sound like it's going to be fast and not a business (boring, I think). Say something like, "You know, I'm in the mood for a cup of coffee. I'd love for you to join me."

Rules are important; here is a summary:

1. Give it a sense that they won't be around long. This will positively affect any doubts you may have about having coffee (or what) with a guy you will meet.
2. Make it sound casual. You don't want her to think of a date in the traditional sense, or else she will get in the traditional nervous dynamics and make you wait for sex (most have a policy of not having sex with a man on the first date.)

If you decide to get her phone number, just say something like, "I enjoyed talking to you, but I have to go now. Maybe we can go out sometime. " If she says something positive like "sounds nice," then ask for a cell phone number.

As an alpha male, you control the frame and do not negotiate if she doesn't want it. It is always better to approach a woman alone, from a woman with typical friends who will not leave her to separate with a guy who barely knows her to separate with an individual as soon as they satisfy her. (If she wants to go, the group will interfere.)

If the woman you board is with a group, I find the best way to handle it is to get her phone number and meet her later.

Telephone Success

In typical relationship books, you'll find all kinds of no-call rules for three days. Since you are an alpha male, you move through life and do not want to play games, So, call whenever you want.

Indeed, I have found from experience that it is better to call EARLIER than LATER. Call her that night or the next day if you want. That way, your conversation with her is still fresh on her mind. When you call, you need to play positively and comfortably with who you are. Remember, you are not forcing on her, but instead, you give the honor and the privilege of talking to you.

Each person is different, there are usually some rules that you should know when you call, but there are some rules. One method I have found to relax and not overthink the conversation is to do some activity while on the phone. Maybe eat a bag of potatoes ... Or call her while you're driving or walking your dog. When you are sitting at home not doing something, you can have seconds of doubts.

When you call, a roommate or family might answer the phone. Most guys say when they call, in a nervous tone of voice, "Hi, is [the girl] there?" When you do that, a lot of people's automatic response is to go defensive and cock-blocky and say something nice (if they're nice), "Who's calling, please?"

350

This makes you take a step back, and when you talk to your girl, you will come across as nervous and therefore unattractive. A better way to deal with your roommate or family is to be relaxed when you call and when someone answers, for example, "Hi, this is [your name]. I'm looking for [your girl's name] to call."

If your girl is the one who answers the phone, that's perfect. Jump down to where you're going. If someone else (who is not your girl), talk to them amicably. Keep the conversation light and lighthearted. It will make your life sort of magnitude easier if you are with friends who live with it. If they tell you the girl is not here, they offer to take a message, say, "Thanks, but I'm leaving a message." Trust me, and they'll say they called her. Not leaving a message adds an air of mystery.

Most dating books are wrong when they say the rush to get to the phone. Unless you're in a rush, don't feel like you have to follow such rules. Continue your comfortable frame as an alpha male. You're calling because you want to chat in confidence, not because you're desperate for a date and have to think to pretend you're busy.

Also, you will find a lot of advice online on how to talk to girls on cell phone numbers, but my advice is to ignore some. Individuals will have to tell stories from their own lives, and you will adopt them as your own. However, this is a huge error because you come across as false. It must be original; Talk about your own life with the girls you call.

When your girl is on the phone, don't force the conversation; instead, just keep chatting about the conversation you had with her when you got her number. Get back to those conversational threads for a little bit. When you do this, you will return her to the state she was in when she met you. Then start telling interesting stories about something that happened to you in your life. Your goal is to be light and witty and just "vibrate" with the girl.

351

Make sure you speak with animated sounds and not filtered. Don't use monotonous things or low volume when speaking. Avoid talking about things that make you nervous when you talk. That includes things such as asking her "WHAT'S SHE UP TO," asking how her day was (instead of telling her how YOUR day was), and tell her that you are the guy who knows her from the bookstore (or wherever you met her)...

Don't try hard to create a report. Better, just assume that the report already exists. This is the way you can relax and have an interesting conversation. After they chatted for a while, meeting the girl will be easy. She will probably always do it indirectly. Just say something like, "Hey, I'm busy with work, but it would be fun to go out for coffee for a minute. When are you free?"

 (Obviously, your goal is not to go out with her for just a little bit, but don't say this to her. You tell her that your time is limited to lower her defenses against having sex on the first date.)

If she gets defensive or gives you a negative answer, don't worry about it. At least you had 10 or 15 minutes practicing how to talk on the phone with a girl; now you hardly know.

Just say, "It was a pleasure talking to you. I guess I'll talk to you later." Don't end up saying, "Hey, I'll call you this week." The former puts you more of a challenge and unpredictable in their eyes. When you are talking to a woman "hand in hand," it is time to escalate the interaction towards sex slightly. Realize that women want sex almost as much as we do, and you just do it. There are five things you are going to focus on:

1)   Stay relaxed as much as possible (that is, the opposite of nervous and insecure).

2)   Feel sexual and hot.

3)   Talk like their old friends.

4) Taking the initiative and persisting towards romance.

The Only Place You Should Take a Woman on a First Date

Take her to a spot that is not traditionally associated with "romance." Because this means you are not taking her to a fancy dinner or doing anything that she associates with a "Date." If you do, inside her is the same "Make her wait" state of mind that she adopted with the previous 100 guys, who bought her a nice dinner. Instead, find any casual place, like a coffee shop or cheap restaurant, for lunch. Don't do the "who pays for the food" big thing, because again, the 100 men from the previous dates paid for the food because it was obvious that they hoped to get to be with her.

As an alpha male, you shouldn't do any of these because "you're hoping to get to be with her." These scents of despair kill the attraction that a woman feels. (A more attractive guy has sex all the time, so sex is not a big deal for him. If a woman wants his attention, she has to earn it ... not the other way around. In other words, he is a challenge to her, not a sure thing.)

As I said earlier, spending money on a woman lowers your value in their eyes. To avoid spending money in the places that you are going to go out with the girl. Although at equal opportunity, you don't want to appear stingy.

My favorite place to meet is in a coffee shop because it is casual, a very public place where women feel safe, and a place where it is never necessary to spend more than a few coins. So if you decide to buy him a coffee, it will never be a big deal. Another great advantage of meeting in the cafe is that you avoid setting a "date," where everyone gets nervous, like when you go to dinner on a first date since a coffee shop is somewhat relaxed and a comfortable place for a meeting.

Relaxation should be a big factor in deciding where to date a girl. If the place is too luxurious, it can be intimidating. Remember, for a woman to become receptive to sex, she needs to feel comfortable. Try to go somewhere that is close to your home. The longer the journey from the meeting venue to your house, the longer the window of time for the woman to begin to realize her hot emotional state and start having bad thoughts that she is on her way to the home of a man on his first date.

Another thing to consider. Become a regular customer wherever you take the girls. In my case, I am a natural at a coffee shop not far from my house. One tip is to befriend employees. Thus, when the girl goes to the site with you, she will see that people know you and like you, which increases your social status. Girls put a lot of emphasis on a man's social status. That helps you because the girl sees that people know you and like you. To her, that means you're normal instead of some weird guy.

While we are on your social status, another suggestion is to take the girls anywhere that you are popular or that people like you. If you're the boss at work, for example, arrange to meet the girl at work before you go on your date. By taking your seat at the rendezvous, do the opposite of what the etiquette books tell you. The place the girl has to sit on the seat by the wall, you must sit.

Turn your back to the wall. You have her sitting in front of the table, so all she can see is you and the wall. This minimizes the distractions with which you have to compete. You will have her focused on you, instead of competing with the other people that she would look at in the place of the appointment, the view of the river, or the buildings on the street, the people in the place of the appointment, etc. You don't want their attention to be interrupted by anything more interesting than you.

By the way, throughout this, keep in mind that I've been talking about where you want to go. This is an important point. You want to control the frame. Let her enter your world, not the other way around. So don't

354

be like those wimpy kids who say, "What place would you like to see?" Have a place in mind, and bring it into your reality.

Later in the relationship, this can and should change. But first, always have a place in mind you want to go and adopt this mindset: "I'm going to be doing something fun, and this woman is just coming for a walk."

How to Convert an Easy Conversation Successful on a Date

You want your conversation to be free, fluid, and not forced, so keep your speech informal, just as if you were talking with a friend. Keep in mind that you are patiently getting to know her a little before taking action. Relax, and don't think too much about what to say.

Here are some amazing recommendations on what to talk about:

Interesting stories from your life.

She will probably start talking about something interesting in her life. If something she says is fascinating to you, tell her you'd like to hear more about it. However, do not pretend to be interested in something, as women can often detect falsehood.

Relevant facts from your past.

Make these relevant events something emotionally huge, just as it was something very interesting that you saw, or something scandalous or out of the place where it happened. She will probably tell her relevant facts.

TV shows, movies, and celebrities.

Even if you don't spend much time watching TV, you can catch up quickly by watching a few minutes on the news channels or the Internet. The Hollywood A-List website at

355

www.thehollywoodalist.com is a celebrity gossip source that can give you an easy conversation with almost most women.

Music.

Look at Rolling Stone magazine to quickly find out about today's music and how you can interestingly talk about music.

Food.

It doesn't matter if a woman is fat or thin; the chances are high that she is obsessed with this topic.

Holidays.

Talk about the most interesting aspects of the places you have been to.

Your passions in life.

Do you have passions? Or not? If you don't have them, develop some. And develop the ability to talk about them.

Differences between men and women.

A lot of girls can talk for hours about this!

Shoes.

Women have a peculiar fascination for shoes, and you can easily have a half-hour of valuable conversation with any woman just by getting her to teach you about shoes.

It's okay if you ask her questions about her, but try to avoid doing it a lot. Why? Why don't you usually ask a lot of questions when you're talking to someone you know. (And remember, you're trying to create within her the feeling that "this guy is nice to talk to, it's like I've known him for years!")

Find out information, make statements instead of asking questions. It's okay to ask, "What kinds of books do you like to read?" But a more reliable way to put it is, "I'd love to hear about the books you like to read." This conveys your vitality and is a more personal statement from the moment you express your feelings and reactions.

What you talk about is not important since a woman will not have sex with you simply based on what you say. However, she will protect herself from you if you talk about the wrong issues. Lots of guys make this mistake, so pay special attention to this list of 14 specific topics that you should never discuss in conversations with a woman you want to have sex with:

1) Negative Issues as it is that she hates her job so much.

Maintain a positive interaction. You want her to join good feelings with you. Also, you are the man she will have sex with; you are not her psychologist! Let your friends listen to your problems instead of you.

If she addresses negative topics, steer the discussion to a topic that you prefer. Be nice before changing the subject, say something like, "I'll help you get your mind off that issue."

2) Extremely Negative Matters About You.

Don't tell him how you spent those two years in prison, how much you hate a dead-end job, or how shy you are that you don't date girls much.

However, she does not know someone perfect, so you should disclose the fewest vulnerabilities from time to time, just as you get nervous when you give a speech in front of large crowds, how bad you are keeping your clean car, or how you have always been afraid your parents will die.

Talking about minor vulnerabilities can increase their affection for you due to:

357

a. It personalizes you and helps you relate to it.
b. Show that you are not trying to win their approval.

3) Controversial Issues.

Sorry, the gunman. If she gets irritated by the number of people who own guns, sex will be the last thing on her mind. It is also possible that you support opinions that disqualify you in her mind (maybe she has very strong opinions about gay marriage ... and it is the opposite of how you see it). Avoid mentioning anything with that potential.

If the woman herself brings up religion or political issues, try to agree as much as you can. Don't be weak and compromise your main ideas, but at the same time, if you disagree with her, you can say something like, "That's a good point... I like that you are well informed. Hey, did you know? And then change the subject to someone else.

4) Issues that point to Boring Women.

Probably a percentage of women have little idea whether the New York Yankees will trade their overpriced pitcher and steroid addict for the Boston outfielder junkie, so save that conversation for your night out with friends. Women also don't care about the new synchronized hydraulic turbocharger you have in your car.

- You almost always get a "me too!" As a reaction when you say this to her ...

- For some reason, most girls might not care how dirty your car is. What matters to them is how clean your house is.

- This is another vulnerability that you can reveal that guarantees you that a woman says, "Me too."

Nor are they interested in how you wasted your time on an electronic game or some other computer-related topic of conversation.

5) Some Technical Issue

Save yourself fussing over your upgraded 1GB RAM for when you're with your nerdy friends. If you need to explain what a RAM is and how it works, save it for your colleagues. I can't always say it, but this must be well framed in your brain. For women to be sexually predisposed, they must be emotionally engaged. When you engage them logically, this stiffens the emotional sector of their mind. So, don't be boring!

6) Vulgar Topics

You don't make yourself sexually more attractive when you explain that you don't like cream in your coffee because it gives you diarrhea. (Sadly, this is a real example of one of the boys I train; surprisingly, he has no idea that this was why the girl lost interest in him.) And don't laugh about how you can fart. Women think things like that aren't fun; they disgust.

7) Issues that could offend women

There are some distinctions between guys and gals on certain issues. Even the most addicted drug users, party girls, have a strongly fed instinct.

Sometimes, sure, this is obvious. A friend of mine told a woman what he thought was funny when he ran over a squirrel, which he then left complaining about the road. (Needless to say, he came home alone that night)

8) Your Ex Crush or Some Other Guy You Still Like.

When this comes up, change the subject IMMEDIATELY AS SOON AS YOU CAN. Even if the girl talks about how she hates her ex, she is still attracted to him. (If not, I would be indifferent and not want to talk about it.) The goal is that you want her to think of you, and only you, not other boys.

9) Sex

Don't verbalize anything about sex because it will ignite that part of his mind that has been trained to think, "Oh, this guy just wants one thing, I better keep him waiting, or others will think I'm just anybody!" Be sexy, but don't verbalize anything about sex, and when she turns you on, expect her to get as horny as you are gradual. (I will explain this concept later in the next section.)

10) Low-Status Indicators.

Go to the chapter on "How to be Nice" to avoid talking about things such as bragging about yourself.

11) Bombard Her With Questions

If you try to bind a connection to it instead of just acting like it already exists, chances are you will fail. Why? Because by acting like someone she just met, you will be placed in that category, which makes sex a very distant possibility. Instead, you should make her think of you as the guy she gets along with from the get-go. So you should talk about things that you would talk about if the two of you felt comfortable and confident.

When you're comfortable with someone, you don't machine-gun them with endless questions. Instead, you make sentences and have normal conversations. So this should apply the same in the case of women.

12) Something Encrypted

If you search the Internet, you will be able to find pages that promise to give you the ability to hypnotize women or alter their emotional states. They include canned phrases and stories designed to make women laugh and throw them into an almost hypnotic state. I'm not saying this stuff doesn't work, but the problem is that unless you have an extremely good shipment, you will look like a phony if you start saying a lot of lines to it.

This book's methods are much simpler and will do a good job of getting you to sleep with girls like any other system. Why waste countless hours memorizing lines when you can just make yourself more attractive and be yourself with women?

13) Romantic Conversation

You heard right. Recite Shakespeare's poems when you are in Spanish class, not when you are on a date. Romance should come after sex, not before. If you set the romance framework, the woman will likely make you wait to have sex.

As you are the dominant male who controls the frame, you prefer to establish the dynamic where sex is something given and not a big thing, not something that you have to endure over long months in anticipation of the great day of deflowering.

14) Too Much Humor

It's good to be naturally witty and funny in the course of your conversation, and many guys who are good with girls are good at making them laugh. Either way, don't overdo it. If you use too much humor, the woman will not take you seriously or see you sexually.

Remember that you control the interaction with a woman, so you want to establish the correct frame of mind. You are a sexual man and an alpha male, not a clown.

initiating the Emotionally Relevant Conversation

When you talk to a girl, it is important to appeal to her emotions. Simply put: a woman committed to her emotions is more receptive to sex.

For example, rather than saying: "I have driven more than 5 miles", as you speak to one of your friends, you should say to her: "You would not believe what I saw early when I was driving" (She will be excited and will ask you what it was) The best way to learn how to talk to a woman in an emotionally relevant way is to just talk about your daily experiences with them in a way that allows them to feel the way you should have felt.

Were you yelled at by your boss? Did you notice an interesting lake that someone made while you were walking on the sidewalk? Did you embarrass yourself this morning in front of many people? Things like that where you felt a strong emotion at the time (no matter what emotion it was) These are the kinds of conversational thread that girls are drawn to.

Do you remember elsewhere in this guide where I recommended that you have at least one good conversation with one woman every day? One of the benefits you will get from this is learning the types of topics that fascinate women. Over time, emotionally relevant topics will come naturally to you. It is also helpful to accompany women and check how they speak to each other. Then you can similarly talk to them (Make sure to be masculine about this, though, so that you don't become their "gay best friend")

The Importance of Laughter

PairFor women, laughing can be a bonding experience, so be the guy who makes her laugh now and then. I don't mean to be a comedian all the time, but instead, make witty comments from time to time. By the way, never act witty, funny, or playful. Avoid all those things, develop your intelligence, and make funny comments or witty remarks as you please.

And realize that if even something sounds a bit funny, the woman will laugh at the simple fact that you two agree. flirting skill comes naturally to women, but most guys have a problem with this, and you will rid yourself of the problem.

Taker's hair. What I mean is, send mixed messages. Women tease us because they love doing it. These women tease with their eyes. They look flirtatiously at the boys and then look away. They provoke their way of dressing, wearing sexy clothes showing us a little, but not too much. Strip club dancers carry out the ultimate goal of the provocation. They grab onto the boy's tie and move so close they could almost kiss him. After all that, they suddenly change, turn around and turn their backs on you. And then they repeat the procedure.

Think about how dancers get to turn you on and then cool you down, turn you on, and cool you down again. These women do it all the time and on a large number of levels. And women do it because they realize that foreplay begins long before you get to the bedroom. Post much so, and he teases a woman playfully because she adores him. Provoke her about:

- Hiss answers to your questions
- The way you saw
- Of its peculiarities and mannerisms.

I got her on the butt when she says offensive things. Roll up a piece of paper and put it in your mouth, looking at her with a mischievous smile. Visualize the entire interaction with a woman almost as if you were her older brother, and she is your comical little sister. Keep everything fun and playful.

Signs Of Attraction

I probably don't need to list the attraction signals that you find in relationship books. The reason is if a woman is clinging around you, talking to you, and being nice, obviously she doesn't dislike you!

Prior it's always possible that she likes you just as a friend (even though the more you keep pushing, the interaction backs off), so my advice is to learn and memorize the following list I have released and then try to forget it. And this is because you will paralyze yourself during conversations if you start by analyzing small details like how forcefully she twirls her hair around her fingers.

Once you have enough experience with women, you will instinctively recognize the signs of attraction. The following list is in no particular order.

1. She compliments you on just about anything.
2. She is nervous around you. Look for signs of nervousness, such as his muscles stretching.
3. She taunts you playfully.
4. She attempts to tell you how much she admires the same things that you like
5. She talks about things you can do in the future. "Do you also like vintage clothing stores? she might say, "We should go someday!" By the way, this is additionally something you should share with the girls. Could you not do it too seriously? Do it like you are playful. "We could go shopping for the tightest purple pimp-looking clothes on Fifth Avenue."
6. When her legs are crossed, see at the foot of her top leg. If he is pointing at you, it is a sign that you have obtained his full attention.
7. She makes an effort to keep the conversation moving forward when it quiets down. (Now and then, you can even test her attraction on purpose by allowing the conversation to pause or end on your part. Then see if she restarts the conversation)
8. She touches her face. When a person touches their face, it is a sign that they are thinking about something. To be sure that she is thinking good thoughts, look for this signal combined with others on the list.
9. She fixes her gaze on your eyes and keeps her gaze
10. .She imitates you. (Being passive by nature, women follow the lead of a man they are attracted to.) Watch to see how she does.

- The posture is similar to yours.

- Modulate the volume of his voice to match yours.

- Modulate the scale of his voice to match yours.

- Match the rhythm of your breathing.

- Laugh when you laugh.

11. Peel a cylindrical object such as a wine glass or pencil from top to bottom with your thumb and index finger. This means that you are having a strong effect on her, big boy!
12. She moves her head back or sides. Watch her hair sway as she does that.
13. She touches his face while he looks at you.
14. She hangs her shoe off her foot or even takes it off.
15. She rubs her fingertips around the top of her chest
16. She rubs her palm on the rear of her head, letting her hair fluff.
17. She plays with her hair while she sees you.
18. She shows a genuine smile rather than a forced one.
19. Her eyes glow because her pupils are large and dilated
20. She raises her eyebrows at times.
21. Her nipples harden. Of course, you can only say this if she is wearing the right clothes.
22. She has a relaxed face. (However, sometimes a non-relaxed face can be fine, like when a woman is so attracted to you that she feels nervous)
23. She fixes her gaze on your eyes. Your pupils dilate (grow)
24. She focuses her attention on you, even when other people are around.
25. She touches you while speaking to you. Even if it is "accidental," Ladies are highly mindful of their bodies, so this will rarely be an accident when they touch you. Watch her touch your arm to emphasize a point or stroke her feet against yours when she laughs at one of your witty comments.
26. She laughs at your comments like they're the funniest things they've ever heard, even if they are only mildly resourceful.
27. She shows her tongue, such as when she touches it with her front teeth or wets her lips
28. With her body bent towards you, she quickly sits upright, her arm muscles tense and her chest lifted.

29. She shows her palms towards you. Open palms indicate that she feels open to you

30. She rubs her wrist or plays with her bracelet.

31. Your skin becomes flushed. Watch particularly to notice if she blushes. (This can also be a sign that she's feeling horny.)

32. She rubs her earlobes or works with her earrings.

33. She asks about herself. They will not be just superficial questions that she has asked anyone ("Where are you from?"), On the contrary, they will be deeper questions to determine what makes you tick (example: What are your passions in life?)

34. She is energetic when she talks to you.

35. Your voice becomes a little lower (half an octave or about)

36. She adjusts her blouse.

There are some signals that a woman gives to indicate that she is not interested in you. Usually, these signals are subconscious; women do not always think about them. Sometimes women do it in an exaggerated way to try to give you a hint.

Beware in your mind as you need to see several of these signals manifesting before drawing any conclusions. A person sometimes crosses their arms simply because they are cold rather than uncomfortable.

As well, try to get a woman to express her rejection of you in words. On multiple occasions, I have had a woman send me signals of rejection. However, I persisted in the conversation and eventually managed to fuck her.

1. A soft hand (shaking hands without strength, without interest).

2. She looks elsewhere, especially when you're talking to her.

3. She makes little effort to talk to you. Give one-word answers.

4. Crossing arms across your chest (putting them as a barrier.

5. Cross your legs at the ankles.

6.   She is continually scratching his nose. When a person is uncomfortable, blood collects in their nose, making them itch.
7.   When you turn your body language towards her, she leans back and away from you.
8.   She seems off talking to you.
9.   She has a neutral tone of voice.

Assume right now that you always attract a woman to you. Not even interpersonal relationships are exact and fulfilled prophecies; they are based on our attitudes, so use that to your advantage. If you have a strong inner attitude that says, "Of course she is attracted to me," then she will catch your wave and be influenced by you.

Why You Must Assume the Attraction

Many of the advice you find on the Internet about choosing the women you find around you to say that you must do several tactics to attract a woman. Telling the memorized stories and other routines will get him to laugh and so on. The problem with all this work to build a woman's attraction is that it comes from a beta male mindset. If you are always trying to say the right things to a woman, you are also trying to approve of you hardly.

The fact is if you have good body language, strong confidence, look better, and have many projects in your life, and you are automatically going to be more attractive to a woman than 95% of the remaining guys. (And make no mistake about this, you'll be in the top 5% of male attraction, virtually all women will potentially find you, someone they want to have sex with.) If you assume the attraction, then you're going to act the right way anyway. For example, when a woman acts like a brat and asks you a certain question like, "Why did you choose to speak to me?" or "do you say that kind of thing to all women?" The best thing you can do is not look for the best answer. And instead, the best way to react is with indifference. That way, you

367

keep control of the frame. (When you take care of and pay attention to what a woman may think, you are giving her control.)

There is never a need to feel like you need to entertain a woman. Doing this makes you a beta. When you chat with a woman, interact with her. Do your research to make sure she can carry on a conversation by going with you. That makes you an alpha male. This is what you always assume that the woman is attracted to you, the most important rule to control the frame's harmony, we will always be willing to go far. When I talk about persistence until you get rejected or have sex, sometimes it's nice to be the only one who walks away first (if it's a girl you don't like), just to know you can.

The state is always willing to go far if the need arises, even if you need to, while being conserved as a challenge for women. If a woman sees a guy as a challenge, she cares about him. It means that she has to work to get you, and win your affection, as it is her reward. If you are always a "sure thing" for a woman, she gives her validation and causes her to lose her attraction to you. If you simply assume the attraction, that ensures that the woman always thinks that she is attracted to you and not you are attracted to her.

Your Behavior

When you feel hot, and you want her to feel hot too, you should sit as close to her as possible. According to anthropologist Edward Hall, friends have to communicate at a distance greater than 18 inches (45.72 cm) between the two of you. People who want to be intimate keep a distance of fewer than 18 inches between the two. When you create an intimate dynamic with the woman you are scoring, you must keep a close distance between the two. Make it a goal to always stay within that intimate 18-inch space. When you establish the dynamics of being within reach of others' personal spaces, you also want the two of you to be comfortable touching each other.

Even though you are touching her for seemingly innocent reasons, human communication research has shown that a person is more likely to accept someone else's touch if they feel affection around them.

Touching a woman, you are:

- Citing the parts of your mind that say, "I like this guy!"

If she reacts negatively, then you know that you are wasting your time holding on to her. And it's also a hallmark of alpha males that they feel free to touch others.

By being so free to play, you communicate non-verbally that you are an alpha male and a man who has confidence in women.

(After all, only a man with a high degree of self-confidence can be relaxed while touching a woman.) Knock woman as if it were something natural without giving much importance to this fact. So, she realizes that you place a lot of importance on touching her (maybe like you're looking at your hands when you touch her), then this dynamic turns into something of yours that energetically tries to get to fuck her causes let her raise her defensive shields.

When you are in public with her, progress like this:

1) Touch her Hand.

You can do this in a fun way by having a "thumb wrestling" competition. If you don't know how to do this, watch the Arnold Schwarzenegger movie Risky Lies in the scene where he and Jaime Lee Curtis said, "One, two, three, four, I declare a thumb war." Once you've started with the idea that touch can be as much fun as this, then you can touch her hand for other times, as if you want to discover that cool ring she's wearing.

2) Touch her wrist

Do this by referring to her bracelet or watch when she touches her wrist.

3) Touch her forearm.

Knock to his forearm when you want to emphasize a point

4) Touch her Arm

Do it when you are saying something that you had thought.

5) Touch her neck

Do it within the context of whispering a secret in your ear. Do it to the point where you both feel good enough to hold his hand.

6) Touch her Lower Back

Knock Behind her when you are next to her, and they start walking at the dating site. One of the several important things in the whole process is that you stay calm and relaxed if you haven't emphasized it. Sit comfortably and enjoy.

Pair to relax, note that the interaction with the girl should not be so important.

To do what you've been doing when you talk to her is knowing about her and establishing a connection before you have a physical connection. Look at her in the eyes, as you speak, but sweetly and gently in a sexual way.

Gently talk to her, with a normal tone of voice, as if you have been in a relationship for a long time, and you already feel completely relaxed and comfortable with her. In other words, speak softly, with a sexy voice. Use the Powerful "Doing the Boyfriend Technique"

Brand reveals an important technique to create well-being that you will not find anywhere else. I call her "Becoming the boyfriend." In short, there is something you can do that is ONLY normally done by a woman's lover. If you do it, too, it's a way to get on a woman's radar and make her feel comfortable with you so that she'll be receptive to having sex without making you wait.

Will sees, for a woman to want to have sex with a man, she must have feelings of comfort/well-being. It is not enough that she is attracted to a boy. Let's say you meet a girl at five in the morning at happy hour. The two of you like each other, and you have a pleasant conversation. She laughs. She is interested. You cast a spell on her by telling fabulous stories about her life. You both seem nice.

At 7:30, you're hungry, and you invite her to get some food. In food, things are also going well. The meal ends now what? And at this moment, a lot of guys don't know how to go on. The goal is to sleep with her, but the road map is often confusing.

Usually, the night ends, and the girl tells you: "I had a great time with you. Giving me a call. Goodbye"

The need for comfort/well-being is why women like to keep boys waiting before having sex. (if he's a lucky guy, he may only need three dates, but with many women, the guy is made to wait for months, as we noted earlier).

Lucky there is a way to short-circuit that barrier. I call it the "grooming technique."

If you observe couples who are intimate, you will notice an interesting phenomenon. The man and the woman are comfortable touching each other. This form of behavior is only done by people who feel good next to each other. Of course, when you have a relationship where you can be comfortable in a woman's eyes, you are long past the time when the two of you feel comfortable having sex.

Do you go along with me? You can use this as a mental weapon to make her feel more comfortable around you. In the middle of a conversation, tell her to stay still and close her eyes. Pretend he has an eyelash and makes him believe you removed it. Later, when you've

371

both eaten and left the restaurant, tell him again to stop. With your finger, brush an imaginary piece of food away from her lower lip.

The result of the "impersonating boyfriend technique" is nuclear, fabulous. First, this communicates subconsciously that the two of you are very comfortable with each other. Second, it involves touching your face, having your heads closer to each other, and progressing toward a session of understanding.

Thirdly, if you touch her lower lip, you are touching an erogenous zone. A woman's lower lip indeed has many nerve endings. Stimulating this part of the body causes a release of sex hormones. Make this seduction technique part of your arsenal, and you will have more success than you have ever had. You should have sex in a matter of hours instead of waiting months.

How do you know when to have her alone with you when the right time to take the opportunity?

When the woman feels comfortable with you and is confident with you, she will feel increasingly sexual herself. Watch her get aroused little by little.

Observe these eight clues that scream: "I want you to put it on me."

1) Look at your mouth and then look back at your eyes.
2) Her eyes are wet and shiny.
3) She touches the mouth.
4) She rubs/touches the neck.
5) The skin on your face alternates between being flushed and pale.
6) Her eyes roam your genitals.
7) She smoothes her skirt, or legs, or stockings.
8) She stares into my eyes with a hungry gaze.

It should be obvious what is on both your mind and hers. At that moment, it is the right time to leave the place where you are (cafeteria, restaurant, bar ...) and go to a place where you are alone. Anyway, you don't want to say, "We're going to have sex." On the first date, the easiest way to get a woman out of her arousal is to verbalize your desire to want to sleep with her.

And instead of saying it, say something innocent and non-sexual to get the two of you to be alone.

As long as a woman is sufficiently aroused, she will be willing to go somewhere where the two of you are alone—usually his house or yours. Generally, women feel more comfortable in their own homes. The excuse you use to get you to stay alone is not important. I like to fake time constraints (I only have a couple of minutes) to overcome any objections.

One plus point is that there is an innocent-sounding reason for both of us to be together (you'll love my stamp collection) When you are going to the place where you will be alone, it would be ideal to continue talking and keep her in that state of excitement. You don't want her to have time to think about what she is doing or for a friend to call and tell her that she is not going to go with you. For this reason, and to date, I like the women of a coffee shop that is in the same distance that I walk on the way home. This way, I could bring my hands with theirs as we walk home "for a few moments."

How To Make A Woman Feel Happy And Very Hot For Sex

what you would like sex to appear in her as if it happened spontaneously. After all, she was only coming to your place for a few minutes, right? If you go to your place or his, save the conversation of the subject you were talking about. When you get out of the car in the parking lot or on the driveway, save the topic.

When you walk to the door, save the conversation. It's his way of keeping her emotionally focused. Do not pause the conversation, or else she will begin to think, and when she thinks about the situation, by logic, it may be that emotion overcomes her; in this case, you will hear the dreaded words, "I need you to give me a clue."

And at this point, you need to give her a comfortable idea that you are alone and in isolation. If you're at home, make him overly fascinated with his library of books and DVD collection. If you are in your home, show him all the cool and interesting stuff you have.

You have cool and interesting stuff in your home, right? If not, get some stuff! Anything that you can have a conversation that you can talk about would be nice to have at the show:

- The table of reserved cafes on the places where you have been traveling.
- Albures made by your great aunt.
- Interesting Reports (of those that have interesting topics to talk about, such as Psychology Today and Hospitality Weekly, not like Maxim and Playboy)
- Floors. Two plants that are tough-killer and that look good are the jade tree and the cast iron plant.

Keep your home safe. It was not necessarily as if it was something made for the eye of a strict guy, but at least having it as if it would not fail a health department inspection. Haver pictures on the wall rather than a poster. Have clean sheets on your bed. Have decent furniture. Clean and sweep your floors with the vacuum cleaner. Wash the dishes. How to demonstrate that, in your home, you can have conversations in each room.

Easy Alpha Male Exercise:

Take a walk around your house and think about the conversational topics that you can have from each place; For example, "you wouldn't believe how I ended up being the owner of the one with the sculpture on the corner."

A friend of mine gave me some good advice about the bedroom, that is, you should avoid calling it a "bedroom." Why? Because the word "bedroom" is a weapon of great proportion programmed in your mind by our purification society to say, "Uh oh, Sex alarm!"

And its place extends its definition. My friend calls his bedroom "the meditation room. I was calling it that, I have observed that as well (you can even make her smile by calling it that, you can get a giggle out of her), and you can talk about how you like to go to your mediation site and to remain silent sometimes thinking-contemplating.

Find an excuse for you to sit very close to each other in your living room or bedroom.

I haven't glad to tell you, "Take a look at my photo album; I have an awesome photograph from my last blah-blah vacation...," which is why you'll be sitting hip-to-hip on your couch as you walk around and peek through the most interesting photos.

These movies are fantastic. They give you an appointment and a half of time on the couch next to her as you progress towards sex. Put on a movie if you can.

It could be any kind of movie that will be pretty, but find light comedies such as Ghostbusters if possible.

By the way, Ghostbusters is a great movie to watch with the girl you just brought into your home because:

1) It is a movie of which everyone has fond memories, during all these years.
2) There are many points about sexual arousal in this movie.

One of the best sex preludes you can encounter with a woman is the standard "getting ready" in the couch position. The other is sitting together to touch hip to hip with your arm behind her with your back resting on the cushions.

Suppose you let a while pass. Sexually, the woman is like iron. She will slowly warm up. Man, however, can be turned on and off in the same way that a light switch is turned on and off. Then, what do you need to do to heat it slowly? You must gradually progress from one level to the next. Be sure not to make very fast moves or plays that she cannot warm up; this way, sex won't happen.

At a certain point when you're with her, touch her lightly on her shoulder with your hand and stretch her back. A bit slower, put your hand on her collar in a more secure way; if she is interested in you, she will hug you or snuggle with you.

If she doesn't do that to herself, don't allow yourself to feel down or upset. Instead, relax and feel good. Now stretch your arm and put it behind her almost, listen to me well, almost touching her (that your arm continued to touch the sofa), and try the former again after a while. Eventually, her feverish state will reach a point where she is dying from putting your arm around her.

Quiet hands. Put your arm around her. Move her silky hair, enjoying the feel of the hair sliding between your fingers. Breathe and smell her hair sensually.

There are things you can do when you are with her to go far. Keep in mind the following parts of her body ... even if they are erogenous zones.

1. Their hair. The best way to warm up a woman is by touching or stroking her hair.
2. Touch your scalp. It's good, and only this is very erogenous.
3. The inside of her elbows. The touch with your fingertips can make her shake.
4. The skin between her fingers. When you hold a woman's hand, the best way to do it is by locking your fingers with hers; it would be to interlock their fingers with yours.

5. Her ears. When you are about to kiss her, and you are very close to her, blow gently into her ears, touch the edges of her ear with the tip of your finger.
6. her shoulders.
7. Her feet.
8. Her toes.

Knock all the mentioned areas on her body,

and she will start to wake up the way we want.

And so things start to get hotter and hotter, move your face to his hair and inhale deeply And say: "Mmmmm, I love the way your hair smells ..." the interaction gets hotter and hotter, and you have your arms around her; the two of you will be looking very deeply into each other's eyes, perhaps with each other's mouths slightly ajar. At this point, you should always lightly brush your bottom lip gently against his, and you will see all his melt in a kiss with you.

continue your kissing process; don't just stick your tongue in his mouth. Expect her to give you a bit of her tongue and then exchange, slowly and then soon, the two of you will be giving each other a passionate kiss.

Have you ever felt very nervous about kissing a girl for the first time and in the direct way that I described it? You, too, can indirectly go to that situation by mentioning this, using what I call the technique: "Rate My Kiss. Yes, that is how the "Tarifa Mi Beso" technique works. When you feel that the moment that has been generated is conducive to the kiss, you have to say, "How much would you score on the scale of 1 to 10 in your ability to kiss?" She can answer you, or she can not answer you, but in 95% of the cases, women will open their lips, and you will be able to move your face towards her.

The Non-verbal Signal That Yells Kiss Me!

Unlike any other technique, this is a great non-verbal cue that says, "Kiss me now, a man of my dreams!"

The technique in a nutshell is:

if you move your face and lips very close to her (after you have inhaled her hair and so on, having done all the rest of the work you should be doing), watch her slowly part her lips in a very gentle way. Generally, the woman will close her eyes as well, although this does not always happen. You move to kiss her, focus not only on kissing her, focus more on brushing your lips with hers. Trust me, she will melt into you, and the two of you will be making out full length without any time limit.

BéLeave for a while, slowly. Keep your mouth open. Wait for your tongue. Only until your tongue enters his mouth. Okay. Now that his tongue entered your mouth, put yours into action.

The most significant point you should know about the kiss

Kissing differs from many other sexual activities; it is one of the few things you do with the woman to let her take the lead or direction. When things like penetrating her happen, you should take the lead, but again, in kissing, she's the one who should take the lead. The greatest murderous modality for women is when the boy puts his tongue in her mouth before she is ready, which, in short, he does not like. Remember she must be ready. So, just relax during the kiss, and watch in a mirror what she does.

Alpha's method of moving, from the first kiss to the "Silver House."

Now, you are not only dating her, but you are also hugging her, and you can touch every part of her and memorize it, slow progress. The entire process generally takes several hours from when you first walk through the door of her place until you have sex.

You carefully peel her shirt down. Button after button, and then kiss her again. Remember, "Two steps forward, one step back." You detach a button, then the 2nd button, and then you massage his hand, and you smell his neck again. Then lightly rub her hair. Then touch her stomach gently, and then go back to the first beat when you French kissed her.

You go towards her breasts, do it slowly. Touch them gently with your fingertips, and then move down to her belly button then start rubbing her stomach.

Generally, she will have her shirt on with the bra. You will slowly want to put your hands under her bra. Once you are completely comfortable touching her breasts, remove her bra. Now go back two steps giving him a French kiss again and repeat the work done initially (smell it, blow the ear, etc.). Then after doing that, he starts sucking on her nipples and the space between her two breasts.

Once you have reached 2nd base (i.e., smelling and sucking on her breasts), your goal is now 3rd base (i.e., towards the bottom of them) almost all women, once you give them oral sex, you are virtually ensuring that you will put your penis inside her.

Some women are fully aware of that fact. So they will put up the barriers of resistance after you have started playing with your fingers on her clit; that is, just when you are ready to penetrate her, she will start her show of resistance.

A womanizing friend of mine told me about an original solution to this problem, which I have tried and found to work. He tells women that he "can't have an erection/sex and then points to his flaccid penis. "Do you see how soft I am?" All I want is to give you oral sex," he says.

Afterward, while giving him oral sex, she touches his penis to make it hard. At this point, because the woman has had a great orgasm from oral sex, she practically begs him to make love to her. So ... he makes love to her!

And this brings up the topic of overcoming a woman's last-minute resistance in general. Sometimes when you move too fast into foreplay, a woman will say things like, "We shouldn't be doing this" or "I don't want to go that far tonight." lots of guys screw up the dynamic by getting upset and arguing with her. You mustn't fall into this trap. Instead, disarm her by saying things like:

- "You're right; we shouldn't be doing this."
- "Okay, we won't go that far. It's nice that we've already done it. "
- "I have limits too."
- "You're right; we shouldn't have so much pleasure on the first night."

As you have verbally disarmed agreeing with her, go back to what you have done before, and then continue slowly climbing. If you go slow enough and keep continually going, gradually a barrier after another fall.

For example, suppose she doesn't have her shirt on, but her bra is still on, and you've been massaging her breasts out of the fabric. So when you start to undo her bra, you hear, "This is too much for the first night."

"you're right, this is too much," you answer. "We will just do what we were doing."

And at this point, go back a few steps. Massage her waist, stroke her hair, kiss her, hug her closely. Gradually increase the intensity, and then after a while, when you are massaging her breasts again, do it so sensually and slowly, and she will surely not resist you taking off her bra.

By the way, when it comes to final penetration, be sure to differentiate symbolic resistance and actual resistance. If a woman says, "No!" then stop what you're doing.

If you force a woman to have sex, then you have committed the crime of rape. It is crucially important that you keep this in mind. Stop when she says no, but at the same time, stay persistent towards sex until you have sex with her or she seriously tells you to stop.

But in any case, don't be shy about taking the lead towards her. (You are the man, and they expect you to be active/energetic). Always make sure to lead the interaction. Be persistent.

By the way, be careful with condoms. The sight of a condom wrapper in your hand can lift a woman out of her sexually aroused state by triggering that portion of her brain that has been programmed to think that sex is "bad."

I put the condom on while I perform oral sex on the woman (and she is too distracted to notice what I am doing with my hands) so that when she is ready for him to penetrate her, everything goes great.

Tomorrow After

To prevent a woman from having buyer's remorse, you need to call her after a night of passion. By buyer's remorse, I mean that sick feeling you get after a pushy salesperson at the electronics store convinces you to pay $ 200 for a warranty you'll never use. Many women go through it, too many if they think they were used for a one-night stand. They, too, feel guilty.

Often what every woman will want is, in fact, a one-night stand. Although women tell a good story when it comes to the fact that men are the only ones interested in such things, it has been my experience that women like to indulge in an affair, perhaps even more than men.

381

Why? Because women put a lot of emotional investment in relationships. When they have the opportunity for an affair with no social consequences, they often go for it.

It is up to you, the next morning, to decide what you want. If you want to continue a relationship with the woman after having passionate sex from the first day the two of you went out is the ideal setting to start. Let him know that sex in your relationship is very common.

I am a huge supporter of relationships. I have standards, and I will not have sex with just any woman. And if I have sex with a woman who meets my standards, why only have sex with her once? Why shouldn't I want to stay with her to have sex?

If you don't want to be in a relationship, you can still keep things in terms of casual "sexual friends" between the two of you.

To do this successfully, make sure you see her no more than once a week to prevent her from seeing you more than a sexual partner. More than once a week, she will start to see you as a potential boyfriend. In the rare case that you never want to see her again (maybe the sex was really bad?), At least have the decency to call her to see how she's doing.

CLOSING WORDS

BECOMING AN ALPHA MALE

It's almost impossible to be an alpha male as long as you follow someone else's orders. When you have someone telling you what to do and do it, you are the beta of that situation. There are only two ways to handle it, and both have their merits.

First, you can play the game. Do your job, take your boss's orders, get paid, and hopefully, you will climb the corporate ladder. The downsides are that you will have to follow office policy to get anywhere, and your boss may fire you if you don't kiss his ass.

Situations like this are not the best in the world for a man's sense of self-worth. And by the way, aggressively flirting with that beautiful secretary can get you off the hook. Top management guys don't like it when lower-level guys go after "their" women. So live your romantic life outside of the workplace. (In fact, the best strategy at work is always to have women working for you. That frees you from trouble.) The second way is to ditch everything and start your own business. This involves a ton more risk, but at least you'll be in charge of your destiny.

That is the path that I chose at age 29, leaving the corporate environment to become an inventor, and I never regretted it. I had some difficult years financially, but I did well, getting the business going. Money aside, the bottom line is that I don't take orders from anyone.

Be the Boss!

To add some leadership positions in your life. It doesn't matter if you're just a graduate aide in a college class. Being in a position of authority somewhere turns women on. Have running your own business and to be the boss of employees are great places to be there. When there are people who are following you, you acquire alpha status.

By the way, a great place to have a meeting with a woman is somewhere where you are the boss. One strategy for this is to say to the woman, "Stop by my office, and we'll go for a coffee there."

When she shows up, she will see that you are an important man who people follow and who is in command, giving her alpha status.

Project Your Ideal Ego By Controlling The Way You Are Seen

None of us truly live in reality. We live in what we think of as reality, but in reality, it is simply our perception of what reality is. Have you ever been surprised when you heard a recording of your voice? Well, that's how the others hear it. It's quite different from how you sound.

When they see it, people do not perceive it as it is but as they think you are.

People project various qualities and traits of his person and then treat him accordingly. This can be great or poor, depending on what your projection is.

However, the important point is that once you understand that people project an identity on you, you can take steps to control what that identity is.

Beta Male Behaviors to Avoid

Here's something we humans can't know: we tend to give negative information about someone more weight than positive information. This is why you may be having a great conversation with someone, and then suddenly, you change your thought about them when they tell you that a UFO abducted them.

It doesn't matter that the person has been smart and resourceful during the last half hour now; you have mentally stamped a file with big red letters that say "CRAZY" based on the UFO question. So, since one bad move can land 100 good guys, it's crucial to avoid negative behaviors characteristic of low-status males or betas if you don't want women to treat you like trash and tell you what to do. These beta features to avoid are:

1) Seek approval by ending sentences with "not true" or "right?" These questions attached to the end of sentences make you sound weak-willed, particularly if your tone of voice is raised. True?

2) Try to dominate. Better, could you do it? Assume a stronger mentality and psychological reality than others. Assume that people are there to follow you because you are the best. Know that you can politely ask people to do what you want them to do instead of bossing them around. (It is interesting to observe military generals who are normally courteous when they get a subordinate to do something.)

3) Be belligerent, either with women or with other men. The alpha male can stay calm under pressure and walk away when he must. Starting a fight is a sign that you are a man of low status. It also implies that fighting to win a woman's affections is the ultimate means of seeking approval, diminishing her attractiveness. That said, though, if some guy violates his limits and comes off with a stream of drool (let's say try to intimidate him), there are times when you need to stand up for yourself. And do it right.

4) Follow other people's agenda and talk about topics they want to discuss, even when you find it boring. Do you remember my story of sitting for two hours with the girl I loved, listening to her tale of sorrows about her neighbor? Bad move. The alpha only talks about what he wants. Look at any alpha in action, and you will recognize this phenomenon. When an alpha man is bored, he

385

doesn't hide his lack of interest. So, please don't pay attention to people until they've earned it.

5) Try to match a person and show that you are smarter than the person you are talking to. When you observe leaders in corporate boardrooms or governor's mansions, you will notice that the best leaders are so self-assured that they can listen to those who are specialists in other matters. You don't have to be smart, and you have to hire smart people.

6) check every pretty woman you see. A man who has an active sex life doesn't have time for this, so you shouldn't do it either. While you notice that you are impressed by the cute bodies around you, notice the difference in the reactions you receive from women. Notice how they start to notice you and want to show themselves or demonstrate something to you.

Alpha males seize the mantle of power as their birthright and act as natural leaders. They don't care what other people think. They do their thing and don't seek approval.

Nevertheless, at the same time, they also offer a profit — be it social status, excitement and excitement, or stimulating conversation — to those who follow them.

People submit to the alpha reality because they want to (since alphas talk about interesting topics) or because everyone else is listening to alpha.

And people — especially women — pay attention because the alpha's style of conversation is interesting. Why? Easy — because he talks about fascinating things. Thus, other people are absorbed in their reality, because consequently, they feel interesting.

So how do you get interesting talking material? It's simple: have an exciting, well-balanced life. If you do, you will naturally be attractive to women. Stay busy with work, your social life, activities, and trying to improve. He does not sit down to play video games. Go snorkeling, take dance lessons, call an old friend and go for a spin. When your life is enjoyable and entertaining, you have tons of stuff to talk about with women.

And when you do talk to a woman, lead the conversation. Captivate their attention.

As you work on your behaviors, you will also work on adopting the alpha mindset. The first thought I notify is that all alpha males have in common is that they assume that people will follow their lead. They aren't bossy because they don't need to be — they have the confidence that comes from knowing that other people will follow.

Being the boss can quickly backfire because few people like to take orders. Do your thing and be passionate, and people will stick to your reality. Just act as if people will follow you, believe that they will, and you will find that what you believe will become a reality.

This raises an important point. Don't look at reality and then adjust to it. Instead, create your reality. This means that you should act as if the events are going the way you would like them to.

Act like you're a good match for any woman. Act like sex isn't a big deal for you, as it isn't for men who have sex all the time. (Although you may not currently have much sex, or not at all, you want to model the mindset of the man who does.) Act as if all your manly desires are - and are - absolutely natural. You have no reason to apologize or cover up your sex drive the way good guys do!

Act as if you are not affected by what a woman thinks, as what you think is much more important. Believe it or not, women will respect him a lot more for this.

Many guys fall into the trap of constantly wondering what the woman is thinking. Stop worrying!

Instead, understand that there is a horny, wild woman inside of her who wants to have strong, passionate sex with you. Just relax. Be an

387

attractive guy, and give her a chance to be attracted to you. If she does not accept this gift of hers, then she misses it.

Be optimistic. Have you noticed how top athletes like Michael Jordan and Tiger Woods know that they will do well? Success comes from confidence. Assume that you will succeed, and your attitude will increase your chances. Assume that you are irresistible to women.

Be powerful and determined. But at the same time, be natural and fun. Be a bit of a bad boy, but not an idiot. Have a devilish smile on your face if you like. You are an exciting man, and women must want it.

Do what you like in life. Be true to your emotions. If you aren't required to do something, then don't do it. Be honest with yourself. Be your own man.

What does this mean? If you want to give a bum some incentive, then go for it. If you want to help, an old lady gets down the street:

1. Feel free to do so. If you want to open the door for your girlfriend to come in, please do so.
2. Just don't feel like you have to do any of those things because you are expected to do them.
3. Do something because you want to do them.

In the end, when you become an alpha male, the man who is loyal to himself, you will encounter the happiest time of your life. Going to bed will be just one of many positive consequences. How about THAT as a side benefit?

Simple Alpha Male Practice - Fixing the Mindset About You.

You need to know that every woman would be lucky to have it. I will ask the following questions. Answer the questions, and write them down.

This exercise can be easy, but it is important because if you have not yet fully internalized the alpha male's mentality, it is essential to remit his thought patterns. Also, it's always helpful to jot down these things so you can reread them later when they need to be remembered on your journey.

- If a woman enters your life, how can you make her feel good in various ways?
- Imagine that you are a man of high value whose time and attention are required by many people. What are your rules for allowing such people to receive the gift of your time and attention?
- What fun things do you like to do those women like too? (Women need emotions to become sexually receptive, so they enjoy emotionally relevant things, like talking on the phone with friends. The easiest way to kill a woman's sexual mood is to talk about logical things like financial statements. .)
- What qualities do you have (or can develop) that women would find attractive?
- What benefits would you need to receive from a woman to allow her to be part of your life?

Come up with your own answers, but keep in mind that there are certain things that women must have, such as great sex, passion, positive emotions, and sensuality.

As long as you provide the benefits to women, you also want to evaluate the quality. As a man, you probably have strong sexual desires (I certainly do!), So you wouldn't want a frigid woman. For me, behaviors that would make me leave a woman are liars, childhood drama, and obesity.

389

The type of woman I like is really like, enjoys life, and knows how to take care of herself. Only you know what you want and what wonderful benefits await the woman who enters your world. I encourage you to complete this exercise before continuing to read this guide.

Okay, now that you've read the questions, thought them through, and jotted down your answers, got your road map written on how to become attractive and safe. Put it another way, you are on your way to understanding how special you are. In the world of love, you are like a Lamborghini. If a woman does not understand her worth, then it is her loss, not yours.

I really like the Lamborghini analogy because of its relevance to men's relationships with women. A Lamborghini has no inherent value — it can be a hunk of metal that consumes a lot of fuel per mile, or it can be an object of beauty and power that you would pay as much for as a house. It all depends on your perception.

Lamborghini dealers have a strong mindset that their cars are highly valuable. As a result, they don't let anyone in for a test ride. They don't bargain for the price they expect to receive, unlike Ford or Chevy dealers who lack the high-value mindset.

Thank you for reading this book.

If you enjoyed it please visit the site where you purchased it and write a brief review. Your feedback is important to me and will help other readers decide whether to read the book too.

Thank you!

Dale Wayne